Birnbaum's 95
Boston

D1807760

A BIRNBAUM TRAVEL GUIDE

Alexandra Mayes Birnbaum
EDITORIAL CONSULTANT

Lois Spritzer
Editorial Director

Laura L. Brengelman
Managing Editor

Mary Callahan
Senior Editor

David Appell
Patricia Canole
Gene Gold
Jill Kadetsky
Susan McClung
Associate Editors

📖 HarperPerennial
A Division of HarperCollins*Publishers*

To Stephen, who merely made all this possible.

BIRNBAUM'S BOSTON 95. Copyright © 1995 by HarperCollins Publishers. All rights reserved. Printed in the United States of America. No part of this book may be used or reproduced in any manner whatsoever without written permission except in the case of brief quotations embodied in critical articles and reviews. For information address HarperCollins*Publishers*, 10 East 53rd Street, New York, NY 10022.

FIRST EDITION

ISSN 0749-2561 (Birnbaum Travel Guides)
ISSN 1056-4357 (Boston)
ISBN 0-06-278184-7 (pbk.)

95 96 97 ❖/RRD 5 4 3 2 1

Cover design © Drenttel Doyle Partners
Cover photograph © Bill Horsman/Stock Boston
Statue of Paul Revere in front of North Church, Boston

Contributing Editors

Brad Durham
Sara Laschever
Anita Peltonen

Elise Nakhnikian
Nancy Roosa
Peter Tietjen

Maps

Mark Carlson
Susan Carlson
B. Andrew Mudryk

Contents

Getting Ready to Go

Practical information for planning your trip.

The City

Thorough, qualitative guide to Boston, highlighting the city's attractions, services, hotels, and restaurants.

Diversions

A selective guide to a variety of unexpected pleasures, pinpointing the best places to pursue them.

Directions

Seven of the most delightful walks through Boston, plus a great driving tour.

Foreword

My sister-in-law lives in Boston—well, actually in Watertown, a suburb. This suggests at least two significant ramifications: First is the fact that as a result of her residence my husband, Steve Birnbaum, and I spent a fair amount of time in New England's most important urban enclave. Second is the dramatic endorsement that her presence implies: My sister-in-law is a charter member of the 1960s flower child generation, educated (at least in part) at the fount in Berkeley, and determined to live in only the most convivial of environments.

I can't tell exactly why my husband's youngest sibling finds Boston and its environs so appealing, but I do know that I think of it as a small town. From a third generation Manhattan dweller that's a meaningful compliment, incorporating concepts of both friendliness and escape. For visitors, Boston has a certain pervasive coziness that is very desirable, an accessibility that makes a traveler feel warmly welcome and at home.

With this sense of well-being very much in the air, it is more than normally nice to explore the historic sites and colonial corners that are Boston's signature. Add the host of truly topnotch hotels and savory restaurants that Boston has spawned in abundance, and you begin to get the impression that this is a town really worth exploring. Where once Boston took a backseat to more exotic urban locales, travelers (like me) have more recently grown up enough to appreciate this marvelous metropolis.

We have tried to create a guide to Boston that's specifically organized, written, and edited for today's demanding traveler, one for whom qualitative information is infinitely more desirable than mere quantities of unappraised data. We realize that it's impossible for any single travel writer to visit thousands of restaurants (and nearly as many hotels) in any given year and provide accurate appraisals of each. And even if it were physically possible for one human being to survive such an itinerary, it would of necessity have to be done at a dead sprint, and the perceptions derived therefrom would probably be less valid than those of any other intelligent individual visiting the same establishments. It is, therefore, both impractical and undesirable (especially in a large, annually revised and updated guidebook *series* such as we offer) to have only one person provide all the data on the entire world. Instead, we have chosen what we like to describe as the "thee and me" approach to restaurant and hotel evaluation and, to a somewhat more limited degree, to the sites and sights we have included in the other sections of our text. What this really reflects is a personal sampling tempered by intelligent counsel from informed local sources.

This guidebook is directed to the "visitor," and such elements as restaurants have been specifically picked to provide the visitor with a representative, enlightening, and, above all, pleasant experience. Since so many extraneous considerations can affect the reception and service accorded a regular restaurant patron, our choices can in no way be construed as an exhaustive guide to resident dining. We think we've listed all the best places, in various price ranges, but they were chosen with a visitor's enjoyment in mind.

Other evidence of how we've tried to tailor our text to reflect modern travel habits is apparent in the section we call DIVERSIONS. Where once it was common for travelers to spend an urban visit seeing only the obvious sights, today's traveler is more likely to want to pursue a special interest or to venture off the beaten path. In response to this trend, we have collected a series of special experiences so that it is no longer necessary to wade through a pound or two of superfluous prose just to find exceptional pleasures and treasures.

Finally, I also should point out that every good travel guide is a living enterprise; that is, no part of this text is carved in stone. In our annual revisions, we refine, expand, and further hone all our material to serve your travel needs better. To this end, no contribution is of greater value to us than your personal reaction to what we have written, as well as information reflecting your own experiences while using the book. Please write to us at 10 E. 53rd St., New York, NY 10022.

We sincerely hope to hear from you.

Alexandra Mayes Birnbaum

ALEXANDRA MAYES BIRNBAUM, editorial consultant to the *Birnbaum Travel Guides,* **worked with her late husband, Stephen Birnbaum, as co-editor of the series. She has been a world traveler since childhood and is known for her travel reports on radio on what's hot and what's not.**

Boston

How to Use This Guide

A great deal of care has gone into the special organization of this guidebook, and we believe it represents a real breakthrough in the presentation of travel material.

Our text is divided into four basic sections in order to present information in the best way on every possible aspect of a vacation to Boston. Our aim is to highlight what's where and to provide basic information—how, when, where, how much, and what's best—to assist you in making the most intelligent choices possible.

Here is a brief summary of what you can expect to find in each section. We believe that you will find both your travel planning and en route enjoyment enhanced by having this book at your side.

GETTING READY TO GO

A mini-encyclopedia of practical travel facts with all the precise data necessary to create a successful trip to Boston. Here you will find how to get where you're going, plus selected resources—including useful publications, and companies and organizations specializing in discount and special-interest travel—providing a wealth of information and assistance useful both before and during your trip.

THE CITY

This individual report on Boston offers a short-stay guide, including an essay introducing the city as a historic entity and a contemporary place to visit; a *Boston At-a-Glance* section that's a site-by-site survey of the most important, interesting, and unique sights to see and things to do; *Sources and Resources,* a concise listing of pertinent tourism information, such as the address of the local tourist office, which sightseeing tours to take, where to find the best nightspot or hail a taxi, which shops have the finest merchandise and/or the most irresistible bargains, and where the best museums and theaters are to be found; and *Best in Town,* which lists our collection of cost-and-quality choices of the best places to eat and sleep on a variety of budgets.

DIVERSIONS

This section is designed to help travelers find the best places in which to engage in a variety of exceptional experiences, without having to wade through endless pages of unrelated text. In every case, our particular suggestions are intended to guide you to that special place where the quality of experience is likely to be highest.

DIRECTIONS

Here are seven walks that cover Boston, its main thoroughfares and side streets, and its most spectacular landmarks and parks. We also suggest a drive to the nearby, history-rich towns of Cambridge, Lexington, Concord, and Lincoln.

————————————————

To use this book to full advantage, take a few minutes to read the table of contents and random entries in each section to get a firsthand feel for how it all fits together. You will find that the sections of this book are building blocks designed to help you put together the best possible trip. Use them selectively as a tool, a source of ideas, a reference work for accurate facts, and a guidebook to the best buys, the most exciting sights, the most pleasant accommodations, and the tastiest foods—*the best travel experience* that you can possibly have.

Getting Ready to Go

Getting Ready to Go

When to Go

Although Boston typically receives the most visitors from June to September, the best time to visit may be in autumn. The nights can be cold, but the days are most pleasant—generally clear and brisk. The brief, cool New England spring also is an attractive time to visit. Summers can be surprisingly hot and humid, and winters can be formidable, with icy winds, snow, and sleet.

Travel during the off-season (from around mid-November through the end of April) and shoulder seasons (the months immediately before and after the peak months) offers relatively fair weather and smaller crowds, and can be less expensive. Room rates also may be lower on weekends, when business travel is slow. Exceptions include the peak fall foliage period (mid-September through October) and college graduation time (late May), when bargains disappear and reservations may be required as much as six months in advance.

If you have a touch-tone phone, you can call *The Weather Channel Connection* (phone: 900-WEATHER) for current weather forecasts. This service, available from *The Weather Channel* (2600 Cumberland Pkwy., Atlanta, GA 30339; phone: 404-434-6800), costs 95¢ per minute; the charge will appear on your phone bill.

Traveling by Plane

SCHEDULED FLIGHTS

Leading airlines offering flights to Boston's *Logan International Airport* include *America West, American, American Eagle, Continental, Delta, Delta Connection, Delta Shuttle, Midwest Express, Northwest, NW Airlink, TWA, TWA Express, United, United Express, USAir, USAir Express,* and *USAir Shuttle.*

FARES The great variety of airfares can be reduced to the following basic categories: first class, business class, coach (also called economy or tourist class), excursion or discount, and standby, as well as various promotional fares. For information on applicable fares and restrictions, contact the airlines listed above or ask your travel agent. Most airfares are offered for a limited time. Once you've found the lowest fare for which you can qualify, purchase your ticket as soon as possible.

RESERVATIONS Reconfirmation is not generally required on domestic flights, although it is wise to call ahead to make sure that the airline has your reservation and any special requests in its computer.

SEATING Airline seats usually are assigned on a first-come, first-served basis at check-in, although you may be able to reserve a seat when purchasing your ticket. Seating charts sometimes are available from airlines and also are included in the *Airline Seating Guide* (Carlson Publishing Co., 11132 Los Alamitos Blvd., Los Alamitos, CA 90720; phone: 310-493-4877).

SMOKING US law prohibits smoking on flights scheduled for six hours or less within the US and its territories on both domestic and international carriers. A free wallet-size guide that describes the rights of nonsmokers under current regulations is available from *ASH* (*Action on Smoking and Health;* DOT Card, 2013 H St. NW, Washington, DC 20006; phone: 202-659-4310).

SPECIAL MEALS When making your reservation, you can request one of the airline's alternate menu choices for no additional charge. Though not always required, it's a good idea to reconfirm your request the day before departure.

BAGGAGE On major airlines, passengers usually are allowed to carry on board one bag that will fit under a seat or in an overhead bin and to check two bags in the cargo hold. Specific regulations regarding dimensions and weight restrictions vary among airlines, but a checked bag usually cannot exceed 62 inches in combined dimensions (length, width, and depth), or weigh more than 70 pounds. There may be charges for additional, oversize, or overweight luggage, and for special equipment or sporting gear. Check that the tags the airline attaches are correctly coded for your destination.

CHARTER FLIGHTS

By booking a block of seats on a specially arranged flight, charter operators frequently can offer travelers bargain airfares. If you do fly on a charter, however, read the contract's fine print carefully. Federal regulations permit charter operators to cancel a flight or assess surcharges of as much as 10% of the airfare up to 10 days before departure. You usually must book in advance, and once booked, no changes are permitted, so buy trip cancellation insurance. Also, make your check out to the company's escrow account, which provides some protection for your investment in the event that the charter operator fails. For further information, consult the publication *Jax Fax* (397 Post Rd., Darien, CT 06820; phone: 203-655-8746; fax: 203-655-6257).

DISCOUNTS ON SCHEDULED FLIGHTS

COURIER TRAVEL In return for arranging to accompany some kind of freight, a traveler pays only a portion of the total airfare (and sometimes a small registration fee). One agency that matches up would-be couriers with courier companies is *Now Voyager* (74 Varick St., Suite 307, New York, NY 10013; phone: 212-431-1616; fax: 212-334-5243).

Courier Companies

Discount Travel International (169 W. 81st St., New York, NY 10024; phone: 212-362-3636; fax: 212-362-3236; and 801 Alton Rd., Suite 1, Miami Beach, FL 33139; phone: 305-538-1616; fax: 305-673-9376).

F.B. On Board Courier Club (10225 Ryan Ave., Suite 103, Dorval, Quebec H9P 1A2, Canada; phone: 514-633-0740; fax: 514-633-0735).

Halbart Express (147-05 176th St., Jamaica, NY 11434; phone: 718-656-8279; fax: 718-244-0559).

Midnite Express (925 W. Hyde Park Blvd., Inglewood, CA 90302; phone: 310-672-1100; fax: 310-671-0107).

Way to Go Travel (6679 Sunset Blvd., Hollywood, CA 90028; phone: 213-466-1126; fax: 213-466-8994).

Publications

Insiders Guide to Air Courier Bargains, by Kelly Monaghan (The Intrepid Traveler, PO Box 438, New York, NY 10034; phone: 212-569-1081 for information; 800-356-9315 for orders; fax: 212-942-6687).

Travel Unlimited (PO Box 1058, Allston, MA 02134-1058; no phone).

CONSOLIDATORS AND BUCKET SHOPS These companies buy blocks of tickets from airlines and sell them at a discount to travel agents or directly to consumers. Since many bucket shops operate on a thin margin, be sure to check a company's record with the *Better Business Bureau*—before parting with any money.

Council Charter (205 E. 42nd St., New York, NY 10017; phone: 800-800-8222 or 212-661-0311; fax: 212-972-0194).

International Adventures (60 E. 42nd St., Room 763, New York, NY 10165; phone: 212-599-0577; fax: 212-599-3288).

Travac Tours and Charters (989 Ave. of the Americas, New York, NY 10018; phone: 800-872-8800 or 212-563-3303; fax: 212-563-3631).

Unitravel (1177 N. Warson Rd., St. Louis, MO 63132; phone: 800-325-2222 or 314-569-0900; fax: 314-569-2503).

LAST-MINUTE TRAVEL CLUBS Members of such clubs receive information on imminent trips and other bargain travel opportunities. There usually is an annual fee, although a few clubs offer free membership. Despite the names of some of the clubs listed below, you don't have to wait until literally the last minute to make travel plans.

Discount Travel International (114 Forrest Ave., Suite 203, Narberth, PA 19072; phone: 215-668-7184; fax: 215-668-9182).

FLY ASAP (PO Box 9808, Scottsdale, AZ 85252-3808; phone: 800-FLY-ASAP or 602-956-1987; fax: 602-956-6414).

Last Minute Travel (1249 Boylston St., Boston, MA 02215; phone: 800-LAST-MIN or 617-267-9800; fax: 617-424-1943).

Moment's Notice (425 Madison Ave., New York, NY 10017; phone: 212-486-0500/1/2/3; fax: 212-486-0783).

Spur of the Moment Cruises (411 N. Harbor Blvd., Suite 302, San Pedro, CA 90731; phone: 800-4-CRUISES or 310-521-1070 in California; 800-343-1991 elsewhere in the US; 24-hour hotline: 310-521-1060; fax: 310-521-1061).

Traveler's Advantage (3033 S. Parker Rd., Suite 900, Aurora, CO 80014; phone: 800-548-1116 or 800-835-8747; fax: 303-368-3985).

Vacations to Go (1502 Augusta Dr., Suite 415, Houston, TX 77057; phone: 713-974-2121 in Texas; 800-338-4962 elsewhere in the US; fax: 713-974-0445).

Worldwide Discount Travel Club (1674 Meridian Ave., Miami Beach, FL 33139; phone: 305-534-2082; fax: 305-534-2070).

GENERIC AIR TRAVEL These organizations operate much like an ordinary airline standby service, except that they offer seats on not one but several scheduled and charter airlines. One pioneer of generic flights is *Airhitch* (2790 Broadway, Suite 100, New York, NY 10025; phone: 212-864-2000).

BARTERED TRAVEL SOURCES Barter—the exchange of commodities or services in lieu of cash payment—is a common practice among travel suppliers. Companies that have obtained travel services through barter may sell these services at substantial discounts to travel clubs, who pass along the savings to members. One organization offering bartered travel opportunities is *Travel World Leisure Club* (225 W. 34th St., Suite 909, New York, NY 10122; phone: 800-444-TWLC or 212-239-4855; fax: 212-564-5158).

CONSUMER PROTECTION

Passengers whose complaints have not been satisfactorily addressed by the airline can contact the *US Department of Transportation* (*DOT;* Consumer Affairs Division, 400 Seventh St. SW, Room 10405, Washington, DC 20590; phone: 202-366-2220). Also see *Fly Rights* (Publication #050-000-00513-5; *US Government Printing Office,* PO Box 371954, Pittsburgh, PA 15250-7954; phone: 202-783-3238; fax: 202-512-2250). If you have safety-related questions or concerns, write to the *Federal Aviation Administration* (*FAA;* 800 Independence Ave. SW, Washington, DC 20591) or call the *FAA Consumer Hotline* (phone: 800-322-7873).

On Arrival

FROM THE AIRPORT TO THE CITY

Logan International Airport is located 3 miles from the center of Boston. A taxi ride from the airport to downtown takes from 10 to 30 minutes (or longer)—depending on the time of day and traffic—and costs $18 to $30. *City Transportation* (phone: 617-321-2282) runs minibuses from *Logan* to

Back Bay hotels from 7:15 AM to 9:15 PM daily; the 25- to 30-minute trip costs $7.50. *Peter Pan Trailways* (phone: 800-343-9999 or 617-426-7838) provides bus service between the airport and the company's bus station at 555 Atlantic Avenue daily from noon to 7:10 PM; the trip takes about 30 minutes and costs $7.

The most practical means of getting from *Logan* to almost anywhere in the Boston area—if you aren't carrying much luggage—is by the *Massachusetts Bay Transportation Authority* (*MBTA;* phone: 800-392-6100 or 617-722-3200) *Blue Line* trains. There are free shuttle buses from airport terminals to the *Blue Line* airport stop; from there the trip to the Government Center station at City Hall Plaza takes under half an hour. Trains are in service weekdays from 5:15 AM to 12:48 AM, and weekends from 6:05 AM to 12:48 AM; the fare is 85¢. The *MBTA*'s "Visitors' Passport," which permits unlimited travel on the subway and bus lines for a period of one, three, or seven days and includes discount coupons for local attractions, can be purchased from the *Greater Boston Convention and Visitors Bureau* (see *For Further Information* for address), as well as at major subway stations in Boston.

The *Massachusetts Port Authority* (*Massport;* phone: 800-23-LOGAN) operates a water shuttle that connects *Logan* with Rowes Wharf (400 Atlantic Ave.) weekdays from 6 AM to 8 PM (Fridays until 11 PM), Saturdays from 10 AM to 11 PM, and Sundays from 10 AM to 8 PM. The trip takes about 7 minutes and costs $8 ($4 for seniors; free for children under 12). Shuttle service is provided between airport terminals and the water shuttle dock.

RENTING A CAR

You can rent a car through a travel agent or national rental firm before leaving home, or from a regional or local company once in Boston. Reserve in advance.

Most car rental companies require a credit card, although some will accept a substantial cash deposit. The minimum age to rent a car is set by the company; some also may impose special conditions on drivers above a certain age. Electing to pay for collision damage waiver (CDW) protection will add to the cost of renting a car, but releases you from financial liability for the vehicle. Additional costs include drop-off charges or one-way service fees.

Car Rental Companies

Adventure Rent-A-Car (phone: 617-783-3825).
Agency Rent-A-Car (phone: 800-321-1972).
Alamo (phone: 800-327-9633).
Avis (phone: 800-331-1212).
Budget (phone: 800-527-0700).
Dollar Rent A Car (phone: 800-800-4000).
Enterprise Rent-A-Car (phone: 800-325-8007).

Hertz (phone: 800-654-3131).

National (phone: 800-227-7368).

Sears Rent-A-Car (phone: 800-527-0770).

Snappy Car Rental (phone: 800-669-4802 or 617-924-7147).

Thrifty (phone: 800-367-2277).

U-Save Auto Rental (phone: 800-272-USAV or 617-254-1900).

NOTE

Rent-A-Wreck (phone: 800-421-7253 for locations of franchises nation-wide; 617-284-9633 for office near *Logan Airport;* 617-267-8888 for Cambridge/North Boston office; 617-576-3700 or 617-492-8182 for Cambridge office) rents cars that are well worn but (presumably) mechanically sound. *Exotic Rentals* (phone: 617-245-9598) rents luxury and sports cars—but not during winter.

Package Tours

A package is a collection of travel services that can be purchased in a single transaction. Its principal advantages are convenience and economy—the cost usually is lower than that of the same services purchased separately. Tour programs generally can be divided into two categories: escorted or locally hosted (with a set itinerary) and independent (usually more flexible).

When considering a package tour, read the brochure *carefully* to determine exactly what is included and any conditions that may apply, and check the company's record with the *Better Business Bureau.* The *United States Tour Operators Association* (*USTOA;* 211 E. 51st St., Suite 12B, New York, NY 10022; phone: 212-750-7371; fax: 212-421-1285) also can be helpful in determining a package tour operator's reliability. As with charter flights, to safeguard your funds, always make your check out to the company's escrow account.

Many tour operators offer packages focused on special interests such as the arts, local history, sports, and other recreations. *All Adventure Travel* (5589 Arapahoe St., Suite 208, Boulder, CO 80303; phone: 800-537-4025 or 303-440-7924; fax: 303-440-4160) represents such specialized packagers. Many also are listed in the *Specialty Travel Index* (305 San Anselmo Ave., Suite 313, San Anselmo, CA 94960; phone: 415-459-4900 in California; 800-442-4922 elsewhere in the US; fax: 415-459-4974). In addition, a number of local companies offer half- or full-day sightseeing tours in and around Boston.

Package Tour Operators

American Airlines FlyAAway Vacations (offices throughout the US; phone: 800-321-2121).

Capitol Tours (PO Box 4241, Springfield, IL 62708; phone: 800-252-8924 for reservations; 217-529-8166 for information; fax: 217-529-5831).

Caravan Tours (401 N. Michigan Ave., Chicago, IL 60611; phone: 800-CARAVAN or 312-321-9800; fax: 312-321-9810).

Certified Vacations (110 E. Broward Blvd., Ft. Lauderdale, FL 33302; phone: 800-233-7260 or 305-522-1440; fax: 305-357-4687).

Collette Tours (162 Middle St., Pawtucket, RI 02860; phone: 800-752-2655 in New England; 800-832-4656 elsewhere in the US; fax: 401-727-4745).

Contiki Holidays (300 Plaza Alicante, Suite 900, Garden Grove, CA 92640; phone: 800-266-8454 or 714-740-0808; fax: 714-740-0818).

Continental Grand Destinations (offices throughout the US; phone: 800-634-5555).

Dan Dipert Tours (PO Box 580, Arlington, TX 76004-0580; phone: 800-433-5335 or 817-543-3710; fax: 817-543-3729).

Delta's Dream Vacations (PO Box 1525, Ft. Lauderdale, FL 33302; phone: 800-872-7786).

Domenico Tours (751 Broadway, Bayonne, NJ 07002; phone: 800-554-8687, 201-823-8687, or 212-757-8687; fax: 201-823-1527).

Globetrotters SuperCities (139 Main St., Cambridge, MA 02142; phone: 800-333-1234 or 617-621-0099; fax: 617-577-8380).

Globus/Cosmos (5301 S. Federal Circle, Littleton, CO 80123; phone: 800-221-0090, 800-556-5454, or 303-797-2800; fax: 303-347-2080).

GOGO Tours (69 Spring St., Ramsey, NJ 07446-0507; phone: 201-934-3759).

Jefferson Tours (1206 Currie Ave., Minneapolis, MN 55403; phone: 800-767-7433 or 612-338-4174; fax: 612-332-5532).

Kerrville Tours (PO Box 79, Shreveport, LA 71161-0079; phone: 800-442-8705 or 318-227-2882; fax: 318-227-2486).

Le Ob's Tours (4635 Touro St., New Orleans, LA 70122-3933; phone: 504-288-3478; fax: 504-288-8517).

Marathon Tours (108 Main St., Charlestown, MA 02129; phone: 800-444-4097 or 617-242-7845; fax: 617-242-7686).

Maupintour (PO Box 807, Lawrence, KS 66044; phone: 800-255-4266 or 913-843-1211; fax: 913-843-8351).

Mayflower (1225 Warren Ave., Downers Grove, IL 60515; phone: 800-323-7604 or 708-960-3430; fax: 708-960-3575).

MLT Vacations and Northwest World Vacations (c/o *MLT,* 5130 Hwy. 101, Minnetonka, MN 55345; phone: 800-328-0025 or 612-989-5000; fax: 612-474-0725).

New England Vacation Tours (PO Box 560, West Dover, VT 05356; phone: 800-742-7669 or 802-464-2076; fax: 802-464-2629).

Panorama Tours (600 N. Sprigg St., Cape Girardeau, MO 63701; phone: 800-962-8687 in Missouri and adjacent states; 314-335-7824 elsewhere in the US; fax: 314-335-7824).

Saga International Holidays (222 Berkeley St., Boston, MA 02116; phone: 800-343-0273 or 617-262-2262).

Tours and Travel Odyssey (230 E. McClellan Ave., Livingston, NJ 07039; phone: 800-527-2989 or 201-992-5459; fax: 201-994-1618).

TravelTours International (250 W. 49th St., Suite 600, New York, NY 10019; phone: 800-767-8777 or 212-262-0700; fax: 212-944-5854).

United Airlines Vacations (PO Box 24580, Milwaukee, WI 53224-0580; phone: 800-328-6877).

Yankee Holidays (435 Newbury St., Suite 210, Danvers, MA 01923-1065; phone: 800-225-2550 or 508-750-9688; fax: 508-750-9692).

Companies Offering Day Tours

The Boston Helicopter Company (151 Tremont St., Boston, MA 02111; phone: 800-55-PILOT in Massachusetts; 617-274-1230 elsewhere in the US; fax: 617-274-1237; flights depart from *Civil Air Terminal,* Hanscom Field, Bedford, MA 01730).

Boston Trolley (PO Box 267, Boston, MA 02132; phone: 617-TROL-LEY; fax: 617-269-8018).

Brush Hill Tours/Gray Line Boston and Beantown Trolley (39 Dalton St., Boston, MA 02199; phone: 617-236-2148; fax: 617-236-5570).

Old Town Trolley (329 W. Second St., S. Boston, MA 02127; phone: 617-269-7010; fax: 617-269-8018).

Sleuth & Company (20 Park Plaza, Suite 510, Boston, MA 02116; phone: 617-542-2525; fax: 617-542-3831).

Insurance

The first person with whom you should discuss travel insurance is your own insurance broker. You may discover that the insurance you already carry protects you adequately while traveling and that you need little additional coverage. If you charge travel services, the credit card company also may provide some insurance coverage (and other safeguards).

Types of Travel Insurance

Automobile insurance: Provides collision, theft, property damage, and personal liability protection while driving.

Baggage and personal effects insurance: Protects your bags and their contents in case of damage or theft at any point during your travels.

Default and/or bankruptcy insurance: Provides coverage in the event of default and/or bankruptcy on the part of the tour operator, airline, or other travel supplier.

Flight insurance: Covers accidental injury or death while flying.

Personal accident and sickness insurance: Covers cases of illness, injury, or death in an accident while traveling.

Trip cancellation and interruption insurance: Guarantees a refund if you must cancel a trip; may reimburse you for additional travel costs incurred in catching up with a tour or traveling home early.

Combination policies: Include any or all of the above.

Disabled Travelers

Make travel arrangements well in advance. Specify to all services involved the nature of your disability to determine if there are accommodations and facilities that meet your needs.

Organizations

ACCENT on Living (PO Box 700, Bloomington, IL 61702; phone: 800-787-8444 or 309-378-2961; fax: 309-378-4420).

Access: The Foundation for Accessibility by the Disabled (PO Box 356, Malverne, NY 11565; phone/fax: 516-887-5798).

American Foundation for the Blind (15 W. 16th St., New York, NY 10011; phone: 800-232-5463 or 212-620-2147; fax: 212-727-7418).

Information Center for Individuals with Disabilities (Ft. Point Pl., 27-43 Wormwood St., Boston, MA 02210; phone: 800-462-5015 in Massachusetts; 617-727-5540 elsewhere in the US; TDD: 617-345-9743; fax: 617-345-5318).

Mobility International (main office: 228 Borough High St., London SE1 1JX, England; phone: 44-171-403-5688; fax: 44-171-378-1292; US office: *MIUSA,* PO Box 10767, Eugene, OR 97440; phone/TDD: 503-343-1284; fax: 503-343-6812).

Moss Rehabilitation Hospital Travel Information Service (telephone referrals only; phone: 215-456-9600; TDD: 215-456-9602).

National Rehabilitation Information Center (8455 Colesville Rd., Suite 935, Silver Spring, MD 20910; phone: 301-588-9284; fax: 301-587-1967).

Paralyzed Veterans of America (*PVA;* PVA/ATTS Program, 801 18th St. NW, Washington, DC 20006; phone: 202-872-1300 in Washington, DC; 800-424-8200 elsewhere in the US; fax: 202-785-4452).

Royal Association for Disability and Rehabilitation (*RADAR;* 12 City Forum, 250 City Rd., London EC1V 8AF, England; phone: 44-171-250-3222; fax: 44-171-250-0212).

Society for the Advancement of Travel for the Handicapped (*SATH;* 347 Fifth Ave., Suite 610, New York, NY 10016; phone: 212-447-7284; fax: 212-725-8253).

Travel Industry and Disabled Exchange (*TIDE;* 5435 Donna Ave., Tarzana, CA 91356; phone: 818-368-5648).

Publications

Access Travel: A Guide to the Accessibility of Airport Terminals (Consumer Information Center, Dept. 578Z, Pueblo, CO 81009; phone: 719-948-3334).

Air Transportation of Handicapped Persons (Publication #AC-120-32; *US Department of Transportation,* Distribution Unit, Publications Section, M-443-2, 400 Seventh St. SW, Washington, DC 20590; phone: 202-366-0039).

The Diabetic Traveler (PO Box 8223 RW, Stamford, CT 06905; phone: 203-327-5832; fax: 203-975-1748).

Directory of Travel Agencies for the Disabled and *Travel for the Disabled,* both by Helen Hecker (Twin Peaks Press, PO Box 129, Vancouver, WA 98666; phone: 800-637-CALM or 206-694-2462; fax: 206-696-3210).

Guide to Traveling with Arthritis (Upjohn Company, PO Box 989, Dearborn, MI 48121; phone: 800-253-9860).

The Handicapped Driver's Mobility Guide (*American Automobile Association,* 1000 AAA Dr., Heathrow, FL 32746-5080; phone: 407-444-7000; fax: 407-444-7380).

Handicapped Travel Newsletter (PO Box 269, Athens, TX 75751; phone/fax: 903-677-1260).

Handi-Travel: A Resource Book for Disabled and Elderly Travellers, by Cinnie Noble (*Canadian Rehabilitation Council for the Disabled,* 45 Sheppard Ave. E., Suite 801, Toronto, Ontario M2N 5W9, Canada; phone/TDD: 416-250-7490; fax: 416-229-1371).

Incapacitated Passengers Air Travel Guide (*International Air Transport Association,* Publications Sales Department, 2000 Peel St., Montreal, Quebec H3A 2R4, Canada; phone: 514-844-6311; fax: 514-844-5286).

Ticket to Safe Travel (*American Diabetes Association,* 1660 Duke St., Alexandria, VA 22314; phone: 800-232-3472 or 703-549-1500; fax: 703-836-7439).

Travel for the Patient with Chronic Obstructive Pulmonary Disease (Dr. Harold Silver, 1601 18th St. NW, Washington, DC 20009; phone: 202-667-0134; fax: 202-667-0148).

Travel Tips for Hearing-Impaired People (*American Academy of Otolaryngology,* 1 Prince St., Alexandria, VA 22314; phone: 703-836-4444; fax: 703-683-5100).

Travel Tips for People with Arthritis (*Arthritis Foundation,* 1314 Spring St. NW, Atlanta, GA 30309; phone: 800-283-7800 or 404-872-7100; fax: 404-872-0457).

Traveling Like Everybody Else: A Practical Guide for Disabled Travelers, by Jacqueline Freedman and Susan Gersten (Modan Publishing, PO Box 1202, Bellmore, NY 11710; phone: 516-679-1380; fax: 516-679-1448).

The Wheelchair Traveler, by Douglass R. Annand (123 Ball Hill Rd., Milford, NH 03055; phone: 603-673-4539).

Package Tour Operators

Accessible Journeys (35 W. Sellers Ave., Ridley Park, PA 19078; phone: 800-846-4537 or 215-521-0339; fax: 215-521-6959).

Accessible Tours/Directions Unlimited (Attn.: Lois Bonnani, 720 N. Bedford Rd., Bedford Hills, NY 10507; phone: 800-533-5343 or 914-241-1700; fax: 914-241-0243).

Beehive Business and Leisure Travel (1130 W. Center St., N. Salt Lake, UT 84054; phone: 800-777-5727 or 801-292-4445; fax: 801-298-9460).

Classic Travel Service (8 W. 40th St., New York, NY 10018; phone: 212-869-2560 in New York State; 800-247-0909 elsewhere in the US; fax: 212-944-4493).

Evergreen Travel Service (4114 198th St. SW, Suite 13, Lynnwood, WA 98036-6742; phone: 800-435-2288 or 206-776-1184; fax: 206-775-0728).

Flying Wheels Travel (143 W. Bridge St., PO Box 382, Owatonna, MN 55060; phone: 800-535-6790 or 507-451-5005; fax: 507-451-1685).

Good Neighbor Travel Service (124 S. Main St., Viroqua, WI 54665; phone: 800-338-3245 or 608-637-2128; fax: 608-637-3030).

The Guided Tour (7900 Old York Rd., Suite 114B, Elkins Park, PA 19117-2339; phone: 800-783-5841 or 215-782-1370; fax: 215-635-2637).

Hinsdale Travel (201 E. Ogden Ave., Hinsdale, IL 60521; phone: 708-325-1335 or 708-469-7349; fax: 708-325-1342).

MedEscort International (*ABE International Airport,* PO Box 8766, Allentown, PA 18105-8766; phone: 800-255-7182 or 215-791-3111; fax: 215-791-9189).

Prestige World Travel (5710-X High Point Rd., Greensboro, NC 27407; phone: 800-476-7737 or 910-292-6690; fax: 910-632-9404).

Sprout (893 Amsterdam Ave., New York, NY 10025; phone: 212-222-9575; fax: 212-222-9768).

Weston Travel Agency (134 N. Cass Ave., Westmont, IL 60559; phone: 708-968-2513 in Illinois; 800-633-3725 elsewhere in the US; fax: 708-968-2539).

Single Travelers

The travel industry is not very fair to people who vacation by themselves—they often end up paying more than those traveling in pairs. There are services catering to single travelers, however, that match travel companions, offer travel arrangements with shared accommodations, and provide information and discounts. Useful publications include *Going Solo* (Doerfer Communications, PO Box 123, Apalachicola, FL 32329; phone/fax: 904-653-8848) and *Traveling on Your Own,* by Eleanor Berman (Random House, Order Dept., 400 Hahn Rd., Westminster, MD 21157; phone: 800-733-3000; fax: 800-659-2436).

Organizations and Companies

Contiki Holidays (300 Plaza Alicante, Suite 900, Garden Grove, CA 92640; phone: 800-466-0610 or 714-740-0808; fax: 714-740-0818).

Gallivanting (515 E. 79th St., Suite 20F, New York, NY 10021; phone: 800-933-9699 or 212-988-0617; fax: 212-988-0144).

Globus/Cosmos (5301 S. Federal Circle, Littleton, CO 80123; phone: 800-221-0090, 800-556-5454, or 303-797-2800; fax: 303-347-2080).

Jane's International and Sophisticated Women Travelers (2603 Bath Ave., Brooklyn, NY 11214; phone: 718-266-2045; fax: 718-266-4062).

Marion Smith Singles (611 Prescott Pl., N. Woodmere, NY 11581; phone: 516-791-4852, 516-791-4865, or 212-944-2112; fax: 516-791-4879)

Partners-in-Travel (11660 Chenault St., Suite 119, Los Angeles, CA 90049; phone: 310-476-4869).

Singles in Motion (545 W. 236th St., Riverdale, NY 10463; phone/fax: 718-884-4464).

Singleworld (401 Theodore Fremd Ave., Rye, NY 10580; phone: 800-223-6490 or 914-967-3334; fax: 914-967-7395).

Solo Flights (63 High Noon Rd., Weston, CT 06883; phone: 800-266-1566 or 203-226-9993).

Suddenly Singles Tours (161 Dreiser Loop, Bronx, NY 10475; phone: 718-379-8800 in New York City; 800-859-8396 elsewhere in the US; fax: 718-379-8858).

Travel Companion Exchange (PO Box 833, Amityville, NY 11701; phone: 516-454-0880; fax: 516-454-0170).

Travel Companions (Atrium Financial Center, 1515 N. Federal Hwy., Suite 300, Boca Raton, FL 33432; phone: 800-383-7211 or 407-393-6448; fax: 407-451-8560).

Travel in Two's (239 N. Broadway, Suite 3, N. Tarrytown, NY 10591; phone: 914-631-8301 in New York State; 800-692-5252 elsewhere in the US).

Umbrella Singles (PO Box 157, Woodbourne, NY 12788; phone: 800-537-2797 or 914-434-6871; fax: 914-434-3532).

Older Travelers

Special discounts and more free time are just two factors that have given older travelers a chance to see the world at affordable prices. Many travel suppliers offer senior discounts—sometimes only to members of certain senior citizens organizations (which provide benefits of their own). When considering a particular package, make sure the facilities—and the pace of the tour—match your needs and physical condition.

Publications

The Mature Traveler (PO Box 50820, Reno, NV 89513-0820; phone: 702-786-7419).

The Senior Citizen's Guide to Budget Travel in the US and Canada, by Paige Palmer (Pilot Books, 103 Cooper St., Babylon, NY 11702; phone: 516-422-2225; fax: 516-422-2227).

Take a Camel to Lunch and Other Adventures for Mature Travelers, by Nancy O'Connell (Bristol Publishing Enterprises, PO Box 1737, San Leandro, CA 94577; phone: 510-895-4461 in California; 800-346-4889 elsewhere in the US; fax: 510-895-4459).

Unbelievably Good Deals & Great Adventures That You Absolutely Can't Get Unless You're Over 50, by Joan Rattner Heilman (Contemporary Books, 1200 Stetson Ave., Chicago, IL 60601; phone: 312-782-9181; fax: 312-540-4687).

Organizations

American Association of Retired Persons (*AARP;* 601 E St. NW, Washington, DC 20049; phone: 202-434-2277).

Golden Companions (PO Box 754, Pullman, WA 99163-0754; phone: 208-858-2183).

Mature Outlook (Customer Service Center, 6001 N. Clark St., Chicago, IL 60660; phone: 800-336-6330).

National Council of Senior Citizens (1331 F St. NW, Washington, DC 20004; phone: 202-347-8800; fax: 202-624-9595).

Package Tour Operators

Elderhostel (75 Federal St., Boston, MA 02110-1941; phone: 617-426-7788; fax: 617-426-8351).

Evergreen Travel Service (4114 198th St. SW, Suite 13, Lynnwood, WA 98036-6742; phone: 800-435-2288 or 206-776-1184; fax: 206-775-0728).

Gadabout Tours (700 E. Tahquitz Canyon Way, Palm Springs, CA 92262; phone: 800-952-5068 or 619-325-5556; fax: 619-325-5127).

Grand Circle Travel (347 Congress St., Boston, MA 02210; phone: 800-221-2610 or 617-350-7500; fax: 617-423-0445).

Grandtravel (6900 Wisconsin Ave., Suite 706, Chevy Chase, MD 20815; phone: 800-247-7651 or 301-986-0790; fax: 301-913-0166).

Interhostel (*University of New Hampshire,* Division of Continuing Education, 6 Garrison Ave., Durham, NH 03824; phone: 800-733-9753 or 603-862-1147; fax: 603-862-1113).

Mature Tours (c/o *Solo Flights,* 63 High Noon Rd., Weston, CT 06883; phone: 800-266-1566 or 203-226-9993).

OmniTours (104 Wilmot Rd., Deerfield, IL 60015; phone: 800-962-0060 or 708-374-0088; fax: 708-374-9515).

Saga International Holidays (222 Berkeley St., Boston, MA 02116; phone: 800-343-0273 or 617-262-2262; fax: 617-375-5950).

Money Matters

CREDIT CARDS AND TRAVELER'S CHECKS

Most major credit cards enjoy wide domestic and international acceptance; however, not every hotel, restaurant, or shop in Boston accepts all (or in some cases any) credit cards. It's also wise to carry traveler's checks while on the road, since they are widely accepted and replaceable if stolen or lost. You can buy traveler's checks at banks and some are available by mail or phone. Keep a separate list of all traveler's checks (noting those that you have cashed) and the names and numbers of your credit cards. Both traveler's check and credit card companies have international numbers to call for information or in the event of loss or theft.

CASH MACHINES

Automated teller machines (ATMs) are increasingly common worldwide, and most banks participate in international ATM networks such as *CIRRUS* (phone: 800-4-CIRRUS) and *PLUS* (phone: 800-THE-PLUS). Cardholders can withdraw cash from any machine in the same network using either a "bank" card or, in some cases, a credit card. Additional information on ATMs and networks can be obtained from your bank or credit card company.

SENDING MONEY

Should the need arise, you can have money sent to you in Boston via the services provided by *American Express MoneyGram* (phone: 800-926-9400 for information; 800-866-8800 for money transfers) or *Western Union Financial Services* (phone: 800-325-6000 or 800-325-4176).

Time Zone

Boston is in the eastern standard time zone. Daylight saving time is observed from the first Sunday in April until the last Sunday in October.

Business and Shopping Hours

Boston maintains business hours that are fairly standard throughout the US: 9 AM to 5 PM, Mondays through Fridays. Although banking hours generally are weekdays from 9 AM to 3 PM, many banks stay open until 5 or 6 PM at least one day a week, and some also offer Saturday morning hours. Most retail stores are open Mondays through Saturdays from 9:30 or 10 AM to 5:30 or 6 PM; some also are open on Sundays (from around noon until 5 PM). Malls and department stores usually are open Mondays through Saturdays from 10 AM to 9 PM, and Sundays from noon to 5 PM.

Mail

Boston's main post office, *Fort Point Station* (25 Dorchester Ave., Boston, MA 02205; phone: 617-654-5327), provides window service 24 hours a day. The *John W. McCormack Station* (90 Devonshire St., Boston, MA 02109; phone: 617-654-5684) is open Mondays through Fridays from 7:30 AM to 5 PM. For other branches, call the main post office or check the yellow pages.

Stamps also are available at most hotel desks, some supermarkets and other stores, and from public vending machines. For rapid, overnight delivery to other cities, use *Express Mail* (available at post offices), *Federal Express* (phone: 800-238-5355), or *DHL Worldwide Express* (phone: 800-225-5345).

You can have mail sent to you care of your hotel (marked "Guest Mail, Hold for Arrival") or to the main post office (sent "c/o General Delivery" to the address above). *American Express* offices in Boston also will hold mail for customers ("c/o Client Letter Service"); information is provided in their pamphlet *Travelers' Companion.*

Telephone

The area code for Boston and its adjoining suburbs is 617. To make a long-distance call, dial 1 + the area code + the local number. The nationwide number for information is 555-1212; you also can dial 411 for local information. If you need a number in another area code, dial 1 + the area code + 555-1212. (If you don't know an area code, dial 555-1212 or 411 for directory assistance.)

Although you can use a telephone company calling card number on any phone, pay phones that take major credit cards (*American Express, MasterCard, Visa,* and so on) are increasingly common. Also available are combined telephone calling/bank credit cards, such as the *AT&T Universal Card* (PO Box 44167, Jacksonville, FL 32231-4167; phone: 800-423-4343). Similarly, *Sprint* (8140 Ward Pkwy., Kansas City, MO 64114; phone: 800-THE-MOST or 800-800-USAA) offers the *VisaPhone* program, through which you can add phone card privileges to your existing *Visa* card. Companies offering long-distance phone cards without additional credit card privileges include *AT&T* (phone: 800-CALL-ATT), *Executive Telecard International* (4260 E. Evans Ave., Suite 6, Denver, CO 80222; phone: 800-950-3800), *MCI* (323 Third St. SE, Cedar Rapids, IA 52401; phone: 800-444-4444; and 12790 Merit Dr., Dallas, TX 75251; phone: 800-444-3333), *Metromedia Communications* (1 International Center, 100 NE Loop 410, San Antonio, TX 78216; phone: 800-275-0200), and *Sprint* (address above).

Hotels routinely add surcharges to the cost of phone calls made from their rooms. Long-distance telephone services that may help you avoid this added expense are provided by a number of companies, including *AT&T* (International Information Service, 635 Grant St., Pittsburgh, PA 15219; phone: 800-874-4000), *MCI* (address above), *Metromedia Communications* (address above), and *Sprint* (address above). Note that even when you use such long-distance services, some hotels still may charge a fee for line usage.

Useful resources for travelers include the *AT&T 800 Travel Directory* (phone: 800-426-8686 for orders), the *Toll-Free Travel & Vacation Information Directory* (Pilot Books, 103 Cooper St., Babylon, NY 11702; phone: 516-422-2225; fax: 516-422-2227), and *The Phone Booklet* (Scott American Corporation, PO Box 88, W. Redding, CT 06896; no phone).

Medical Aid

In an emergency: Dial 911 for assistance, 0 for an operator, or go directly to the emergency room of the nearest hospital.

Hospitals

Boston City Hospital (818 Harrison Ave.; phone: 617-534-5000).

Massachusetts General Hospital (55 Fruit St., off Cambridge St.; phone: 617-726-2000).

24-Hour Pharmacies

CVS (35 White St., Cambridge; phone: 617-876-5519).

CVS (155 Charles St.; phone: 617-523-4372 or 617-523-1028). Store open 24 hours daily; prescription department open from 7 AM until midnight.

Additional Resources

International SOS Assistance (PO Box 11568, Philadelphia, PA 19116; phone: 800-523-8930 or 215-244-1500; fax: 215-244-2227).

Medic Alert Foundation (2323 Colorado Ave., Turlock, CA 95382; phone: 800-ID-ALERT or 209-668-3333; fax: 209-669-2495).

Travel Care International (*Eagle River Airport,* PO Box 846, Eagle River, WI 54521; phone: 800-5-AIR-MED or 715-479-8881; fax: 715-479-8178).

Legal Aid

If you don't have, or cannot reach, your own attorney, most cities offer legal referral services maintained by county bar associations. These services ensure that anyone in need of legal representation gets it and can match you with a local attorney. For legal assistance in Boston, contact the *Boston Bar Association Lawyer Referral Service* (phone: 617-742-0625; fax: 617-523-0127) or the *Massachusetts Bar Association Lawyer Referral Service* (phone: 800-392-6164 in Massachusetts; 617-542-9103 elsewhere in the US). If you must appear in court, you are entitled to court-appointed representation if you can't obtain a lawyer or can't afford one.

For Further Information

For tourist information on Boston, contact the *Greater Boston Convention and Visitors Bureau* (Prudential Tower, PO Box 490, Boston, MA 02199; phone: 617-536-4100 in Massachusetts; 800-888-5515 elsewhere in the US; fax: 617-424-7664). Tourist information also is available from the *Massachusetts Office of Travel and Tourism* (100 Cambridge St., 13th Floor, Boston, MA 02202; phone: 800-447-MASS or 617-727-3201; fax: 617-727-6525). For additional sources of local tourist information, see *Sources and Resources* in THE CITY.

The City

Boston

No matter how you approach Boston, you'll be struck by the beauty of its location. Jutting into the island-studded harbor, the city graces the banks of the Charles River with riverside parks and a distinctive skyline. Here are the narrow cobblestones where Boston's colonists walked, the *Common* where their cattle grazed, the churches where they prayed, and the tiny burial grounds that shelter their bones. Here, too, are the bold buildings of government, the fortresses of finance, the colorful chaos of the open market, and the free-wheeling spirit of the waterfront.

Anyone walking briskly could traverse this history-soaked terrain in an afternoon, but take the time to explore Boston at leisure, keeping an eye out for odd quirks of architecture and bright spots of whimsy. Spend a couple of hours in the North End, wandering along twisting streets barely wider than the ancient cowpaths they follow, or in Back Bay, strolling down the broad avenues lined with stately townhouses. Look for the famous brass nameplates and gas lamps of Beacon Hill, the intricate wrought-iron balconies along Commonwealth Avenue, the bronze trash set into the pavement near *Haymarket,* and the grasshopper atop *Faneuil Hall*—the site of many Revolutionary protest meetings.

The 19th century saw the rise of commerce in Boston and a simultaneous flowering of arts and letters—represented by such figures as Emerson, Hawthorne, Longfellow, and Thoreau. The boom of population and wealth prompted the city fathers to fill in the increasingly noxious Back Bay wetlands to provide land for the city's expansion. Today, that barren landscape has been transformed by a century's growth of elms, magnolias, and fruit trees, and early Back Bay homes are prized as exceptional examples of Victorian architecture in America.

After surviving half a century of neglect and deterioration, Boston experienced a renaissance, beginning in the 1960s with the creation of *Government Center* and the restoration of the city's historic neighborhoods. During the 1970s, *Faneuil Hall Marketplace* became the prototype for a new concept of urban retail development (see *Special Places,* below). More recently, *Copley Place* and Cambridge's *Charles Square* have added vitality to the city.

Yet a civilized sense of ease combined with an abundance of opportunity remains. Boston's art museums are among the finest in the world, and its galleries—on Newbury Street, along Fort Point Channel, and the up-and-coming South Street and South End—are worth a day in themselves. Its music scene is thriving as well, and the *Boston Symphony* is only the beginning. Baroque chamber music concerts often are sold out, jazz fans can sit through three sizzling sets in intimate cafés, and the biggest names in folk, country, and rock return faithfully to sing in the clubs that gave them their start. There's also the ever-popular *Boston Pops,* a symphony orchestra with a crowd-pleasing repertoire of popular and classical music.

The *Boston Ballet* is world-renowned, and a variety of contemporary dance companies present frequent, innovative programs. Many Broadway shows get their start here, and local theater groups stage everything from Shakespeare to experimental plays. Besides the many commercial movie houses showing first- and second-run films, local colleges and cultural centers are always sponsoring film festivals where you can catch obscure movies from Eastern Europe or your favorite Chaplin, D. W. Griffith, or Bogart classics.

These same colleges and cultural centers provide virtually unlimited opportunities for education and self-improvement, from the large academic communities of *Harvard,* the *Massachusetts Institute of Technology (MIT),* and *Boston University* to the dozens of smaller institutions. The list of lectures open to the public on any given day is overwhelming.

For many people, Boston is, above all, a sports town. It's easy for *Red Sox* fans to indulge themselves at *Fenway Park*—one of the last of the great old urban ballparks. Basketball and hockey fans have their beloved *Celtics* and *Bruins,* and football followers have the *New England Patriots.* Visitors should bear in mind that loyalties are intense in Boston. If you must cheer for the opposition, do so softly.

Politics often seems like another favorite sport in Boston. Mayor James Michael Curley will live forever in the novel *The Last Hurrah,* and the grandson of another mayor, "Honey Fitz" Fitzgerald, became the 35th President of the US, John F. Kennedy. Such names as Elliot Richardson and Henry Cabot Lodge loom large in our national consciousness, as does that of the late Thomas P. "Tip" O'Neill, a North Cambridge native and formidable Speaker of the *House of Representatives.*

Boston has long been known as "the home of the bean and the cod," but it isn't easy to find authentic baked beans. Local fishermen, however, provide Boston's tables with plenty of fresh fish and shellfish, and scrod (as cooked cod filets are called here) is found on many menus. Ethnic eateries of all kinds have proliferated in recent years, complementing the long-established restaurants and groceries in Chinatown and the Italian North End with Thai, Japanese, Portuguese, Indian, Mexican, and Greek foods, among others. There are also many restaurants dedicated to creative nouvelle cuisine using seasonal produce. Bostonians bargain for their own at *Haymarket* (see "Blackstone Block" in *Special Places*).

Thanks to the genius of Frederick Law Olmsted, Boston enjoys several miles of continuous parkland known as the *Emerald Necklace,* an 8-mile chain of parks that is the longest stretch of urban parkland in the United States. Perhaps the prettiest jewel of them all is the *Public Garden,* with its ever-changing displays of luxuriant blooms and its graceful Swan Boats cruising the quiet pond. Next to the *Public Garden* is *Boston Common,* the nation's oldest public park. The path along the *Charles River Esplanade,* which provides plenty of aquatic as well as terrestrial scenery, is a fine place for jogging. In summer, it is the site of performances in the *Hatch Shell,* among them the famous *July Fourth* extravaganza of the *Boston Pops Orchestra* (see *Special Events*).

At first inhabited largely by descendants of the very first Puritans, the city was then settled by Irish- and Italian-Americans. With the more recent arrival of Eastern European, Asian, and African emigrés, Boston's ethnic texture has grown richer over the years. In making the journey from its staid, Puritanical beginning to its vibrant, cosmopolitan present, Boston has learned to treasure its past while remaining eager to experience the new.

Boston At-a-Glance

SEEING THE CITY

There are two unparalleled posts from which to view Boston: the *John Hancock Tower*'s 60th-floor *Observatory* (Copley Sq.; phone: 247-1977) and the 50th-floor *Prudential Center Skywalk* (800 Boylston St.; phone: 236-3318). The recently renovated *Observatory* offers a spectacular panorama that even includes the mountains of southern New Hampshire (weather permitting). It also has telescopes, recorded commentaries, a topographical model of Boston in 1775 (this is a must—we promise you'll be surprised), and a seven-minute film of a helicopter flight over the city. The *Skywalk* also offers an excellent 360° view. Both are open daily and charge admission.

Boston also has several fabulous rooms with views where you can relax with a drink and watch the sun set over the city. The most elegant is the *Bay Tower Room* on the 33rd floor of the 60 State Street tower, near *Faneuil Hall.* Though it is a private club and a favorite of the working lunch crowd, the elegant restaurant and piano bar on the top floor are open to the general public after 4:30 PM. The menu features creative American cooking; the baked stuffed lobster is especially succulent. A jacket is required for men. Enjoy free hors d'oeuvres, live music on weekends, and a dizzying view of the city's waterfront through three-story-high windows (phone: 723-1666). For a 360° view, visit the revolving restaurant on top of the *Hyatt Regency Cambridge* (see *Checking In*) or the *Top of the Hub* restaurant (phone: 536-1775; open daily) on the 52nd floor of the *Prudential* tower, two floors above the *Skywalk.*

SPECIAL PLACES

Boston is best seen on foot; the city is compact, and driving, even for residents, is often hair-raising.

DOWNTOWN

The confusing crisscross of narrow streets that gives Boston its charm is no more evident than in the city's cradle, the downtown area, which now consists of *Faneuil Hall, Government Center,* and the financial, retail, and waterfront districts. (See also *Walk 6: Downtown* in DIRECTIONS.)

BOSTON COMMON This pastoral green, established in 1634, is the nation's oldest park. The earliest Bostonians brought their cows and horses here to graze. Today, you'll find their descendants engaging in free-form pastimes that range from playing music to playing baseball. We suggest starting your tour of the city here—but don't walk alone at night, as the *Common* is often inadequately patrolled. The lovely *Public Garden* is adjacent to the *Common*, across Charles Street. For information about activities on the *Common*, call 536-4100. (Also see *Walk 4: Boston Common* in DIRECTIONS.) You can park at *Motor Mart* on Stuart Street or at the *57 Park Plaza* hotel.

FREEDOM TRAIL The city has made it both easy and fun to track down the important sites from its colonial and Revolutionary past. Just follow the red brick (or red paint) line set into the sidewalks, which leads through downtown Boston and the North End, then crosses the river into Charlestown. The trail may be followed only on foot; it takes about two hours to walk its length without stops or side trips. To begin, take the *Green* or *Red Line* to Park Street and walk down Tremont Street to the visitors' information center on the *Common*, which has maps.

PARK STREET CHURCH Built in 1809, the church witnessed William Lloyd Garrison's famous first anti-slavery address in 1829 and heard the first singing of "My country, 'tis of thee" three years later. It's open Tuesdays through Saturdays in July and August; otherwise by appointment. 1 Park St. (phone: 523-3383). (Also see *Historic Churches* in DIVERSIONS.)

OLD GRANARY BURYING GROUND In this 1660 cemetery, next door to the *Park Street Church*, are the graves of such Revolutionary notables as John Hancock, Samuel Adams, Paul Revere, and the victims of the Boston Massacre, as well as the parents of Benjamin Franklin. Open daily (phone: 635-4505, ext. 6516). (Also see *Historic Churches* in DIVERSIONS.)

DOWNTOWN CROSSING A great meeting place. Winter meets Summer Street, the *Red Line* meets the *Orange Line*, and the display windows of the two giants of Boston retailing, *Filene's* and *Jordan Marsh*, face each other across a brick, pedestrians-only street. On Saturdays, when the shoppers, vendors, and street performers are out in force, this intersection resembles Mecca at the end of *Ramadan*, which may be why a good proportion of the world's lesser-known religions are represented here, looking for new members or donations. Business is brisk for the vending carts, which sell everything from T-shirts to llama-skin luggage. At the intersection of Winter and Washington Sts.

KING'S CHAPEL AND BURYING GROUND Founded as the Massachusetts Bay Colony's first Anglican church in 1686, *King's Chapel* was the place of worship for British officers and the royal governor. Since the colonists had fled England to escape the Anglican Church, the church's founding was taken as an insult. The ornate *Governor's Pew*, the church's centerpiece, was removed from the church in 1826, only to be restored a century later after it was clear that the colony had rid itself of British elitism. The cemetery next door, established in 1631, is the city's oldest and contains the graves and tombstones of many revered old Bostonians, including John Winthrop, the first governor of the Massachusetts Bay Colony; William Dawes, who was Paul Revere's companion on his famous ride; and Mary Chilton, the first woman Pilgrim from the Plymouth Colony to go to Boston. The church hosts free chamber music and other concerts on Tuesdays just after noon. Open Mondays through Saturdays mid-June through *Labor Day;* Mondays, Fridays, and Saturdays mid-March through mid-June and *Labor Day* through October; Saturdays only the rest of the year. Tremont St. at School St. (phone: 227-2155). (Also see *Historic Churches* in DIVERSIONS.)

OLD SOUTH MEETING HOUSE Though this well-preserved church was built in 1729 to serve Boston's Puritan congregation, its greatest hour was secular. When dissent began to rumble in the colonies before the Revolution, it was here that patriots flocked to debate the issues of the day. It was here that, after failing to persuade the royal governor to send back to England three ships that were filled with dutiable tea and moored in the harbor, Samuel Adams announced in December 1773, "Taxation without representation is tyranny." And it was from here that an incensed mob, some disguised as Indians, set out to dump the tea in the harbor and write a crucial chapter in the birth of this nation. In addition, Ben Franklin, who was born across the street, was baptized here when he was only hours old. An award-winning permanent audio exhibit re-creates the Tea Party and other exciting moments from Boston's past. Also on display are rare colonial artifacts and a scale model of early Boston. Costumed players reenact a town meeting on Saturday evenings in the summer, and from October through April, there's a Thursday lunchtime lecture series on American history. Open daily; admission charge. 310 Washington St. (phone: 482-6439).

GLOBE CORNER BOOKSTORE Formerly the *Old Corner Bookstore,* this venerable landmark was long the hub of Boston's literary scene. The building that first stood on this site belonged to the family of Anne Hutchinson, a religious dissident whose unorthodox beliefs became so popular in the 1630s that she was banished from the colony by an intimidated Governor Winthrop (he later conceded that he was about the only one in town who didn't like her opinions). The present building was constructed in 1718 after the Hutchinson home was destroyed in the Great Boston Fire of 1711. For years, it was the office of eminent publishers *Ticknor and Fields,* where editor Jamie Fields attracted such names as Emerson, Hawthorne, Holmes, Longfellow, Lowell, and Thoreau to his stable of writers. Fields's office was a center of literary discussion. It is now a working bookstore with abundant travel titles, as well as books about New England and by New England authors. 1 School St. (phone: 523-6658).

OLD STATE HOUSE Boston's 18th-century seat of government served both the English colony and the American state of Massachusetts until the *State House* was completed in 1798. Now dwarfed by modern towers of law and finance, the present building was erected in 1713. The *Old State House* served as the council chambers of the royal governors sent from England. As the conflict between England and the colonies became more pointed, so did the goings-on about the *Old State House.* When edicts and proclamations were read from the east balcony, the colonists would adjourn to local taverns to work themselves into a fury and then return, emboldened, to protest. The Boston Massacre was staged in front of the building's east side. It's now a museum, tracing Boston's history from early to contemporary times. Open daily. Admission charge. 206 Washington St. (phone: 720-3290). (Also see *Walk 6: Downtown* in DIRECTIONS.)

CITY HALL The focal point of the *Government Center* plaza, Boston's looming, concrete *City Hall* (1968), designed by Kallman, McKinnell & Knowles, is considered a landmark of modern architecture, although the local populace loves to revile it. *City Hall* sits in the middle of an eight-acre plaza that is often the scene of civic celebrations and politicking. Congress St. (phone: 725-4000).

FANEUIL HALL MARKETPLACE The market takes its official name from adjacent *Faneuil* (pronounced *Fan*-yool) *Hall,* a historic meeting house. It is also known as *Quincy Market,* which is the name of the main market building. When it opened in 1826, this was the site of the city's meat and produce markets (11 of the original tenants still do business here). Redesigned between 1976 and 1978 by Benjamin Thompson and the Rouse Company, the market has become a much-copied prototype of urban renewal. Now a lively gathering place, it has performers and street vendors outside and eateries, trinket shops, and boutiques inside. Over a million people a month visit its stalls, restaurants, and shops. Open daily. Off I-93 between Clinton and Chatham Sts. (phone: 338-2323). (Also see *Walk 6: Downtown* in DIRECTIONS.)

WATERFRONT

There's much to do and see along Boston's waterfront. Walk along *Waterfront Park,* with its invigorating views of the harbor; browse in the many new shops set in the renovated wharf buildings; or take a sightseeing tour by water from Long Wharf (see *Getting Around,* below). Also here is the *Aquarium* (see below). Just over the Congress Street Bridge, past the *Boston Tea Party Ship and Museum* and into the commercial district of South Boston—some call it Wallpaper Row—are the wildly popular *Computer Museum* and *Children's Museum.* They are located on the park-like *Museum Wharf,* home of the enormous red-and-white H. P. Hood Milk Bottle, a vintage 1930s highway lunch stand that is 40 feet high. (Also see *Walk 6: Downtown* in DIRECTIONS.)

NEW ENGLAND AQUARIUM One of the world's top collections of marine life—more than 2,000 species in all—it houses exhibits re-creating a tide pool, northern waters, and tropical marine environments. Of particular note is the four-story saltwater tank, girded by a spiral viewing ramp from which visitors can view the resident sharks, sea turtles, moray eels, and wide variety of fish. Divers regularly feed the underwater multitudes so they don't dine on each other. Penguins cavort in their own habitat, and seals and dolphins perform aboard the floating pavilion *Discovery,* next door to the main building. Films are shown in the auditorium, and there's an interesting gift shop. Open daily. Admission charge except for children under three and on Thursdays after 3 PM. Central Wharf, Waterfront (phone: 973-5200).

BOSTON TEA PARTY SHIP AND MUSEUM Board the *Brig Beaver II,* a full-size working replica of one of the three original ships at the Boston Tea Party, and throw a little tea into Boston Harbor. The adjacent museum houses documents relevant to the period as well as films and related exhibits. Open daily March through mid-December. Admission charge. Congress Street Bridge at Fort Point Channel (phone: 338-1773).

CHILDREN'S MUSEUM Formerly an old woolens warehouse, this kid-pleasing place has a number of hands-on exhibits, including *Grandmother's Attic,* a petting zoo, and an assembly line that teaches children how a factory operates. Open Tuesdays through Sundays; closed Mondays except during school holiday weeks and between July 1 and *Labor Day.* Admission charge. 300 Congress St., *Museum Wharf* (phone: 426-8855).

COMPUTER MUSEUM The first and only one of its kind in the US, this museum harbors several floors of gadgetry, interactive exhibits, and educational programs that trace the history and the future of what is probably the 20th century's greatest contribution to technology. A veritable circus of computerized equipment performs dazzling feats: coloring a map of the US at your verbal command, providing your piano playing with the appropriate orchestral accompaniment, even altering the contours of your face on screen. A walk-through computer allows a visitor to examine a computer's components from the inside bit by bit (or is that byte by byte?). Open daily in July and August; closed Mondays the rest of the year. Admission charge; free for children under four. Half price on Saturdays before noon. Within sight of the *Boston Tea Party Ship* at 300 Congress St., *Museum Wharf* (phone: 426-2800 or 423-6758).

BEACON HILL

Here is the heart of old Boston, including the *State House* and Mt. Vernon Street, with its stately old townhouses that were (and still are) the pride of the first families of Boston. The cobblestone Acorn Street, parallel to Mt. Vernon and Chestnut Streets, is the most photographed street in town. (Also see *Walk 5: Beacon Hill* in DIRECTIONS.)

BLACK HERITAGE TRAIL This 1.6-mile walking tour explores the history of Boston's black community throughout the 18th and 19th centuries. Free guided tours, led by *National Park Service* rangers, pass 14 sites of historic importance on Beacon Hill, including the *African Meeting House,* the oldest black church in the country, and the homes of well-known abolitionists. (The tour also may be self-guided; pick up the brochure from the *National Park Service Visitor Center* at 15 State St. or 46 Joy St.) Guided tours begin in front of the *State House* at the corner of Beacon and Park Streets, at the *Robert Gould Shaw Memorial.* The memorial honors the first US black regiment, which served under Shaw during the Civil War. Tours are conducted daily from *Memorial Day* through *Labor Day;* by appointment at other times of the year. Registration is not required, but it's advisable to call ahead (phone: 742-5415).

STATE HOUSE Designed by Charles Bulfinch, the gold-domed *State House* dates from 1795. Oliver Wendell Holmes (the author and doctor, not his son, the justice) remarked that the "Boston State House is the hub of the solar system," a remark that spawned the city's nickname, "the Hub." The original *State House* building is the ornate, red brick structure with white marble trim and a great golden dome. The various wings-come-lately are uninspired afterthoughts by comparison. If you squint just right you can block them out of view and see the building as James Monroe did in 1817. The president was so impressed that he put Bulfinch in charge of the reconstruction of the nation's *Capitol* in Washington, DC, where the architect repeated the rotunda and dome motif. Some final notes about the dome: Its original whitewashed shingles were replaced with copper in 1802 by a Grand Master of the Masons, a fellow by the name of Paul Revere. Gold leaf was added to the dome in 1866, though it was painted gray during World War II to hide the building from possible Axis bomb attacks. Enter through the side door of the right wing (the main door is hardly ever used). Pick up informational pamphlets or join a guided tour in *Doric Hall,* which features busts, statues, memorials, and paintings of famous Americans. Also worth a visit are *Memorial Hall* (also known as the *Hall of Flags*), the *Chamber of the House of Representatives,* the *Senate Chamber,* the *Senate Reception Room,* and a library (phone: 727-2590). Closed weekends. No admission charge. On Beacon St. facing the entrance to the *Common* (phone: 727-3676).

BOSTON ATHENAEUM One of the oldest libraries in the country, founded in 1807, is now housed here. This five-story National Historic Landmark building (the first three floors date from 1847–49; the top two from 1913–15) is a temple to civility. From its marble, mahogany, and ornate table lamps to its endless sea of volumes, the *Athenaeum* has the feel of a study in a colonial mansion, sumptuous yet studious. Once an art gallery whose exhibits were the foundation of the collection that became the *Museum of Fine Arts,* the *Athenaeum* still has a permanent collection of American and European works and displays the works of local artists and artisans in its second-floor gallery. In addition, it contains more than 600,000 titles, including the *King's Chapel Library* collection, sent in 1698 by England's William III; works from the *John Quincy Adams Library;* and part of George Washington's personal library. Look for a book written by Oliver Wendell Holmes, a former member of the *Athenaeum,* that has been edited in spots with a pen. The author, it is said, made a couple of later-than-last-minute corrections while leafing through the volume on a visit to the library. Asked why a visitor to the city should come here, a library administrator said it all: "Because it's just so darned Bostonian." Guided tours of the library are given Tuesday and Thursday afternoons (reservations necessary). At other times, the library is open only to members, scholars, and qualified researchers. There's no admission charge. 10½ Beacon St. (phone: 227-0270).

MT. VERNON STREET Henry James once called it the "only respectable street in America." This Beacon Hill street, which runs from behind the *State House* to Charles Street and beyond, is lined with homes that have rich historical associations—and owners. Look for the famous brass knockers, the charming carriage houses, and the intimate backyard gardens. A few blocks down is Louisburg Square, a rectangle of terribly proper houses facing a tiny park that was once home to Louisa May Alcott and Jenny Lind. The most history-intensive part of this area is between Louisburg Square and Joy Street, where you will find the *Nichols House Museum,* the only Beacon Hill home open to the public. Open Mondays, Wednesdays, and Saturdays from 1 to 5 PM in summer; hours vary during other seasons. Admission charge. 55 Mt. Vernon St. (phone: 227-6993).

CHARLES STREET Beacon Hill's one true commercial street stretches from Beacon Street to Cambridge Street. The street began as a seawall; before the Back Bay was filled in, Charles Street marked Beacon Hill's western shoreline, where tides rose nearly 15 feet. Along with lower Chestnut Street, Charles Street today forms Beacon Hill's "Antiques Row" and is home to a number of restaurants, shops, and pubs. The street's most interesting building, the *Charles Street Meeting House,* was built in 1807 as a Baptist church (it has since been converted into retail space). George Grant, the first black graduate of *Harvard* and the inventor of the wooden golf tee, lived at 108 Charles Street. (Also see *Antiques: Boston's Best Hunting Grounds* in DIVERSIONS.)

NORTH END

The *Paul Revere House* and *Old North Church* are both snugly tucked away among the narrow red brick streets of the North End, a colorful, Italian-American community with a lively street life and some excellent little restaurants (see *Eating Out*). To experience *la dolce vita,* stop at the *Caffè Dello Sport* (308 Hanover St.; phone: 523-5063) for cannoli, cappuccino, and good people watching. (Also see *Walk 7: North End* in DIRECTIONS.)

PAUL REVERE HOUSE Home to the legendary Revolutionary War hero, this is the oldest wooden house in Boston. Revere moved here in 1770 with his wife, mother, and five children. He had eleven more children with his second wife, which is why his house was the only one on the block that didn't have to quarter British soldiers. On the night of April 18, 1775, after getting the nod from Joseph Warren in Boston that British troops were moving (British troops had already mustered in North Square), Revere quietly slipped into his house to change into his boots. From here he was rowed by friends across the Charles River, within sight of a British gunship. Borrowing a horse from Deacon John Larkin in Charlestown, the silversmith-cum-patriot galloped off on the ride that earned him a permanent place in American history. William Dawes and Samuel Prescott also rode forth with the news (as did many other area patriots). Although Revere completed his mission, which was to bring word to the town of Lexington, he decided to ride on to Concord; on the way he was captured by the British, questioned, then released. The exhibits inside the house, which include Revere's saddlebags, revolver, portraits, and the account of the ride in his own words, are sure to clear up some misconceptions about the man and his famous ride. Closed Mondays January through March; open daily except major holidays the rest of the year. Admission charge. 19 North Sq. (phone: 523-2338 or 523-1676).

OLD NORTH CHURCH Affectionately known as "Old North," this structure, built in 1723, is officially named *Christ Church.* On the night of April 18, 1775, sexton Robert Newman hung two lanterns outside to warn Bostonians that the British were coming by sea. His action and Paul Revere's famous ride were later immortalized by Henry Wadsworth Longfellow's poem. (The line you will want to remember is: "One if by land, two if by sea.") The church's original clock still ticks in the back, and services are still held every Sunday. Open daily. 193 Salem St. (phone: 523-6676). (Also see *Historic Churches* in DIVERSIONS.)

BLACKSTONE BLOCK On the other side of the expressway, near *City Hall,* the city's first commercial district was named after Boston's first settler, William Blaxton (or Blackstone). Though most of the original 17th-century dwellings are gone, several from the 18th century remain, including the *Union Oyster House* restaurant (41 Union St.; phone: 227-2750) and the *Ebenezer Hancock House* (10 Marshall St.). Ebenezer's brother, John Hancock, actually owned the building; Ebenezer lived there from 1764 to 1785. As paymaster of the colonial troops, Ebenezer kept in the basement the two million silver crowns sent by France to help pay the Revolutionary troops (a deal artfully crafted by Benjamin Franklin). The *Boston Stone,* a millstone brought from England by a painter in the 1600s, is set in the foundation of a shop on Marshall Street. Originally used to grind colored powder into paint, it became to Boston what its counterpart, the London stone, was to that city—the official point from which all distances from Boston were measured. In back of the block is Blackstone Street, a malodorous thoroughfare that should be avoided except on Fridays and Saturdays, when it is the site of *Haymarket,* the city's colorful outdoor produce market. Just north of *Faneuil Hall.* (Also see *Walk 7: North End* in DIRECTIONS.)

BACK BAY

Arlington is the first of an alphabetically ordered series of streets created when the Back Bay was filled in during the mid-1800s. Broad streets and avenues were laid out in an orderly fashion, and along them wealthy Bostonians built palatial homes, churches, and public institutions. This area is a joy to walk and gives a better feeling of Victorian Boston than any other part of the city. (Also see *Walk 3: Back Bay* in DIRECTIONS.)

PUBLIC GARDEN A gem among city parks and a Boston treasure since 1861, the garden has fountains, formal gardens, and a variety of native and European trees that are labeled for identification. Abundant flowers grow along the garden's many footpaths and in plots near the Arlington Street entrance. The carefully tended beds are changed with the seasons—the spring tulips are particular favorites among locals and visitors alike. The flowers are not the only providers of color here: From the dark suits of the financiers en route between office and home to the brilliant hues of the tie-dyed T-shirts worn and sold here in summer, the *Public Garden* attracts an array of humanity that represents all of Boston. Treat yourself to a ride on the fabled, pedal-driven Swan Boats, which leisurely cruise the pond, past the geese and ducks on the lagoon. Rides are offered daily, from mid-April to mid-September except on extremely windy or rainy days. There's a fee for rides; group rates are available. Whether boating or walking, you may want to bring bread scraps for the resident ducks. In the winter, hardy locals tour the lagoon on ice skates. Adjacent to *Boston Common,* bordered by Beacon, Charles, Boylston, and Arlington Sts. (phone: 522-1966). (Also see *Quintessential Boston* in DIVERSIONS.)

COMMONWEALTH AVENUE Intended to replicate the broad boulevards of 19th-century Paris, with their stately, mansard-roofed homes, Commonwealth Avenue ("Comm. Ave." to the locals) has fulfilled its early promise. Stroll down the shady mall, with its statues of famous Bostonians. In April, the magnolias are magnificent. On the corner of Clarendon Street stands the *First Baptist Church,* a splendid Romanesque structure designed by H. H. Richardson and completed in 1872. Open Tuesdays through Fridays, 11 AM to 2 PM, or by prior arrangement. No admission charge. 110 Commonwealth Ave. (phone: 267-3148).

ESPLANADE This strip of parkland runs between Storrow Drive and the Charles River in the vicinity of Back Bay. Formerly just a 2-mile walkway, it was expanded into a park with money donated by Mrs. James Storrow, widow of a wealthy Boston banker. A plush, clean, and relatively safe stretch of parkland, it is a convenient place for runners, bikers, roller skaters, and the rest of the Back Bay cardiovascular crowd—not to mention sunbathers. Several footbridges lead to the *Esplanade* from the Back Bay, over Storrow Drive, where Bostonians display their maniacal driving habits. (Also see *Quintessential Boston* in DIVERSIONS.)

COPLEY SQUARE Seagoing vessels used to drop anchor in Copley Square; now it harbors Richardson's magnificent 19th-century *Trinity Church,* where there are free organ recitals every Friday at noon (phone: 536-0944). A perfect reflection of the church can be seen in the blue glass façade of the *John Hancock Tower,* a mirrored marvel designed by I. M. Pei that contains more than 13 acres of glass. When the building opened in 1975, the glass windows began popping out, much to the alarm of pedestrians who had to traverse the streets below. Just as all the glass was finally replaced, employees in the upper floors complained of a terrifying sway when the wind blew. The building underwent a massive shoring up, but the saga continued when the construction of the tower was found to have done serious structural damage to the beloved *Trinity Church.* Nonetheless, the *Tower's* 60th floor *Observatory* offers spectacular views of the city and beyond (see *Seeing the City*). Across Dartmouth Street from the square is the main branch of the *Boston Public Library,* the oldest municipally supported library in the country (it was founded in 1852). Completed in 1895, the building is considered one of the first outstanding examples of the Renaissance Beaux Arts style in the US. The huge bronze doors just inside the outer doors were created by Daniel Chester French, sculptor of the *Lincoln Memorial.* But the oldest section is under renovation (scheduled to continue until the end of the century), so visitors must enter through the blocky new addition, designed by Philip Johnson and built in 1972. Step inside the Copley Square entrance for a quiet moment in the library's lovely central courtyard. Closed Sundays (phone: 536-5400). Also on Dartmouth Street (on the other side of Huntington Ave.) is *Copley Place* (phone: 375-4400), a complex of hotels, fashionable shops (*Neiman Marcus, Tiffany, Godiva Chocolatiers,* and the like), restaurants, an 11-screen movie theater (phone: 266-1300), and an indoor waterfall.

NEWBURY STREET This is where fashionable Bostonians shop. There are many art galleries and boutiques, as well as a variety of restaurants and several outdoor cafés. Is all begins, sedately enough, where Arlington Street borders the *Public Garden* and the *Ritz* and the *Giorgio Armani* store hold sway. (Just one block away from the *Ritz,* at the end of Boylston Street, is the *Heritage on the Garden* complex, which has high-end, international stores, such as *Escada, Hermès,* and *Waterford-Wedgwood.* Here's where you also find *Biba,* one of Boston's trendiest restaurants, and *The Spa* at the *Heritage,* the perfect antidote to a hard day of shopping.) But continue down Newbury Street to Massachusetts Avenue and the boutiques gradually give way, ending in the mammoth *Tower Records* and the outrageous *Allston Beat.*

NEW ENGLAND HISTORIC GENEALOGICAL SOCIETY Since Bostonians are extremely curious about their lineage, it is fitting that one of the country's most exhaustive collections of family history is located here. The collection, which covers primarily the 17th through 19th centuries, includes 17th-century diaries and journals documenting the lives of New Englanders, and some documentation on other parts of the US and Canada. Closed Sundays and Mondays. There's no admission fee to look around; there is a small fee for using the society's research facilities. 101 Newbury St. (phone: 536-5740).

INSTITUTE OF CONTEMPORARY ART Exciting contemporary artwork by local artists as well as touring exhibitions in several media can be seen at the *ICA,* one of Boston's most important showplaces. An interesting film series is shown in the gallery, which was converted from a 19th-century police station. Open Wednesdays through Sundays. Admission charge. 955 Boylston St. (phone: 266-5151/2).

KENMORE SQUARE Formerly a fashionable area, this square is now notorious for traffic jams and college students (*Fenway Park* and *Boston University* are nearby). A cherished Boston landmark, the *Citgo* sign, has evaded demolition several times and it looks as if it is here to stay. Except when it was turned off during the energy-conservation drive of the late 1970s, it has splashed Kenmore Square with blue, white, and red lights for decades.

THE FENWAY

Some of the city's finest medical, educational, and cultural institutions are located in this former marshland in southwest Boston. The *Museum of Fine Arts* and the *Isabella Stewart Gardner Museum* are located on *The Fens,* as are *Simmons College, Emmanuel College,* and branches of *Northeastern University. Symphony Hall,* home of the *Boston Symphony Orchestra* and the *Boston Pops Orchestra,* is here as well, and the *New England Conservatory of Music* and *Harvard Medical School* (located in the world-renowned Longwood Medical Area) are nearby. (Also see *Walk 1: The Fens* in DIRECTIONS.)

THE FENS PARK Landscape designer Frederick Law Olmsted crafted this serene park out of mud flats, while preserving some of the area's original environment. In this 12-acre, marshy park are footbridges, statuary, reed-bound pools, rows of magnolias, a rose garden, community gardens, and a running path, all surrounded by the still-marshy Fens.

MUSEUM OF FINE ARTS This is one of the world's great art museums, with comprehensive exhibits from every major period and in every conceivable medium. Noteworthy are the collection of Impressionist paintings (with more Monets than anywhere outside Paris); the decorative arts and sculpture from the colonial period to the present; an outstanding assemblage of Egyptian art; the greatest collection of Asiatic art under one roof; an exhaustive gathering of American art, including numerous works by Homer, Copley, Sargent, and Hopper; and an impressive classical collection with artifacts from the

6th, 5th, and 4th centuries BC, and the early Roman Imperial period. The wares of silversmiths on display at the *MFA* will prove that the patriot Paul Revere had many valuable talents on top of riding fast on a horse and disturbing the peace. The main building was built in 1909; the airy West Wing, designed by renowned architect I. M. Pei, was added in 1981. It houses additional exhibition space, as well as a cafeteria, restaurant, café, and museum shop; special shows are often mounted here. Outside is the *Tenshin Garden,* which features New England flora and Japanese landscape design. Closed Mondays, open late Wednesdays (certain wings also open late Thursdays and Fridays). Admission charge except Wednesdays from 4 to 6 PM. Directly in back of *The Fens,* 465 Huntington Ave. (phone: 267-9300).

ISABELLA STEWART GARDNER MUSEUM This marble Venetian palazzo houses one of the world's magnificent private art collections. Isabella Stewart came to Boston in 1860 to marry John Lowell Gardner, a wealthy Brahmin industrialist. While she was a friend of some of the most famous folks of the era—art critic Bernard Berenson advised her on her collection, and artist John Singer Sargent painted her portrait—her flashy dress and spirited manner quickly made her suspect in the eyes of most proper Bostonians. The art Gardner collected during her worldwide travels is housed in a 15th-century–style Italianate mansion, built between 1899 and 1903, that remains furnished as it was during her lifetime. As a result, objects with as much sentimental as aesthetic value are exhibited next to several Rembrandts, Titian's *Rape of Europa,* a number of Tintorettos, Manets, Botticellis, Whistlers, and one Corot. (Because the art is arranged haphazardly and the museum signs and labels are not particularly detailed, it's a good idea to purchase the museum guide, sold at the main entrance.) When your feet are tired, you can take lunch or tea at a pleasant café on the premises. Every Sunday and Tuesday afternoon, except during the summer, the museum hosts classical concerts. Closed Mondays. No admission charge for children under 12. 280 The Fenway (phone: 566-1401 or 734-1359 for concert information). (Also see *Walk 1: The Fens* in DIRECTIONS and *Quintessential Boston* in DIVERSIONS.)

SOUTH END

Though it contains few recognizable tourist attractions, this reclaimed wetland is interesting for its beautiful architecture and its ethnic diversity. (Also see *Walk 2: South End* in DIRECTIONS.)

THE FIRST CHURCH OF CHRIST, SCIENTIST, IN BOSTON (CHRISTIAN SCIENCE CHURCH WORLD HEADQUARTERS) The world headquarters of the religion founded in the 19th century by the American religious reformer Mary Baker Eddy, this 15-acre complex houses several interesting attractions. Mrs. Eddy's original granite *First Church of Christ, Scientist,* built in 1894, is visible, although enveloped by an overpowering Byzantine and Renaissance edifice erected in 1906. The rectangular reflecting pool, tucked between two modern buildings designed by I. M. Pei, is good for a quiet walk and a view of the Boston skyline. Most interesting is the *Mapparium,* a 30-foot stained glass globe built in 1935 (and reflecting the world as it was in 1935, with only 70 countries), through which you walk on a glass bridge that is also an echo chamber. The *Mapparium* is located in the *Christian Science Publishing Society Building,* the editorial home of the *Christian Science Monitor,* a newspaper with a truly global focus. The *Mapparium* is closed Sundays and Mondays June through mid-October and Saturdays through Mondays mid-October through May. Tours of the complex are available. Massachusetts and Huntington Aves. (phone: 450-3790).

SOUTHWEST CORRIDOR This pleasant, well-manicured footpath stretches from the Back Bay station on the *Orange Line* (just behind *Neiman Marcus*) to Massachusetts Avenue and beyond, affording a leisurely sampling of South End architecture, good people watching, and a view of Boston's skyline.

UNION PARK A residential block of Victorian townhouses that were among the first built during the mid-19th-century development of the South End, this is many Bostonians' favorite spot in the Hub. There are fountains, foliage, and a strip of greenery dividing the two rows of houses that give this pocket of civility a quiet, lazy feel. It is studded with magnolias during the summer months.

CHARLESTOWN

The Puritans first settled here in 1629 in their quest for a "city upon a hill." Charlestown's Breed's Hill was thought to be just fine, until a scarcity of safe drinking water forced the settlers to cultivate the marshy peninsula to the south that became Boston. The Battle of Bunker Hill was fought here, and Monument Hill and Winthrop Square are laced with excellent examples of 18th- and 19th-century architecture. City Square is where Paul Revere began his famed midnight ride. Nearby are the *Charlestown Navy Yard* and the USS *Constitution.*

BUNKER HILL MONUMENT This 221-foot granite obelisk was built in the 1800s to mark the site of the first major battle of the Revolutionary War. On June 17, 1775, on this hill overlooking the Boston Harbor, the British won the Battle of Bunker Hill—but hundreds of their soldiers were killed or wounded. Climb the 294 steps to the top of the monument (there's no elevator), or visit the information center below, which has exhibits and dioramas on the battle and the monument. Open daily; no admission charge. On Breed's Hill, in the center of town off Monument Square (phone: 242-5641).

USS CONSTITUTION This it the famous "Old Ironsides," the oldest commissioned ship in the US Navy and proud victor in 40 sea battles. An adjacent shoreside museum (phone: 426-1812) displays related memorabilia and a slide show. City Square bus stop. Open daily. Admission charge for museum; none for the *Constitution. Charlestown Navy Yard,* Charlestown (phone: 242-5670).

BUNKER HILL PAVILION Witness a vivid multimedia reenactment of the Battle of Bunker Hill on 14 screens, with seven sound channels. Open daily, with shows every half hour from April through December. Admission charge. Adjacent to USS *Constitution* (phone: 241-7575).

CAMBRIDGE

HARVARD SQUARE Just across the Charles River from Boston, Cambridge has always had an ambience all its own. Catering to the academic and professional communities, the square is a lively, "upscale" combination of the trendy and the traditional. It has the greatest concentration of bookstores in the country, many of which are open until late into the evening; movie options that range from vintage films to the latest from Hollywood and abroad; and the ever-present street musicians. When hunger pangs strike, everything from muffins to nouvelle cuisine awaits—with an authentic Italian ice to top it off. Take the *Red Line* toward Alewife and get off at the Harvard Square stop.

HARVARD YARD This tree-filled enclave is the focal point of the oldest (1636) and most prestigious university in the country (the *Law School* is nearby, the *Business School* just across the river, and the *Medical School* a bus ride away in Boston). Notice especially *Massachusetts Hall* (1720; *Harvard*'s oldest building), Charles Bulfinch's *University Hall,* and, in the adjoining quadrangle, *Widener Library* and H. H. Richardson's *Sever Hall.* Campus tours are given year-round; check at the information office in *Holyoke Center* (phone: 495-1573).

WEEKS MEMORIAL BRIDGE This graceful footbridge was built to link *Harvard*'s Cambridge campus with the school's *Graduate School of Business Administration,* on the Boston side. It offers a splendid view of the white, crimson, and gold *Harvard* steeples and the *Harvard* crew team's practices on the Charles River.

HARVARD UNIVERSITY ART MUSEUMS *Harvard*'s impressive collection of paintings, drawings, prints, sculpture, and silver is housed in three fine museums. The *Arthur Sackler Museum* (485 Broadway) houses ancient Roman, Egyptian, and Islamic antiquities, as well as traveling exhibitions, in a 1985 post-modern building designed by James Stirling. Nearby is the neo-Georgian building of the *Fogg Museum* (32 Quincy St.), which features European and American art from the Middle Ages to the present. Connected to the *Fogg* is the *Busch-Reisinger Museum,* the only museum in the US that specializes in the art of Germanic language–speaking countries. All three are closed Mondays and charge admission (phone: 495-9400).

HARVARD UNIVERSITY MUSEUMS On a short block parallel to Oxford Street is this complex housing the *Comparative Zoology, Peabody, Mineralogical and Geological,* and *Botanical* museums. The *Peabody* houses extensive anthropological and archaeological collections, with an emphasis on South

American Indians, as well as a fine gift shop. The *Botanical* houses a famous collection of glass flowers handmade for *Harvard* between 1887 and 1936 by Leopold and Rudolph Blaschka, a German father and son, and renowned for their scientific accuracy as well as their beauty. Renowned *Harvard* professor Stephen Jay Gould often lectures at *Comparative Zoology,* a natural history museum, and the *Mineralogical and Geological Museum* displays rocks of all kinds. Reservations must be made for either group (phone: 495-2341) or individual (phone: 495-3045) tours for any of the museums. Open daily. Admission charge except on Saturdays from 9 to 11 AM. 26 Oxford St. (phone: 495-2341).

RADCLIFFE YARD One of the Seven Sister colleges, *Radcliffe* has evolved from its historical role as "*Harvard*'s Annex" to its current position, with its under-graduates fully integrated with *Harvard*'s. *Radcliffe* offers alternative programs for women at the graduate level and those interested in career changes. Its *Schlesinger Library* has one of the country's top collections on the history of women in America, as well as an important culinary collection. Closed weekends. No admission charge. 3 James St. (phone: 495-8647).

OLD BURYING GROUND This historic cemetery, also known as *God's Acre,* is on Garden Street just past *Christ Church.* The graves date back to 1635, and a number of Revolutionary War heroes and *Harvard* presidents are buried here. On the Garden Street fence, there's a mileage marker dating to 1754.

BRATTLE STREET This elegant Cambridge street was known in the 1770s as "Tory Row" because seven mansions owned by supporters of King George were located here (a couple still stand today). William Brattle, a Loyalist who fled Boston in 1774, lived at 42 Brattle, an 18th-century gambrel-roofed Colonial home that later became the home of Margaret Fuller, an early feminist. The building is now the headquarters of the *Cambridge Center for Adult Education* (phone: 547-6789). The yellow clapboard *Pratt House* at No. 56 is where Dexter Pratt, Longfellow's "Village Blacksmith," lived and plied his trade. It now houses the tiny *Blacksmith House Café and Bakery* (phone: 354-3036). Though the "spreading chestnut tree" that Longfellow referred to is long gone, a plaque on the corner of Brattle and Story Streets preserves its memory. Longfellow lived just down the street from 1837 until his death in 1882. That house (105 Brattle St.; phone: 876-4491), built in 1759, served as the headquarters for General Washington during the British siege of Boston. Concerts are now held there in summer, and guided tours are available. It's open daily; there's an admission charge.

MASSACHUSETTS INSTITUTE OF TECHNOLOGY The foremost scientific and technological school in the country, *MIT* opened its doors in Boston in 1865 and moved across the river to its present Cambridge campus in 1916. In addition to its world-famous laboratories and graduate schools in engineering and science, its professional schools include the *Sloan School of Management,* the *Joint Center for Urban Studies* (with *Harvard*), and the

School of Architecture. Architect I. M. Pei is an alumnus; next to his *Green Building* for the earth sciences stands Calder's stabile *The Big Sail,* one of a superb collection of outdoor sculptures on the campus. Also worth noting are Eero Saarinen's chapel and his *Kresge Auditorium,* just across from the main entrance on Massachusetts Avenue. The main *MIT Museum* (265 Massachusetts Ave.; phone: 253-4429 or 253-4444) contains permanent collections and changing exhibits of contemporary art and technology. Closed Mondays; admission charge. The *Compton Gallery* (77 Massachusetts Ave.; phone: 258-9118) features changing technical exhibitions. Closed weekends; no admission charge. The *Wiesner Building* (20 Ames St.; phone: 253-4680) is another I. M. Pei landmark, worth a visit for its arresting interior and the often provocative changing exhibitions. The *List Visual Arts Center* is located in this building. Open daily; no admission charge (phone: 253-4680). *MIT* campus tours are given year-round on weekdays at 10 AM and 2 PM. *Red Line,* Kendall Square/MIT stop, or No. 1 Dudley bus, headed toward Harvard Square. 77 Massachusetts Ave. (phone: 253-4795).

MT. AUBURN CEMETERY The first garden cemetery in the United States, this rural retreat in the midst of Cambridge is bliss to the senses. Founded in 1831, *Mt. Auburn*'s 170 beautifully landscaped acres include hills, ponds, more than 3,500 magnificent trees (including 575 varieties), and an observation tower. An hour's stroll here might be the pinnacle of a sightseeing day—especially for bird watchers. Among the many famous people buried here are Mary Baker Eddy, Henry Wadsworth Longfellow, Julia Ward Howe, Oliver Wendell Holmes, and Winslow Homer. Open daily during daylight; tower open in fair weather from early spring to late fall. Stop for a map at the north entrance. 580 Mt. Auburn St. (phone: 547-7105).

OTHER SPECIAL PLACES

CHINATOWN This neighborhood has one of the largest Chinese-American populations in the country. Tucked between the *Combat Zone* (the city's rapidly shrinking enclave of pornography shops, clubs, and theaters), the leather merchants' district, and the Southeast Expressway, Chinatown is a pocket of faithfully preserved Chinese culture. There are frequent festivals in celebration of Chinese holidays, including a big bash for *Chinese New Year* (see *Special Events*). This is an interesting place for strolling, although most visitors are attracted by Chinatown's many restaurants, which garner most of the city's late-night business. Try *Ho Yuen Ting* (13A Hudson St.; phone: 426-2316) or *Chau Chow* (52 Beach St.; phone: 426-6266) for excellent Cantonese food served with minimal fuss and minimalist decor. The latter stays open until 4 AM on weekends. The best approach to the neighborhood is through the Chinese arch at the head of Beach Street, where it meets Atlantic Avenue.

JOHN F. KENNEDY LIBRARY Designed by architect I. M. Pei, this presidential library sits on the edge of a point of land projecting into Dorchester Bay, with a magnificent view of the Boston skyline and out to sea. There's an exhibit of documents, photographs, films, and memorabilia that may conjure up a bit of nostalgia even if you voted for Nixon. JFK's famed rocking chair is here, as are the desk at which he presided over nearly three years as president and the documents of the Kennedy administration. The museum also houses a section devoted to Robert F. Kennedy and, by special arrangement, the papers of Ernest Hemingway, which occupy an entire floor. Open daily except major holidays. Admission charge for adults; children under 16 free. By car, take the Southeast Expressway south to the JFK Library/UMass exit. Or take the *MBTA Red Line* (Ashmont train to the JFK/UMass stop; a shuttle bus will take you the rest of the way). Off Morrissey Blvd., next to the *University of Massachusetts* campus, in Dorchester (phone: 929-4567).

COMMONWEALTH MUSEUM Next door to the *John F. Kennedy Library,* this museum has audiovisual presentations on the history of the people, places, and politics of Massachusetts. The state archives are also stored here; several are always on a rotating display. Closed Sundays. No admission charge. 220 Morrissey Blvd. (phone: 727-9268).

MUSEUM OF SCIENCE AND THE CHARLES HAYDEN PLANETARIUM Sitting astride the Charles River Dam and overlooking its boat docks is a cluster of modern buildings that make up one of Boston's greatest educational institutions. The *Museum of Science* includes over 400 interactive exhibits covering every aspect of science from medicine to geology to space exploration. Old favorites include the "Transparent Woman," whose internal organs light up as their functions are explained; the lightning exhibition, where lightning—and a resulting clap of thunder—is created before your very eyes; and the *Charles Hayden Planetarium.* The planetarium features a $2-million Zeiss planetarium projector and a multi-image program on cosmic discoveries, as well as laser light shows with computer animation and brilliant laser graphics. At the museum's *Omni Theater,* a 70-foot domed screen envelops the viewer in the ultimate film experience. The museum has a wonderful gift shop and a couple of cafeterias. Take the *MBTA Green Line* to *Science Park.* Closed Mondays. Admission charge for the museum; additional charge for the *Omni Theater;* advance reservations are advised for the *Omni Theater. Science Park,* on O'Brien Hwy. at the eastern end of Storrow Dr. (phone: 723-2500).

ARNOLD ARBORETUM Contained in these 265 acres of beautifully landscaped woodland and park are over 14,000 trees, shrubs, and vines, most of them labeled by their assiduous *Harvard* caretakers. The visitors' center shop has a large selection of books on botany and horticulture. Open daily, sunrise to sunset. No admission charge. By car, the main gate and visitors' center are 100 yards south of the rotary junction of Routes 1 and 203. Or take the *E* train (*Green Line*), the Arborway bus No. 39 from the Copley Square stop, or the *Orange Line,* Forest Hills stop. Six miles southwest of downtown Boston on The Arborway, Jamaica Plain (phone: 524-1717/8). (Also see *Quintessential Boston* in DIVERSIONS.)

FRANKLIN PARK ZOO The highlight of this facility is an exciting rain forest exhibit in which jungle animals prowl in areas resembling their natural habitats. In the middle of the huge, climate-controlled, hangar-like structure is the gorilla area, where six mountain gorillas frolic over the rocky terrain and where birds fly free (sort of) under the soaring roof. Other animals—dwarf forest buffalos, crocodiles, a dwarf hippo, storks, and even scorpions—roam in a separate space; the zoo also boasts four waterfalls and the largest collection of tropical plants in New England. Other sections include *Bird's World, Hooves and Horns,* and a *Children's Zoo.* Open daily; admission charge except on Tuesdays after noon. Take Route 1 (VFW Parkway) to Route 203 East, or take Bus No. 16 from the Forest Hills stop on the *Orange Line* or the Andrew stop on the *Red Line.* Rte. 203, *Franklin Park,* Dorchester (phone: 442-4896 or 442-2002).

FREDERICK LAW OLMSTED NATIONAL HISTORIC SITE This house was occupied by Olmsted, the premier 19th-century landscape designer, and his two sons after the death of his wife. Best known as the designer of New York City's *Central Park,* Olmsted also designed Boston's 8-mile *Emerald Necklace* of green spaces, which ties the city to the suburbs. Tours are conducted of the house and of the grounds, which illustrate the principles of Olmsted's designs, and archives on the site include plans, drawings, and photographs of his work. Open Fridays through Sundays from 10 AM to 4:30 PM. No admission charge. 99 Warren St., Brookline (phone: 566-1689).

Sources and Resources

TOURIST INFORMATION

For tourist information, maps, and brochures, visit the visitors' information center at *Boston Common.* It's open daily. The *Boston Convention and Tourist Bureau* (*Prudential Center*; phone: 536-4100) has multilingual maps and brochures and is open daily. The *Massachusetts Office of Travel and Tourism* (100 Cambridge St.; phone: 727-3201) also can provide maps, calendars of events, health updates, travel advisories, and other tourist information; it's open weekdays. Another good source is the *Boston National Historical Park Downtown Visitors Center* (15 State St.; phone: 242-5642), located across from the *Old State House,* which has maps, brochures, books, and a slide show on the historic sites of Boston. In addition, park rangers here answer questions, offer advice, and lead walking tours. It's open daily.

The 24-hour *Visitor's Channel* of the Panorama Television Network, Channel 12 on local hotel television sets, provides weather updates every

15 minutes as well as travel advisories, traffic information, and half-hour bulletins on attractions within Boston and day trips outside the city.

LOCAL COVERAGE *Boston Globe,* morning daily; *Boston Herald,* morning daily; *Christian Science Monitor,* weekday mornings; *Boston Phoenix,* weekly; *The Tab,* weekly; *Boston* magazine, monthly; *Bostonia* magazine, quarterly.

Useful guidebooks include *Access Boston* (HarperCollins; $18), *In and Out of Boston (With or Without Children)* by Bernice Chesler (Globe Pequot Press; $15.95), and *Historic Walks in Old Boston* by John Harris (Globe Pequot Press; $12.95). For restaurant listings, see the *1995 Zagat Boston Restaurant Survey* (Zagat Survey, NY; $9.95), or *Robert Nadeau's Guide to Boston Restaurants* by Mark Zanger (World Food Press; $3.95).

TELEVISION STATIONS WBZ Channel 4–NBC; WCVB Channel 5–ABC; WHDH Channel 7–CBS; WGBH Channel 2–PBS; WXNE Channel 25–Fox; WSBK Channel 38; WLVI Channel 56.

RADIO STATIONS AM: WRKO 680 (talk); WHDH 850 (adult contemporary); WBZ 1030 (pop); WEEI 590 (sports). FM: WBUR 90.9 (classical/National Public Radio); WROR 93.5 (pop); WJIB 98 (pop); WFNX 101.7 (contemporary/new wave); WBCN 104.1 (rock/pop).

TELEPHONE The area code for Boston is 617. All numbers listed here are in the 617 area code unless otherwise indicated. *Note:* Some areas surrounding Boston are served by the 508 area code. For further information, see GETTING READY TO GO.

SALES TAX The city sales tax is 5%; there also is a 9.7% hotel tax.

GETTING AROUND

BUS, TROLLEY, AND TRAIN The *Massachusetts Bay Transit Authority (MBTA)* operates a network of trolleys and subways (referred to by locals as "the *T*") with four major lines, the *Red, Blue, Green,* and *Orange.* The *MBTA* also runs the city's bus system. *MBTA* service is fairly frequent during the day, less frequent at night, and nonexistent after about 12:30 AM. *MBTA* stations are marked with large, white circular signs bearing a giant "T." For schedules, directions, timetables, maps, and help in planning travel routes, call the *Travel Information Center* at 722-3200 or 800-392-6100 between 6 AM and 11:30 PM on weekdays and until 9 PM on weekends.

Compared to the mass transit systems in most major American cities, Boston is still a bargain: 60¢ for buses and 85¢ for the *T*. Exact change is required for the buses. Three-day visitors' passes are $9, and seven-day passes are $18. They entitle holders to free rides on all *MBTA* conveyances—trolleys, subways, trains, and buses—and to $50 worth of discounts on entertainment, restaurants, and other attractions around the city.

The *T* is the cheapest and often the fastest way to travel between downtown and the airport. Take the *Blue Line* to the airport stop; from there, a free *MBTA* shuttle bus will take you to your terminal. Warning: Don't try this at rush hour with several suitcases. *MBTA* commuter trains are an excellent way of getting to Boston's suburbs. From *South Station* (Atlantic Ave. at Summer St.; no phone), a gorgeous and sprawling train station inside an ornate 19th-century façade, there are commuter trains to points south and west of Boston, including Framingham, Stoughton, and Providence, Rhode Island. *South Station* is also Boston's link with *Amtrak* (phone: 482-3660), which makes frequent runs to Providence, Rhode Island, Connecticut, and New York City. *North Station* (on Causeway St., just behind the *Boston Garden;* no phone) is the point of departure for commuter trains north and west, including Concord, Gardner, Lowell, Ipswich, and other points on the North Shore.

CAR RENTAL For information on renting a car, see GETTING READY TO GO.

SIGHTSEEING CRUISES *Bay State Cruise Company* (phone: 723-7800) provides service from *Memorial Day* through *Columbus Day* (and sometimes on warm weekends during the winter) out of two locations, Long Wharf and Commonwealth Pier. Boats take passengers on day trips to Georges Island (the site of *Fort Warren,* which was used as a Civil War prison) and the Inner Harbor; to Nantasket Beach and the Outer Harbor; on whale watching trips; and across Cape Cod Bay to Provincetown.

Boston Harbor Cruises (phone: 227-4320) runs whale watches from May through September, and harbor cruises of historical sites from April through mid-October, departing from Long Wharf. It also runs the *Navy Yard* water shuttle to Charlestown year-round. For $1, this is a great way to get from the *Aquarium* to the *Charlestown Navy Yard.*

Massport (phone: 800-235-6426) runs a water shuttle from Rowes Wharf to *Logan Airport* (a seven-minute ride) year-round except Saturdays and holidays.

SIGHTSEEING TOURS Boston's various trolley sightseeing tours have gained a reputation for colorful—albeit not always accurate—information. The major ones are *Old Town Trolley Tours* (phone: 269-7010), fully narrated tours of more than 100 historic Boston sites; *Boston Trolley* (phone: TRO-LLEY; fax: 269-8018), which has a number of boarding and reboarding stops at major Boston hotels; and *Brush Hills Tours/Gray Line Boston* and *Beantown Trolley* (phone: 236-2148; fax: 236-5570). *Sleuth & Company* (phone: 542-2525; fax: 542-3831) offers evening trolley tours built around crimes and misdeeds from the city's past; the tours are narrated by performers who act out the parts of various miscreants. You also can see the city from 500 feet in the air, with *The Boston Helicopter Company* (151 Tremont St.; phone: 800-55-PILOT in Massachusetts; 274-1230 elsewhere in the US; fax: 274-1237), which departs daily from the *Civil Air Terminal* at Hanscom Field in Bedford. For further information on companies offering tours in and around Boston, see GETTING READY TO GO.

TAXI You can hail a taxi on the street, pick one up at a taxi stand downtown, or call *Boston Cab* (phone: 536-5010); *Independent Taxi Operators Association* (phone: 426-8700); *Town Taxi* (phone: 536-5000); *Checker Taxi* (phone: 536-7000); *Yellow Cab* (Cambridge; phone: 547-3000); or *Ambassador/Brattle Taxi* (Cambridge; phone: 492-1100).

COMPUTER GUIDES

Interactive video machines placed on various street corners assist visitors trying to get their bearings. Enter the name of a particular spot in the area or ask for a selection of shops and restaurants, and the machine will display detailed information. Other computer terminals located at *Logan Airport* provide information on cultural and tourist events throughout New England.

LOCAL SERVICES

For information about local services not listed here, call the *Boston Chamber of Commerce* (phone: 227-4500).

AUDIOVISUAL EQUIPMENT *Massachusetts Audio Visual Equipment Co.* (phone: 646-5410).

BABY-SITTING For Boston proper, call *Child Care Choices of Boston* (178 Tremont St.; phone: 357-6020, ext. 17) between 10 AM and 1 PM. For surrounding communities, call *Child Care Resource Center* (552 Massachusetts Ave., Cambridge; phone: 547-9861) or *Parents in a Pinch* (45 Bartlett Crescent, Brookline; phone: 739-5437).

BUSINESS SERVICES *Bette James & Associates* (678 Massachusetts Ave., Cambridge; phone: 661-2622) offers word processing, desktop publishing, mailing, packing and shipping, faxing, and photocopying services. *OfficePlus* (8 *Faneuil Hall Marketplace;* phone: 367-8335) rents office space and provides access to a wide range of office services. *Headquarters Business Centers* (*HQ;* 100 Federal St.; phone: 342-7000) provides word processing, telex and facsimile services, and conference rooms; *Meeting House Offices* (121 Mt. Vernon St.; phone: 367-7171) offers office space and word processing and photocopying services.

DRY CLEANER/TAILOR *Sarni Original Dry Cleaners* has a dozen locations. Try the one at 122 Milk St. (phone 338-9133).

LIMOUSINE *Carey of Boston* (phone: 623-8700); *Classic Limo* (phone: 266-3980); *Waites Transportation, Inc.* (phone: 567-5867 or 567-0420).

MECHANIC Ray Magliozzi (one of the amusing hosts of National Public Radio's "Car Talk"), at the *Good News Garage* (between Central Sq. and MIT at 75 Hamilton St., Cambridge; phone: 354-5383), will repair anything. But fame has its price—namely, $45 an hour.

MEDICAL EMERGENCY For information on area hospitals and pharmacies, see GET-TING READY TO GO.

MESSENGER SERVICES *Beacon Hill Courier Service* (phone: 742-1358); *Boston Cab Association,* 24-hour service (phone: 536-5010); *Central Delivery Service,* 24-hour service (phone: 395-3213); *Town Taxi,* 24-hour service (phone: 536-5000).

PHOTOCOPIES *Copy Cop* has many locations, including 815 Boylston St. (phone: 267-9267) and 85 Franklin St. (phone: 451-0233).

POST OFFICES For information on local branch offices, see GETTING READY TO GO.

PROFESSIONAL PHOTOGRAPHER *Atlantic Photo Service* (669 Boylston St.; phone: 267-7480); *Fay Foto Service* (45 Electric Ave.; phone: 267-2000).

SECRETARY *A-Plus Secretarial Office,* 4 Brattle St., Cambridge (phone: 491-2200).

TELECONFERENCE FACILITIES The *Charles; Colonnade; Hyatt Regency, Cambridge;* the *Marriott* hotels in Cambridge, at *Copley Place* and on Long Wharf; the *Meridien; Omni Parker House;* and the *Royal Sonesta* (see *Checking In*).

TRANSLATOR *Berlitz* (437 Boylston St.; phone: 266-6858); *Boston Language Institute* (636 Beacon St.; phone: 262-3500).

TRAVELER'S CHECKS *American Express* has several offices providing traveler's checks and travel agency services, including those at 1 Court St., Boston (phone: 723-8400); 44 Brattle St., Cambridge (phone: 661-0005); and 55 Boylston St., Chestnut Hill, Newton (phone: 964-0622). *Thomas Cook Currency Services* has offices at 160 Franklin St., Boston (phone: 426-0016); 800 Boylston St., Boston (phone: 247-3121); and 39 JFK St., Cambridge (phone: 868-6605).

WESTERN UNION/TELEX *Western Union* (phone: 800-325-6000 or 268-6700) has offices throughout the city. For information on money transfers, see GET-TING READY TO GO.

SPECIAL EVENTS

The *Chinese New Year* is celebrated annually on every street in Chinatown in January or February, depending on the Chinese calendar. The one-day event, from noon to 6 PM, features a dragon and lion dance, firecrackers, and lots of food. Don't miss the *International Cultural Festival* at the *Ritz-Carlton* (see *Grand Hotels*) from the first week in January through the third week in March, featuring cuisine by various chefs and political and cultural lectures; each week a different country is highlighted. *St. Patrick's Day* and *Evacuation Day* (when the British fled Boston) are both celebrated in South Boston on March 17. *Patriots Day,* featuring a number of parades, reenactments of revolutionary skirmishes, and other events, is observed in and around Boston (in Concord, Lexington, and so on) on the third Monday in April and the weekend before. The *Boston Marathon,* the oldest and most celebrated marathon in the US, is also held that Monday, with the front-runners usually crossing the finish line in Copley Square around 2 PM. The *Big Apple Circus,* sponsored by the *Children's Museum* (phone: 426-8855), comes to town from early April through mid-May, giving two performances daily. *Lilac Sunday,* the annual viewing of over 300 varieties of lilacs at the *Arnold Arboretum* (phone: 524-1717), is held on the third Sunday in May. The *Cambridge International Fair,* a celebration of summer and the arts with theater, dance, music, and food, is held in Central Square in early June (phone: 349-4380). June is also the month of colorful neighborhood street fairs, with the *Back Bay Street Fair* and the *Bay Village Fair* on the first Saturday, and the *St. Botolph Street Fair* in the South End on the third Saturday. The *Boston Globe Jazz Festival* (phone: 929-2651), a week-long series of jazz performances and free midday concerts, is held each year in mid-June, kicking off in the plaza of the *Charles* hotel in Cambridge and concluding at the *Hatch Shell* on the *Esplanade.* Boston is filled with color and pageantry during the annual *Fourth of July* celebrations. On July 4, the waterfront comes alive with *Harborfest,* a series of events on land and water: The Declaration of Independence is read from the balcony of the *Old State House* at 10 AM; the annual turnaround of USS *Constitution,* "Old Ironsides," commences at 10:30 AM; and the *Boston Pops* holds its beloved annual holiday concert at the *Hatch Shell* in the evening, which features a sing-along of all-American favorites and culminates with its rousing rendition of the *1812 Overture* underneath a dazzling display of fireworks (phone: 800-858-0200). North End *Italian Festas,* a series of saint's day celebrations, always begin and end with religious services and processions, and feature a lot of food, games, dancing, and general festivity in between. They are held on nearly every weekend throughout July and August. The oldest American professional tennis championship, the nine-day *US Pro Tennis Championships at Longwood,* begins the third week of July and features many tennis greats (phone: 731-4500). Rowers from around the world and from a variety of American colleges compete in the annual *Head of the Charles Regatta*—which starts on the Charles near the Boston University Bridge and goes upstream to *Harvard* and beyond—on the last Sunday in October. In even-numbered years, the *Harvard-Yale Football Game* is held in Cambridge (phone: 495-2207). Boston's best *Christmas* tradition, the presentation of the *Handel & Haydn Society's Messiah,* is on five evenings in early December (phone: 266-3605). At the *Tea Party Reenactment* (Congress St. Bridge; phone: 338-1773), uniformed participants throw chests of tea off the *Tea Party Ship* on the Sunday closest to December 16. The *First Night Celebration,* a series of musical, culinary, theater, and film events that draws more than 500,000 people to Boston's Back Bay and downtown, is held on *New Year's Eve* (phone: 524-1399).

MUSEUMS

In addition to those described in *Special Places,* other fine museums worth visiting include the following:

BOSTON CENTER FOR THE ARTS This multi-use arts complex occupies an entire block of historic buildings, the highlight of which is the *Cyclorama Building,* built in 1884 to house a 400-foot-long circular painting of the *Battle of Gettysburg* by Paul Philippoteaux, a famed chronicler of the Civil War (the painting is now in Philadelphia). The complex also houses the *Millis* gallery, three theater spaces, and artists' studios. Open Wednesdays through Sundays from noon to 4 PM. No admission charge. 539 Tremont St. (phone: 426-5000 or 426-7700).

CARPENTER CENTER FOR THE VISUAL ARTS Part of *Harvard University,* this is Le Corbusier's only building in the US. Rotating exhibitions and film series are presented throughout the school year. The center is open daily; the *Sert Gallery* on the third floor is open Tuesday through Sunday afternoons. No admission charge. 24 Quincy St., Cambridge (phone: 495-3251).

FIRST HARRISON GRAY OTIS HOUSE The house was designed in the late 18th century by Charles Bulfinch for Otis, a lawyer, congressman, and Boston mayor. It is now the headquarters of the *Society for the Preservation of New England Antiquities.* Guided tours are available Tuesdays through Saturdays. Admission charge. 141 Cambridge St. (phone: 227-3956).

GIBSON HOUSE Built in the mid-1800s, this home contains the Victorian-era fixtures and furniture of the original owners. Among its 19th-century features are a basement kitchen and a butler's pantry complete with a dumbwaiter. The house is shown by guided tour only. Open Wednesdays through Sundays May through October, and on weekends only from November through April. Admission charge. 137 Beacon St. (phone: 267-6338).

MUSEUM OF AFRO-AMERICAN HISTORY The museum's changing exhibits focus on both historical and contemporary issues and personalities. It's located in the *African Meeting House,* the oldest black church in the country, which was built by free black labor in 1806. Closed weekends. No admission charge. 46 Joy St. (phone: 742-1854).

MUSEUM OF THE ANCIENT AND HONORABLE ARTILLERY COMPANY OF MASSACHUSETTS Chartered in 1638 to protect the early settlers, the *Ancient and Honorable* is America's oldest military outfit. On display are firearms, artifacts, flags, cannons, uniforms, and other memorabilia. Closed weekends. No admission charge. *Faneuil Hall,* third floor (phone: 227-1638).

MUSEUM OF THE CONCORD ANTIQUARIAN SOCIETY Here are 15 period rooms with contents dating from the 17th to the 19th centuries. Open Tuesdays through Sundays from April through December; daily from January through March. Admission charge. 200 Lexington Rd., Concord (phone: 508-369-9609).

MUSEUM OF OUR NATIONAL HERITAGE A museum and library of American history, it often hosts traveling exhibits of folk art and other artifacts. Open daily. No admission charge. 33 Marrett Rd., Lexington (phone: 861-6559).

RALPH WALDO EMERSON MEMORIAL HOUSE Here the essayist, philosopher, and poet moved and raised a family with his second wife. Some of their original furnishings are still on display. The guided tour includes a biography of Emerson and stories about his family's days in the house. Open Thursdays through Sundays, mid-April through October; closed the rest of the year. Admission charge. 28 Cambridge Tpke., Concord (phone: 508-369-2236).

SPORTS MUSEUM Features memorabilia, photographs, equipment, temporary exhibits, interactive video presentations, and other artifacts of New England's rich sports history. Open daily. Admission charge. In the *Cambridgeside Galleria,* Memorial Dr., Cambridge (phone: 787-7678).

MAJOR COLLEGES AND UNIVERSITIES

Boston is the country's consummate college town, with literally dozens of educational institutions. Check college bulletin boards and newspapers for listings of campus events. *Harvard University,* in Cambridge (see *Special Places*), is one of the most prestigious in the country. *MIT* (see *Special Places*), another premier American university and also in Cambridge, produces scientists in all fields. In Boston itself, *Boston University,* with its many colleges and graduate schools, sprawls along Commonwealth Avenue, west of Kenmore Square (phone: 353-2000). *Boston College,* located to the west in Chestnut Hill, is a large Jesuit university with a variety of undergraduate and graduate programs and a loyal following of sports fans (phone: 552-8000). Other schools in the area include *Brandeis University* (415 South St., Waltham; phone: 736-2000); *Emerson College* (100 Beacon St.; phone: 578-8500); *Emmanuel College* (400 The Fenway; phone: 277-9540); *Endicott College* (376 Hale St., Beverly; phone: 508-927-0585); *Lesley College* (29 Everett St., Cambridge; phone: 868-9600); *Simmons College* (300 The Fenway; phone: 738-2000); *Suffolk University* (8 Ashburton Pl.; phone: 573-8000); *Tufts University* (Medford-Somerville; phone: 628-5000); *University of Massachusetts/Boston* (Park Sq. and Columbia Point; phone: 287-5000); *Wellesley College* (Wellesley; phone: 235-0320); *Wheaton College* (Norton; phone: 508-285-7722); and *Wheelock College* (150 The Riverway; phone: 734-5200). In addition, there are numerous aristocratic New England prep schools and specialized institutions such as the *Berklee College of Music* (138 Massachusetts Ave.; phone: 266-1400) and the *New England Conservatory (NEC)/Jordan Concert Hall* (30 Gainsborough St.; phone: 536-2412).

SHOPPING

Boston is a browser's paradise, with plenty of elegant and one-of-a-kind stores in a small area. Newbury Street is the place to go if your tastes run to art galleries, designer clothing, fine jewelry, expensive antiques, and outdoor cafés. Even if your preferences are more eclectic than elegant, don't rule out this pretty, European-looking venue. For atmosphere, walk the length of Charles Street, just across the *Public Garden* from the *Ritz.*

The winding, gaslit street contains antiques shops, art and print galleries, and several intimate cafés. Newbury and Charles Streets are also a paradise for antiques aficionados (for more information, see *Antiques: Boston's Best Hunting Grounds* in DIVERSIONS). Just two blocks south of Newbury Street is *Copley Place,* a glitzy shopping mall near Copley Square (see *Special Places*). And finally, the *Downtown Crossing* area has the city's two best-known department stores—*Jordan Marsh* and *Filene's*—surrounded by blocks of so-so shops. Below is a list of some of the city's best emporia.

Allston Beat Blue jeans, leather, and metal, much loved by teens and collegians. 348 Newbury St. (phone: 421-9555).

Autre Fois The focus here is on French country furniture, although there is also furniture from Italy and England, plus a variety of decorative accessories. 125 Newbury St. (phone: 424-8823).

Avenue Victor Hugo Offers a wide range of used books and magazines. 339 Newbury St. (phone: 266-7746).

Betsey Johnson The wild, 1960s-inspired fashions of this New York designer enliven this street. 201 Newbury St. (phone: 236-7072).

Body Sculpture An unpretentious-looking little place that sells some of the city's most creative jewelry—gorgeous, handcrafted stuff. Be sure to ask to see everything, since some of the most interesting designs are in drawers. 127 Newbury St. (phone: 262-2200).

Brattle Book Shop This Dickensian-style bookstore, located near the *Boston Common,* is an antiquarian book lover's Elysian Fields. More than 350,000 used, out-of-print, and rare books populate the three-story building, with original manuscripts and authors' autographs for sale. Closed Sundays. 9 West St. (phone: 542-0210 or 800-447-9595).

Brooks Brothers *The* place for proper and durable men's attire. 46 Newbury St. (phone: 267-2600).

Le Chapeau A delightful little store that carries hats, caps, boaters, beanies, and other assorted headgear. *Copley Place* (phone: 236-0232).

Chocolate by Design Wander in to see the offbeat designs at this company, which will shape chocolate for you in almost any way you can imagine. 134 Newbury St. (phone: 424-1115).

Cole-Haan Classic men's and women's shoes and leather goods are showcased in a new store that feels more like a Victorian home. 109 Newbury St. (phone: 536-7826).

Cuoio Shoes This little shop (pronounced *kwao*) has some of the most unusual and elegant women's shoes around. 115 Newbury St. (phone: 859-0636).

DeLuca's Market When almost every food emporium is now either part of a chain or homogenized to anonymity, here's a friendly, family-run food market devoted to high quality and personal service. 11 Charles St. (phone: 523-4343) and 239 Newbury St., Back Bay (phone: 262-5990).

Escada Elegant, colorful clothing by German designer Margaretha Ley. 308 Boylston St., at *Heritage on the Garden* (phone: 437-1200).

Essence The master perfumer here custom-makes scents to match your skin's special needs and your olfactory preferences. He also mixes up great imitations of various well-known fragrances. 223 Newbury St. (phone: 859-8009).

FAO Schwarz This huge children's funhouse is almost as large as the New York City flagship. The centerpiece is the singing, two-story clock with moving figurines, a singing giraffe, and a bear tea party on top. If you're lost, ask Spanky, the talking bear, for assistance. 440 Boylston St. (phone: 262-5900).

Filene's A fine department store with a full line of clothing, accessories, and housewares. It is located above the famous *Filene's Basement,* but the two stores now have different owners. *Downtown Crossing,* 426 Washington St. (phone: 357-2100).

Filene's Basement Here you'll find the best bargains in town, with markdowns from every state in the union and nearly every country in the world. *Downtown Crossing,* 426 Washington St. (phone: 542-2011).

Firestone and Parsons An elegant jewelry store in the *Ritz,* this establishment carries what may be the city's finest estate gems. Newbury and Arlington Sts. (phone: 266-1858).

George Gravert Orderly and uncluttered, this establishment specializes in 18th- and 19-century continental antiques. There's a good selection of French country furniture, decorative accessories, and even some 19th-century garden statuary. 122 Charles St. (phone: 227-1593).

Giorgio Armani This understated emporium is a fitting venue for this Italian designer's understated and elegant clothing for men and women. 22 Newbury St. (phone: 267-3200).

Godiva Chocolatiers This store for chocolate fanciers sells wonderful confections that look like tiny—and edible—works of art. *Copley Place* (phone: 437-8950).

The Gods Buddhas, pharaohs, flying dragons, icons, madonnas, and all manner of other religious relics are packed into this fascinating little shop. 253 Newbury St. (phone: 859-3034).

Hermès Elegant and expensive French apparel and accessories for Boston's Brahmins. 22 Arlington St., at *Heritage on the Garden* (phone: 482-8707).

HMV There is a vast selection of CDs here, but for other types of music, it may be worth going elsewhere, as prices are on the high side. 1 Brattle St., Cambridge (phone: 868-9696).

Joan & David The well-known shoe designers have a boutique stocked with their beautiful, unique shoes and a small line of their clothing. *Copley Place* (phone: 536-0600).

Jordan Marsh New England's largest department store, this 19th-century landmark carries clothing, including most of the top designer labels, accessories, and housewares. There's a bargain basement, but it is not as highly esteemed as *Filene's Basement* across the street. 450 Washington St. (phone: 357-3000).

Joseph Abboud Native Bostonian Abboud went to New York, went national with his line of classic, earthy menswear, and returned to build this lovely, three-story boutique. 37 Newbury St. (phone: 266-4200).

Kakas Furriers An elegant fur and leather store near the *Public Garden* where older fashionable Bostonians like to shop. 93 Newbury St. (phone: 536-1858).

Louis, Boston Trendy, elegant menswear designed to make a statement. Also in the graceful old building is a floor of women's clothing, *Café Louis,* a continental bistro, and a hair salon called *The Cutting Room.* 234 Berkeley St., Back Bay (phone: 262-6100).

Marika's Antiques Loaded with tapestries, paintings, vases, and furniture from the US, Europe, and the Orient, this shop specializes in jewelry. 130 Charles St. (phone: 523-4520).

Museum of Science Gift Shop For children who have everything, here are intriguing toys and other gifts. *Science Park* (phone: 723-2500).

Neiman Marcus Glitzy merchandise with outrageous price tags characterizes this Dallas-spawned specialty store at *Copley Place* (phone: 536-3660).

Newbury Comics All kinds of comic books, from classic to counterculture. 332 Newbury St. (phone: 236-4930) and seven other locations.

Nostalgia Factory A huge collection of original vintage ads, collectible prints, posters, and postcards is for sale here; there are also monthly exhibitions of such specialities as elections memorabilia and sheet music. 336 Newbury St. (phone: 236-8754).

Oilily Rainbows look dull next to the brightly colored children's clothing in this Dutch company's Boston store. 31 Newbury St. (phone: 247-9299).

Out of Town News A periodical lover's dream, staffed by folks who know when and where every journal under the sun is published, from a Des Moines Sunday paper to a magazine from Cairo. Harvard Sq. (phone: 354-7777).

Priscilla: The Bride's Shop This exclusive bridal shop has been making gowns for society brides for decades. 137 Newbury St. (phone: 267-9070).

Rose Garden Head to this florist for the city's best roses at the best prices. A dozen cost from $10 to $25, depending on season and stem length. 110 Newbury St. (phone: 859-9800).

Rosie's Bakery and Dessert Shop A brightly lit storefront bakery in Cambridge's Inman Square, it's known for its prize-winning brownie, an indescribably rich concoction delicately named a "Chocolate Orgasm," and the best poppyseed cake you'll find anywhere. A great place to order cakes for special occasions, too, should you find yourself in Boston with something to celebrate. 243 Hampshire St., Cambridge (phone: 491-9488).

Sharper Image An amusement park of adult "toys"—talking scales, massaging chairs, tiny pool tables, duck-shape telephones—and all manner of gadgets and contraptions. *Copley Place,* near the crosswalk over Huntington Ave. (phone: 262-7010).

Shreve, Crump & Low One of Boston's oldest and finest jewelry stores, it also stocks crystal, clocks, silver, and a fine collection of American and English antiques from the 18th and 19th centuries. 330 Boylston St. (phone: 267-9100).

Society of Arts and Crafts Talented craftspeople have always gravitated to New England, and for the past 95 years, the *Society* has been carrying their works of furniture, jewelry, housewares, and clothing. 175 Newbury St. (phone: 266-1810) and 101 Arch St. (phone: 345-0033).

Strutters Fans of vintage clothing and accessories should check out the high-quality goods here. 257 Newbury St. (phone: 247-7744).

Sweet Enchantments Kids love walking over the bridge and through the fake forest in this unique candy store, especially since each tree knot is filled with a sweet surprise. 229 Newbury St. (phone: 236-2282).

Tiffany & Co. The prestigious house for jewelry and more. *Copley Place* (phone: 353-0222).

Toscanini's Ice cream heaven. Rumor has it that Bostonians eat more ice cream per capita than the residents of any other city, and this is one of their favorite places to get it—in a blizzard or in balmy weather, it's packed. The ice cream is made on the premises and features exotic foreign flavors such as Italian *nocciòla* (hazelnut) and *gianduia* (chocolate cream), and Indian cardamom-pistachio, mango, and saffron. 899 Main St., Central Sq., Cambridge (phone: 491-5877), and also in the *MIT Student Center* (phone: 494-1640).

Tower Records CDs, tapes, and LPs are housed in this dazzling three-story space at 360 Newbury St., on the corner of Massachusetts Ave. (phone: 247-5900). A second *Tower* store is near *Harvard* at 95 Mt. Auburn St. (phone: 876-3377).

Victorian Bouquet Ltd. More than just another flower shop, it has spectacular flower arrangements and a cordial, thoughtful staff. 53A Charles St. (phone: 367-6648).

Vose Galleries The specialty here is 18th-, 19th-, and early 20th-century American paintings. 238 Newbury St. (phone: 536-6176).

Waterford-Wedgwood This classy store features a full line of the classic brands of Irish crystal and English china. 288 Boylston St. (phone: 482-8886).

Waterstone's Booksellers Housed in an ornate old theater building, with about 150,000 titles, this is one of the largest bookstores in the city. 181 Newbury St. (phone: 859-7300).

Wenham Cross Country-style antiques, including hand-painted furniture, wooden toys, and hooked rugs, are for sale here. 179 Newbury St. (phone: 236-0409).

Women's Educational and Industrial Union Since 1877, the *WEIU* has been providing training and support for working women. Despite its age, the gift shop has a modern collection of housewares, children's clothes and toys, and knickknacks. There is an extensive needlework and crafts section, too. 356 Boylston St. (phone: 536-5651).

Wordsworth Bookstore A bookworm and gift-giver's paradise packed with every hard- and softcover book you can imagine, all discounted 10%-30%. 30 Brattle St., Cambridge, near Harvard Sq. (phone: 354-5201).

SPORTS AND FITNESS

No doubt about it, Boston is one of the all-time great professional sports towns.

BASEBALL The *Red Sox* play at *Fenway Park* (4 Yawkey Way; phone: 267-1700). *Green Line,* Kenmore stop.

BASKETBALL Beginning this fall, the *Celtics* play their home games at the *Shawmut Center* (150 Causeway St.; *Ticketmaster* phone: 931-2000). *Green* or *Orange Line, North Station* stop.

BICYCLING Although a flimsy, two-wheeled vehicle is not the safest mode of city transportation, Bostonians have long loved cycling and refuse to give it up. The city, in response, has built bicycle paths that are safe and extremely popular. A good place to rent a mountain or touring bicycle is the *Community Bike Shop* (490 Tremont St.; phone: 542-8623), which offers 12-speed Nishiki and Jakara bikes. (You'll need identification.) Bicycle tours in and beyond the city are conducted by *American Youth Hostels* (phone: 731-5430), the *Charles River Wheelmen* (phone: 625-0610), and the *Appalachian Mountain Club* (phone: 523-0636), among others. Paths are marked with the international symbol of a cyclist. You can pick up a map of local trails from local bike shops or from the *Department of Public Works* (*Transportation Building,*

10 Park Plaza; phone: 973-8000). *Lincoln Guide Service* (152 Lincoln Rd., Lincoln; phone: 259-9204) and *Pro-Motion* (111 South St., Bedford; phone: 275-1113) offer lessons to those interested in refining their biking skills. The following are two of the better routes for seeing Boston by bike.

BEST BIKE ROUTES

Greenbelt Bikeway This path originates at *Boston Common* and traces the entire length of Boston's celebrated *Emerald Necklace,* an 8-mile chain of parkland stretching from the *Common* to *Franklin Park.* Along the way, cyclists pass magnolia-lined Commonwealth Avenue Mall; Kenmore Square; the *Fens Park;* the *Arnold Arboretum,* with its 14,000 species of trees and shrubs, lilacs, rhododendrons, and magnolias; and finally, *Franklin Park,* where the *Franklin Park Zoo* is located (see *Other Special Places*). The trip, along with a stop for a picnic at the *Arnold Arboretum,* is a great way to spend a warm spring day.

Dr. Paul Dudley White Bikeway Named after the late President Eisenhower's personal physician, a heart surgeon and biking enthusiast, this path begins along the *Charles River Esplanade* and stretches through sections of Boston, Cambridge, Newton, and Watertown Square. In Watertown, the path crosses the Charles River (it's actually more like a creek at this point), and heads back to Boston on the river's other side. The 18-mile round trip offers rich and varied scenery and only a modicum of interference from auto traffic (you walk your bike across a couple of intersections). There are several footbridges that span Storrow Drive, the most handy being the Fiedler Footbridge at the intersection of Arlington and Beacon Streets, near the *Public Garden.* This allows the cyclist to get from Back Bay to the *Esplanade,* while avoiding a harrowing encounter with six lanes of traffic.

BILLIARDS Some know it or its variations as pool or even snooker. Whatever the nomenclature, it is making a glorious comeback in Boston. The city's best-known place for billiards is *Jillian's Billiard Club* (145 Ipswich St.; phone: 437-0300), a staid pool hall near *Fenway Park* that is furnished like an English gentleman's library. Some think the *Boston Billiard Club* (126 Brookline Ave.; phone: 536-7665) is even classier. Both offer cocktail service, snacks, billiards, pool, snooker, darts, and backgammon.

FISHING *Boston Harbor Fishing* (619 E. Broadway, South Boston; phone: 268-2244) offers fishing charters, clambakes, and evening cruises; *Yankee Fishing Fleet* (75 Essex Ave., Gloucester; phone: 508-283-0313 or 800-942-5464) runs charters from April through November; *Boston Sail* (Long Wharf; phone: 742-3316) organizes deep-sea fishing excursions; and *Captain's*

Fishing Parties and Boat Livery (Plum Island Pier, Newburyport; phone: 508-465-7733) features half- and full-day charters. (Also see *Gone Fishing* in DIVERSIONS.)

FITNESS CENTERS Try *Fitcorp Fitness and Physical Therapy Center* (133 Federal St.; phone: 542-1010), which has a track and workout equipment; *Wellbridge Center* (1079 Commonwealth Ave., Brighton; phone: 254-1711; and 695 Atlantic Ave., Boston; phone: 439-9600), which has workout equipment, a pool, and a steam room and sauna; or *Le Pli*, at the *Charles* (5 Bennett St., Charles Sq., Cambridge; phone: 547-4081), which has workout equipment, a sauna, a pool, and steamrooms. Many Boston hotels have fitness centers for guests. The *Boston Athletic Club* (653 Summer St.; phone: 269-4300) offers daily memberships to those with a local hotel room key. The *Greater Boston YMCA* (316 Huntington Ave.; phone: 536-7800) operates branches at nine locations around the city; different branches have different equipment. All are open to nonmembers for a fee.

FOOTBALL Football (*New England Patriots*) and some soccer matches are played at *Foxboro Stadium* (Rte. 1, Foxboro; phone: 508-543-0350).

GOLF There's a city course in *Hyde Park,* where the *Parks and Recreation Department* offers golf instruction. Contact *George Wright Pro Shop* (420 West St., *Hyde Park;* phone: 361-8313 or 361-9679); you also can play or take lessons at the *Fresh Pond Golf Club* (691 Huron Ave., Cambridge; phone: 354-9130). (Also see *Great Golf Outside the City* in DIVERSIONS.)

HOCKEY Beginning this fall, the *Bruins* hockey team faces off at the *Shawmut Center* (150 Causeway St.; phone: 931-2000 for tickets), which replaces the *Boston Garden. Green* or *Orange Line, North Station* stop.

JOGGING Run along the banks of the Charles River on Memorial Drive (in Cambridge) or along Storrow Drive (in Boston). Many bridges over the river make loops of varying lengths possible.

RACING Greyhounds race at *Wonderland Park,* Revere (on the *Blue Line;* phone: 284-1300).

SAILING Befitting its history as a port city, Boston offers several options for visitors interested in skippering their own skiffs on the Charles or serving as crew members on larger vessels in the harbor and beyond. Instruction is always available for those not sure of their skills. The following are several of Boston's best sailing experiences.

TAKING TO THE WATERS

Boston by Sail *Boston by Sail* rents 23-foot Sonars and 27-foot O'Day sailboats for tooling about the harbor. You may take these out alone if you are a licensed sailor; otherwise a captain will accompany you.

Larger boats, from a 47-foot vessel to a 95-foot schooner that can ferry more than 50 people comfortably, are available for larger parties, tour groups, or business functions. The proprietors remain flexible: They offer tailor-made sunset and moonlight cruises, voyages up the Charles River, and trips to the Harbor Islands and ports of call on the North Shore. Located on Long Wharf near the *Marriott* hotel and the *New England Aquarium.* 66 Long Wharf (phone: 742-3313).

Boston Sailing Center Specializing in sailboat charters, this outfit charts courses for tourists. For history buffs, there's the water tour of Boston's historic sites, including a close inspection of the USS *Constitution;* for speed demons, they'll unfurl the spinnaker for some swift sailing far from shore; for families, there are picnic cruises to the Harbor Islands; for couples, sunset and moonlight cruises. Other "theme" sailing excursions are also available. The basic rate for the 23-foot Sonar is $50 per hour (minimum of two hours); trips on the 29-foot craft are $70 per hour, and the *Center* has access to hundreds of other sailboats and yachts moored on Boston Harbor. Lewis Wharf (phone: 227-4198).

Community Boating Thanks to *Community Boating Inc.,* visiting and local sailors alike can find themselves skimming along the Charles River at the helm of a 15-foot Mercury or 13-foot Laser sailboat. The city's most popular sailing organization, *Community Boating* aims to promote sailing as an activity that should be enjoyed by all—not just the rich. Two- or seven-day memberships are available for out-of-towners. Brush up on your nomenclature and points of sail since, in order to get going, you may have to answer a question or two about the operation of your boat. Lessons are available. The boathouse is located on the *Esplanade* near the Fiedler Footbridge and the Charles Street *T* stop on the *Red Line.* 21 Embankment Rd., (phone: 523-1038).

SHIP AHOY!

Launched in 1973, the Harvey Gamage, a 95-foot schooner, is one of the most technologically advanced of all the windjammers. The two showers aboard are cold, but only a few windjammers have any at all. The ship is also unusual in welcoming children of any age among its 30 passengers. Special rates are available for senior citizens. Cruises take in the New England coast in summer, the Virgin Islands during the winter. Sailing instruction is provided. Booked by *Dirigo,* which also represents other vessels, such as the ketch *Angelique* (with a deck lounge equipped with a piano and a fireplace), the *Nathaniel Bowditch* (bring your own beer for a lobster and clam cookout), and tall ships. Information: *Dirigo Cruises,* 39 Waterside La., Clinton, CT 06413 (phone: 203-669-7068 or 800-845-5520).

SKIING There's cross-country skiing at Weston Ski Track on *Leo J. Martin Golf Course* (Park Rd., Weston; phone: 894-4903). *Lincoln Guide Service* (152 Lincoln Rd., Lincoln; phone: 259-9204) and *Pro-Motion* (111 South St., Bedford; phone: 275-1113) offer lessons daily. Within a two-hour drive of the city are a number of small downhill skiing areas: *Blue Hills Ski Area* in Canton (phone: 828-5070); *Boston Hill* in North Andover (phone: 508-683-2734); *Wachusett Mountain Ski Area* in Princeton (phone: 508-464-2300); and *Nashoba Valley Ski Area* in Westford (phone: 692-3033).

TENNIS There are courts at the *Charles River Park Tennis Club* (35 Lomasney Way; phone: 742-8922). The *Metropolitan District Commission (MDC)* also operates a number of well-maintained tennis courts throughout the city. All are available on a first-come, first-served basis except the *Charlesbank Courts,* which include two unlit courts on the bank of the Charles River and two lighted courts on the southwestern section of *Boston Common.* These require a permit, which may be picked up a few days in advance; for more information, contact *MDC Lee Memorial Pool* (20 Somerset St.; phone: 354-9523). *Hyde Park,* another cluster of *MDC* courts, has six tennis courts, four of which are lighted. Unlit courts are open until dusk, lighted courts until 11 PM. For further details, contact the *MDC* (phone: 727-8865).

Only members and their guests may play at the *Longwood Cricket Club,* but, as the home of the *US Pro Tennis Championships at Longwood,* this is Boston's primary site of competitive tennis. The championship, which takes place for approximately nine days in the latter half of July, draws some of the top names in tennis. Information: *Longwood Cricket Club,* 564 Hammond St., Brookline, MA 02167 (phone: 731-2900; 731-4500 for tickets to the *US Pro* matches).

THEATER

Catch a Broadway show before it gets to Broadway. Trial runs often take place at the *Shubert Theater* (265 Tremont St.; phone: 426-4520), the *Colonial Theatre* (106 Boylston St.; phone: 426-9366), the *Wilbur Theater* (246 Tremont St.; phone: 423-4008), and the *Wang Center for the Performing Arts* (270 Tremont St.; phone: 482-9393). Or check out the *Charles Playhouse* (74 Warrenton St.; phone: 426-6912), a much smaller and often livelier place that hosts interesting contemporary plays. Currently in an open-ended run here is the long-running hit play *Shear Madness,* a participatory thriller in which the audience is invited to guess whodunit. The *New Theater* (755 Boylston St.; phone: 247-7388) features new works with provocative themes. The *Lyric Stage* (140 Clarendon St.; phone: 437-7172) performs first-time, experimental works—often satiric and political—with aplomb. The *American Repertory Theater* (64 Brattle St., Cambridge; phone: 547-8300), one of the

East Coast's premier repertory companies, is based at *Harvard's Loeb Drama Center* and performs both classic and new plays during the school year. In addition, there are dozens of smaller theater groups, including several affiliated with colleges, such as the *Huntington Theatre Company* (264 Huntington Ave., Back Bay; phone: 266-3913 or 266-0800) at *Boston University.* The *Boston Ballet Company* gives performances at the *Wang Center* (see above; call 695-6950 for ballet information). Tickets for theatrical and musical events can be purchased through the *Out of Town Ticket Agency* (on the mezzanine level of the *Red Line's Harvard Square Station;* phone: 492-1900); *TicketMaster* (phone: 244-8400 for *TicketMaster* locations; 931-2000 to order tickets by phone); or, on the day of the play, from *Bostix* (*Faneuil Hall Marketplace;* phone: 723-5181). For information on performance schedules, check the local publications listed above. (Also see *Inside Boston's Theaters* in DIVERSIONS.)

CINEMA

Boston features an array of movie theaters that screen everything from first-run action/suspense movies to zillionth-run classics and foreign films. The *Boston Globe's* Thursday "Calendar" section is an invaluable source for current attractions and reviews. For a complete listing of times and locations of films showing in the area, call 333-FILM.

Several theaters specialize in showing eclectic, hard-to-find films. Two of the best are *Nickelodeon Cinemas* (606 Commonwealth Ave.; phone: 424-1500), which features foreign films and other first-run movies not intended to be blockbusters; and the beloved *Coolidge Corner Cinema* (290 Harvard St., Brookline; phone: 734-2500), which has been saved from the wrecking ball on several occasions and continues to feature foreign, classic, and avant-garde treasures.

In Cambridge, the *Brattle* (40 Brattle St.; phone: 876-6837) features oldies and the avant-garde; and *Harvard Square* (10 Church St.; phone: 864-4580) often screens non-mainstream movies. The *Harvard Film Archive* at the university (24 Quincy St.; phone: 495-4700) also shows classics and foreign films. In a struggle to compete with multiplex cinemas, the grand old *Somerville Theater* (55 Davis Sq., Somerville; phone 625-5700) hosts first-run foreign and repertory films, classic Disney animation festivals, and performances by local musicians.

MUSIC

Almost every evening, Bostonians can choose from among several classical and contemporary musical performances, ranging from the most delicate chamber music to the most ferocious alternative rock. The *Boston Symphony Orchestra,* usually under the baton of director Seiji Ozawa, performs at *Symphony Hall* (301 Massachusetts Ave.; phone: 266-1492) September through April; in summer, it's at the *Tanglewood Music Festival* in Lenox, Massachusetts. Selected members of the *Boston Symphony* make up the *Boston Pops Orchestra*, which performs less weighty orchestrations of popular music. In addition to performing at *Symphony Hall* (see above) from April through July, the *Boston Pops* gives free outdoor concerts in the *Hatch Shell* on the *Charles River Esplanade* in June and July. Both the *Handel & Haydn Society* (300 Massachusetts Ave.; phone: 266-3605) and *Boston Baroque* in Cambridge (phone: 641-1310) perform historically correct music on period instruments. The *Boston Lyric Opera* performs a full season of classical operas at the *Emerson Majestic Theater* (219 Tremont St.; phone: 248-8660). Several colleges and universities also offer classical concerts: *Harvard*'s *Sanders Theater* (Kirkland and Quincy Sts., Cambridge; phone: 495-5595); *MIT*'s *Kresge Auditorium,* in a peculiar building on the West Campus that has a curved roof resting on only three points (77 Massachusetts Ave., Cambridge; phone: 253-2826); and the *Boston University Concert Hall* (855 Commonwealth Ave.; phone: 353-3345).

Soothing piano music can be found in the *Plaza* bar of the *Copley Plaza* hotel and energetic sing-alongs at *Diamond Jim's Piano Bar* at the *Lenox* hotel (see *Checking In* for both hotels). The premier jazz club in the area is the super-elegant *Regattabar* in Cambridge's *Charles* hotel (see *Checking In*), which showcases both local and national talent. Top-name blues and pop musicians play here, too. For more jazz, try the classy, two-level *Nightstage* (823 Main St., Cambridge; phone: 497-8200); the bustling, intimate *Ryles* (Inman Sq., Cambridge; phone: 876-9330); or the mixed bag, from avant-garde to be-bop, at *Scullers Jazz Lounge* in the *Guest Quarters Suite* (see *Checking In*), which showcases both national and local talent.

The *Paradise* (967 Commonwealth Ave.; phone: 254-2053) is an intimate room that regularly books top-name rock musicians. The *Rathskeller,* a.k.a. "The Rat" (528 Commonwealth Ave.; phone: 536-2750), is a head-banging Boston institution (many would contend its patrons belong in institutions) that relishes its role as the scourge of Kenmore Square. Here you'll find an endless stream of such bands as *The Queers* or *Slaughter Shack,* as well as nearby *Boston University*'s "existential" crowd. For some of the finest Irish music this side of Dublin, go to the *Purple Shamrock* (1 Union St.; phone: 227-2060); the *Black Rose* (160 State St.; phone: 742-2286); or the *Green Briar* (304 Washington St., Brighton; phone: 789-4100) on Monday nights. The *Tam O' Shanter* (1648 Beacon St., Brookline; phone: 277-0982) is an excellent venue for folk, blues, and the occasional jazz performance, as is the *Plough and Stars* (912 Massachusetts Ave., Cambridge; phone: 492-9653), where they pack them in cheek-to-jowl and serve some of the finest ales in the city. For folk music in a coffeehouse atmosphere, visit *Passim* (47 Palmer St., Cambridge; phone: 492-7679); for bluegrass, drop in at *Harpers Ferry* (158 Brighton Ave.; phone: 254-9734). The *Western Front* (343 Western Ave., Cambridge; phone: 492-7772) is Boston's focal point for reggae music. Once you step in the door, you'll think you're in Kingston, Jamaica.

NIGHTCLUBS AND NIGHTLIFE

A sophisticated and well-heeled crowd gathers nightly in the elegant *Plaza* bar at the *Copley Plaza* hotel (see *Checking In*) or at the *Palm Court* at *Cricket's* (101 *Faneuil Hall Marketplace;* phone: 720-5570). If dancing disco is your passion, try the sumptuous *Roxy* (279 Tremont St.; phone: 338-7699). *The Last Hurrah,* downstairs at the *Omni Parker House* (see *Checking In*), also has live jazz bands on weekends, with no cover charge. Thursday through Saturday nights, there's dancing to pop music at *Club Nicole,* a spot in the *Back Bay Hilton* (see *Checking In*) reminiscent of the old *Stork Club* in New York. Among the trendiest clubs are *Avalon* (15 Lansdowne St.; phone: 262-2424); *Alley Cat* (1 Boylston Pl.; phone: 457-6200); *Venus de Milo* (7 Lansdowne St.; phone: 421-9595); *Zanzibar* (1 Boylston Pl., off Boylston St.; phone: 351-7000); and the *Harbor Club* (145 Northern Ave.; phone: 426-8600). A rather disheartening sight is the *Bull & Finch* pub (84 Beacon St.; phone: 227-9605) of television's "Cheers" fame, which still draws crowds of tourists despite an expansion from the basement to the first floor and a general lack of atmosphere. Only the façade of this tourist trap was used for the show; the interior is filled with kitsch.

COMEDY CLUBS

Sometimes it seems that nearly everybody in Boston is a comedian—or wants to be. Those who have decided to turn professional can be found at one of the area's many comedy clubs. Big-name comics can be found at **Nick's Comedy Club** (100 Warrenton St.; phone: 482-0930). Other laugh joints include **Duck Soup** at **Faneuil Hall Rotunda** (phone: 248-9700), the city's largest comedy club; **Dick Doherty's Comedy Club** at **Remington's Eating & Drinking Exchange** (124 Boylston St.; phone: 337-6920); and the **Comedy Connection** at the **Charles Playhouse** (76 Warrenton St.; phone: 426-6339).

Best in Town

CHECKING IN

Boston has some gracious old hotels with the history and charm you'd expect to find in this dignified New England capital. But Boston experienced a hotel building boom in the 1980s, and there are now many modern places as well, offering standard contemporary accoutrements. Expect to pay $150 or more for a double room (including private bath, air conditioning, TV set, and phone, unless otherwise indicated) at those places noted as expensive; between $100 and $150 for those in the moderate category; and under $100 in places listed as inexpensive. Many of these hotels offer special weekend packages for relatively low rates. Reservations always are required, so write or call well in advance. Most of Boston's major hotels have complete facilities for the business traveler. Those hotels listed below as having "business services" usually offer such conveniences as meeting rooms, photocopiers, computers, translation services, and express checkout, among others. Call the hotel for additional information. All telephone numbers are in the 617 area code unless otherwise indicated.

For bed and breakfast accommodations in the Boston area, write to the *Massachusetts Division of Tourism* (100 Cambridge St., 13th Floor, Boston, MA 02202) for its *Spirit of Massachusetts Bed & Breakfast Guide* or contact *Bed & Breakfast Associates of Bay Colony* (PO Box 166, *Babson Park,* Boston, MA 02157; phone: 449-5302); *Greater Boston Hospitality* (Box 1142, Brookline, MA 02146; phone: 277-5430); *Bed and Breakfast Cambridge & Greater Boston* (Box 665, Cambridge, MA 02140; phone: 576-1492); *Host Homes of Boston* (Box 117, Boston MA 02168; phone: 244-1308); *New England Bed and Breakfast, Inc.* (1753 Massachusetts Ave., Cambridge, MA 02138; phone: 498-9819); or *Bed & Breakfast Agency of Boston* (47 Commercial Wharf, Boston, MA 02110; phone: 720-3540).

For an unforgettable experience in Boston, we begin with our favorites, followed by our recommendations of cost and quality choices of accommodations, listed by price category.

GRAND HOTELS

Boston Harbor This distinctive, 16-story property, one of Boston's best hostelries, offers the most dramatic entry to the Hub. From *Logan Airport,* visitors are whisked by water taxi across Boston Harbor to dock within an anchor's throw of the hotel at Rowes Wharf, with its enormous eight-story golden arch that opens onto Atlantic Avenue and downtown Boston. The shopping district, the North End, and the *Faneuil Hall Marketplace* are all within walking distance. The property's 230 spacious guestrooms (some with balconies) have views of either the city or the harbor. *Foster's Rotunda,* a copper-domed observatory atop the arch, boasts mesmerizing views. Amenities include a spa, saunas, and a 60-foot indoor pool, as well as 24-hour room service and a concierge. There's also the glass-enclosed *Harborview Lounge,* a casual, outdoor café (in summer), and the elegant *Rowes Wharf* bar and restaurant, specializing in seafood prepared in unusual ways. Business services also are available. 70 Rowes Wharf (phone: 439-7000 or 800-752-7077; fax: 330-9450).

Copley Plaza This historic bowfront property, part of Copley Square's triangle of turn-of-the-century elegance, is on everybody's short list of Boston hotels. Although it has 373 splendid guestrooms, its public areas are what make this hotel truly great. Corporate Boston fills the seats of the *Plaza* bar, which has been compared to a British officers' club in India. Adjacent to the bar is the airy tea court, which is painted in the precise Victorian technique of photographic realism, creating the illusion that you're outdoors. There are two restaurants: The elegant *Plaza* (see *Eating Out*) has a French menu, and *Copley's* serves excellent American/New England fare in richly decorated Victorian-style rooms. The multilingual staff is refined and helpful. Other amenities include 24-hour room service, a concierge, and business services. 138 St. James Ave., Copley Sq. (phone: 267-5300; 800-223-7434; fax: 267-7668).

Four Seasons Service is this refurbished hotel's strong suit—which is not to say that the place is lacking in ambience. On the contrary: The 288 guestrooms, each with a bar and two to three phones, resemble a gracious Beacon Hill residence, with cherry furniture, floral prints, and marble vanities. This is one of only two Boston hotels that overlook the *Public Garden;* half the guestrooms enjoy leafy (or snow-swept) garden views. The hotel's formal restaurant, *Aujourd'hui* (see *Eating Out*), features an American-continental menu. The more informal *Bristol Lounge* offers live entertainment most nights and a Viennese dessert buffet Friday and Saturday nights. The location is convenient as well as attractive: Most of the city's popular sites are within walking distance. The full-service health club includes a pool, sauna, and whirlpool baths. Children get their own bathrobes, board games, Nintendo, milk and cookies, and food for the *Public Garden* ducks. Other amenities include 24-hour room service, a concierge, and business services. 200 Boylston St. (phone: 338-4400; 800-332-3442; fax: 423-0154).

Meridien The stylish French-owned hotel chain has created a small and delightful Gallic world in this splendid 1922 Renaissance Revival structure in downtown's Post Office Square. The 326 guestrooms, each with a small sitting area with a writing desk, are decorated in 150 different styles, from fin de siècle to modern. The elegant *Julien* restaurant offers a classical Gallic-inspired menu (see *Eating Out*)—the creation of consulting chef Marc Haeberlin of the three-Michelin-star *L'Auberge de L'Ill* in Alsace. Also on the premises is *Café Fleuri,* a French bistro housed in a leafy six-story atrium. The hotel hosts a delectable all-you-can-eat buffet of chocolate desserts on Saturday afternoons; Sunday brunch is wonderful here as well. *La Terrasse,* an informal outdoor café, serves breakfast, lunch, and cocktails. There's also a health club, an indoor pool, lobby shops, 24-hour room service, and a concierge. Business services also are available. 250 Franklin St., Post Office Sq. (phone: 451-1900; 800-543-4300; fax: 423-2844).

Omni Parker House When it opened in 1855, the elegant *Parker House* became a Boston institution almost immediately; it was here that Charles Dickens would dwell during his heavily publicized Boston visits. The 540 rooms are richly decorated with dark wood and tapestries, and the building, located on the historic Freedom Trail, is within walking distance of the *King's Chapel,* the *Park Street Church,* Beacon Hill, *Boston Common,* and the *Faneuil Hall Marketplace.* Boston cream pie and Parker House rolls were born at *Parker's,* the hotel's main restaurant (which still features both on its contemporary continental menu). The restaurant was once the meeting place of the *Saturday Club,* a 19th-century literary association whose members included such luminaries as Longfellow, Emerson, and Oliver Wendell Holmes. Other amenities include room service until midnight, a concierge, and business services. 60 School St. (phone: 227-8600; 800-THE-OMNI; fax: 742-5729).

Ritz-Carlton This grande dame of Boston hotels has reigned since 1927. Strategically located near most of Newbury and Boylston Streets' smart shops, it overlooks the *Public Garden,* with the windows on the north side of the building offering views of the magnolia-lined Commonwealth Avenue Mall. All 278 guestrooms are traditionally furnished and decorated with 17th- to 19th-century paintings. The rooms in the hotel's older section are the fanciest. Afternoon tea in the upstairs lounge is a Boston institution (see *Quintessential Boston* in DIVERSIONS). The large and lovely *Ritz* dining room serves excellent continental fare (see *Eating Out*), and the serene *Ritz* bar makes the best martini in town; both look out over the garden. Legions of staff members do their best to serve you. Other amenities include 24-hour room service, a concierge, and business services. 15 Arlington St. (phone: 536-5700; 800-241-3333; fax: 536-1335).

EXPENSIVE

Back Bay Hilton The rooms in this 26-story hostelry, conveniently located near the *Hynes Convention Center* and *Prudential Center,* are known for their peace and quiet; each of the 336 rooms is soundproofed. If you don't mind a little street noise, the bay windows actually open. *Fitcorp,* a health club with fitness machines and a swimming pool, is available to guests, and *Club Nicole* plays popular dance music. Children stay free in their parents' rooms, and there are some moderately priced rooms. Business services also are available. Dalton and Belvedere Sts. (phone: 236-1100; 800-874-0663; fax: 267-8893).

Bostonian Understated and small (152 rooms), this beautifully appointed hotel is across from *Faneuil Hall Marketplace* and just two blocks from the North End and the revitalized waterfront. Its glass-enclosed, rooftop *Seasons* restaurant, which serves fine continental fare, discreetly overlooks the colorful bustle below. Other amenities include 24-hour room service, a concierge, and business services. North and Blackstone Sts. at *Faneuil Hall Marketplace* (phone: 523-3600; 800-343-0922; fax: 523-2454).

Charles Between the Charles River and Harvard Square, this handsome red brick building is the centerpiece of the *Charles Square* complex. The 296 rooms are well decorated, and those on the 10th floor have teleconferencing and telecommunications facilities. Relaxation can be sedentary in the pleasant *Bennett Street Café* or elegant *Rarities* restaurant (see *Eating Out*), or more active at the lavish *Le Pli* health spa, complete with an indoor pool. The *Regattabar* features live jazz. Business services also are available. One Bennett St., Cambridge (phone: 864-1200; 800-882-1818; fax: 864-5715).

Colonnade This distinguished property near the *Prudential Center,* Copley Square, and Newbury Street offers 288 large rooms, a (seasonal) rooftop pool, the classy *Promenade Café,* and *Zachary's,* a bar that features jazz on weekend nights. Business services also are available. 120 Huntington Ave. (phone: 424-7000; 800-962-3030; fax: 424-1717).

Eliot This all-suite Back Bay establishment was built in 1925 (a $4.3 million renovation was completed in the early 1990s) as the nearby *Harvard Club*'s guest facilities. The elegant lobby and all the rooms shine in a classic European manner; each of the 93 suites has a marble bath, antique furnishings, French doors between rooms, and a private pantry. Guestrooms away from bustling Commonwealth Avenue are quieter. Dual-line room telephones include modems, and writing desks are larger than usual. Amenities include continental breakfast, mini-bars, and concierge service. Business services also are available. The popular bar of the same name next door is not part of the hotel. 370 Commonwealth Ave. (phone: 267-1607; 800-44-ELIOT; fax: 536-9114).

Guest Quarters Suite A distinctive property on the Charles River, it has 10 conventional guestrooms and 310 luxurious suites. There's a restaurant, and complimentary breakfast is served on weekends. Its *Scullers Jazz Lounge* is one of the city's premier jazz venues, and there's a health club with a pool, a whirlpool bath, a sauna, and exercise machines. Other amenities include room service until 11 PM, a concierge, and business services. 400 Soldiers Field Rd., at the Cambridge/Allston exit of I-90, the Massachusetts Turnpike (phone: 783-0090; 800-424-2900; fax: 783-0897).

Hyatt Regency, Cambridge Surrounding the atrium and glass-walled elevators are 469 rooms. The revolving rooftop restaurant offers a spectacular view of Boston, especially at sunset. The health club includes an indoor pool, a sauna, a whirlpool bath, and a steamroom. Other amenities include 24-hour room service, a concierge, and business services. On the Charles River, near *MIT* and *Harvard* (not easily accessible by public transportation). 575 Memorial Dr., Cambridge (phone: 492-1234; 800-233-1234; fax: 491-6906).

Lafayette Although the ambitious *Lafayette Place* complex has sunk to dismal lows, the hotel within maintains classic European standards of elegance and service. The 497 beautifully appointed rooms are grouped around four atriums. As befits a member of the Swissôtel group, one dining room is called the *Café Suisse;* for dinner, the *Lobby Lounge* serves informal American fare. A lap pool, a sun terrace, and saunas also are available. Other amenities include 24-hour room service, a concierge, and business services. 1 Ave. de Lafayette (phone: 451-2600; 800-621-9200; fax: 451-2198).

Lenox Built in 1900 and modeled after New York City's *Waldorf-Astoria,* this property has 222 guestrooms with high ceilings and rocking chairs (the corner rooms have fireplaces). Each is decorated in either French provincial or colonial style. The lobby is handsomely decorated in blue with gold trim and a fireplace—always blazing in the winter—that evokes the feel of a country inn. *Diamond Jim's Piano Bar* features sing-alongs starring musically talented waiters and waitresses. There also are two restaurants—the casual *Lenox Pub* and the more formal *Lenox Grill.* Other amenities include room service until midnight, a concierge, and business services. 710 Boylston St. (phone: 536-5300).

Logan Airport Hilton Just 10 minutes from downtown Boston and the only hotel located at *Logan Airport* (the rooms are soundproofed), it has a restaurant, a lounge, an outdoor pool, and a health club. There's free limousine service to your airline. Business services also are available. 75 Service Rd., E. Boston (phone: 569-9300; fax: 569-3981).

Marriott, Cambridge The fifth Marriott in Greater Boston is in the heart of the Kendall Square construction boom near *MIT.* This understated yet posh 431-room property features a comfortable restaurant and lounge, an indoor pool, and a health club with a whirlpool bath and saunas. Business services also are available. 2 Cambridge Center (phone: 494-6600; 800-228-9290; fax: 494-6600).

Marriott, Copley Place This 1,147-room giant is a focal point of the *Copley Place* development, with three restaurants, three bars, and the largest ballroom and most expansive exhibition area in any Boston hotel. For relaxation, there's an indoor pool, health club, and gameroom. Business services also are available. 110 Huntington Ave. (phone: 236-5800; 800-228-9290; fax: 236-9378).

Marriott, Long Wharf A striking five-story atrium is the centerpiece of this big downtown property (412 rooms) at the foot of State Street. The *Harbor Terrace Sea Grille* requires a jacket and tie; the more casual *Rachel's Lounge* provides taped contemporary music for dancing nightly. A ballroom, indoor-outdoor pool, and health club offer diversions. Other amenities include room service until midnight, a concierge, and business services. 296 State St. (phone: 227-0800; 800-228-9290; fax: 227-2867).

Park Plaza Just south of the *Public Garden,* between Back Bay and the theater district, this venerable establishment has a large and bustling lobby and spacious rooms. *Legal Sea Foods,* with good seafood (see *Eating Out*), and *Café Rouge,* with respectable American dishes, are here. Other amenities include 24-hour room service, a concierge, and business services. One Park Plaza at Arlington St. (phone: 426-2000; 800-225-2008; fax: 426-5545).

Royal Sonesta This flagship of the Sonesta chain boasts 400 tastefully decorated rooms and five eye-catching suites, along with an outpost of *Davio's* (see *Eating Out*), one of the area's best northern Italian restaurants. There's also a fully outfitted health club with a pool. Business services also are available. 5 Cambridge Pkwy. (near Kendall Sq.), Cambridge (phone: 491-3600; 800-SONESTA; fax: 661-5956).

Sheraton Boston A huge, 1,252-room modern hotel in the *Prudential Center,* it's surrounded by fine places to shop. Three restaurants, two cocktail lounges, and a year-round pool and health club provide plenty of diversion. Business services also are available. 39 Dalton St., *Prudential Center* (phone: 236-2000; 800-325-3535; fax: 236-1702).

Sheraton Commander A comfortable 176-room hotel directly on the *Cambridge Common,* within walking distance of *Harvard University* and Harvard Square, this is where many visiting scholars stay. The lobby is formal and elegant, with gold trim and a large chandelier. There's a fitness room and sun deck with lovely views of Cambridge. Business services also are available. 16 Garden St., Cambridge (phone: 547-4800; 800-325-3535; fax: 868-8322).

Westin, Copley Place This opulent 36-story, 804-room property is one of two hotels in burgeoning *Copley Place.* Its *Turner Fisheries* restaurant serves award-winning clam chowder in a town renowned for its chowder. There's also a fully outfitted health club with a pool, saunas, and masseuse. Other amenities include 24-hour room service, a concierge, and business services. 10 Huntington Ave. (phone: 262-9600; 800-228-3000; fax: 451-2750).

MODERATE

57 Park Plaza Howard Johnson's They're pretty much the same everywhere. This one offers 353 rooms, free parking, a year-round pool, and a location convenient to downtown. Business services also are available. 200 Stuart St. (phone: 482-1800; 800-654-2000; fax: 451-2750).

Holiday Inn–Boston Government Center In Boston's old West End, convenient to Beacon Hill, the Freedom Trail, *Faneuil Hall Marketplace,* and the *Massachusetts General Hospital* medical complex, this familiar replica of the national chain offers 301 guestrooms (including some on a deluxe Executive Level), an outdoor pool, two restaurants (notably, the *James Michael*), and a top-floor lounge. A movie theater is next door. All rooms are air conditioned and have cable TV. 5 Blossom St. (phone: 742-7630; 800-HOLIDAY; fax: 742-4192).

Howard Johnson's Cambridge On the Charles River 10 minutes from downtown Boston, this modern, 205-room facility is a few minutes' drive from both Harvard and MIT and is popular with tour groups and parents visiting their student offspring. It's not easily accessible by public transportation. A few rooms have balconies, and all have good views. There's a pool and free parking. Business services also are available. 777 Memorial Dr. (phone: 492-7777; 800-654-2000; fax: 492-7777, ext. 1799).

Inn at Harvard This modern building juts into an intersection near Harvard Square, its style echoing that of the Georgian and Federal brick dormitories that surround it. With 113 rooms and a central atrium, it has a homey, distinctly collegiate feel. Each room is hung with replicas of art from Harvard's museums. Although it was built by the university to host its many visitors, the inn is also open to the public. Updated New England–style food is served in the atrium for breakfast and dinner. Business services also are available. 1201 Massachusetts Ave., Cambridge (phone: 491-2222; fax: 496-5020).

Newbury A brick and brownstone townhouse that has been converted into an urban bed and breakfast establishment. Its location—in the heart of Back Bay, on a street of boutiques, cafés, and galleries—is perfect for city-philes who prefer country living. The 15 rooms are decorated in a simple, 19th-century style. A continental breakfast is served in the parlor and on the street-side patio in the summertime. 261 Newbury St. (phone: 437-7666).

Tremont House Set in the heart of Boston's theater district, this 281-room property was built as the national headquarters of the *Elks Club* in 1925. The resplendent lobby features a marble staircase, a mammoth crystal chandelier, and lots of gold leaf. There are two nightclubs—the *Roxy* offers big band and 1940s music, and the *Juke Box* has a 1950s and 1960s theme— and a famous eatery, the *Broadway Deli*. The double rooms have queen-size beds. Business services also are available. 275 Tremont St. (phone: 426-1400; 800-228-5151; fax: 482-6730).

267 Commonwealth A stay in this nine-room urban inn in the middle of Boston's Back Bay can be a memorable experience. Built in an 1880 townhouse, it was restored several years back (by Bob Vila, former host of the "This Old House" series on public television). The suites all feature kitchens, working fireplaces, and gorgeous woodwork. The helpful staff provides guests with a variety of personal services, from dry cleaning to tour arrangements. Even if you don't stay here, you may want to incorporate this place into your tour of the Victorian buildings of the Back Bay (see *Walk 3: Back Bay* in DIRECTIONS). No credit cards accepted. 267 Commonwealth Ave. (phone: 267-6776).

INEXPENSIVE

Chandler Inn Modest and comfortable, and conveniently located between Copley and Park Squares, near *Copley Place,* it has 56 rooms and provides a complimentary continental breakfast in the lobby. 26 Chandler St. at Berkeley St. (phone: 482-3450; 800-842-3450).

Howard Johnson's Fenway A perfect location for *Fenway Park,* the *Museum of Fine Arts,* the *Isabella Stewart Gardner Museum,* and the *Prudential Center.* There is a restaurant, lounge, outdoor pool, valet service, bellhops, and a multilingual staff. 1271 Boylston St. (phone: 267-8300; fax: 267-8300, ext. 151).

Howard Johnson's Kenmore Square Ideally situated near *Boston University,* it features a restaurant, two lounges, an indoor rooftop swimming pool, valet service, and free parking. Business services also are available. 575 Commonwealth Ave. (phone: 267-3100; fax: 267-3100, ext. 40).

Midtown In Back Bay, across the street from the *Christian Science World Headquarters* and near the *Prudential Center,* this low-rise property, flanked by ritzier lodgings on either side, is a darling of tour groups. All rooms feature cable TV. 220 Huntington Ave. (phone: 262-1000; 800-343-1177; fax: 262-8739).

Ramada Inn/Airport Conveniently located just over a mile from *Logan Airport.* There is a pub, a restaurant, a glass-enclosed swimming pool, health facilities with sauna, and free shuttle to the airport. Business services also are available. 225 McClellan Hwy. (phone: 569-5250; 800-228-2323; fax: 569-5159).

EATING OUT

Boston doesn't have a reputation as a culinary capital, but the 1980s brought a wealth of sophisticated restaurants—both expensive and moderately priced—opened by talented young chefs, many of whom actively sought to develop a new New England–style cuisine. Bostonians' appetites and culinary standards rose to the occasion, and the city now supports a vital restaurant community. Visitors have their pick of many wonderful dining spots. Expect to pay $100 or more for two at one of the places we've noted as expensive; between $50 and $100 at those rated moderate; and $50 or under at those listed as inexpensive. Prices do not include drinks, wine, or tips. All telephone numbers are in the 617 area code unless otherwise indicated. Unless otherwise noted, restaurants are open daily for lunch and dinner. Where they are accepted, *reservations are advised.*

For an unforgettable dining experience, we begin with our culinary favorites, followed by our cost and quality choices, listed by price category.

Biba Owner Lydia Shire inspires intense feelings among foodies. Most rave; some think she tries too hard. But all keep coming back to see what she will do next. The surprises start with the six-part menu: Instead of the typical divisions of appetizer, entrée, and dessert, here you'll find meat, fish, legumina (salads and vegetables), starch, sweets, and offal (sweetbreads and other animal parts, such as tongue and kidneys, prepared in a variety of tasty ways). Entrées draw on the spices and flavors of many cultures—the kitchen makes good use of its tandoori and wood-burning ovens. The street-level bar, with its light menu, has become the place to see and be seen. The striking photos of exotic lands that grace its walls were taken by Shire on her many travels. The decor throughout—bold geometric patterns in burnt reds and golds—is the handiwork of noted designer Adam Tihany. Closed for lunch on Saturdays. Reservations necessary. Major credit cards accepted. 272 Boylston St. (phone: 426-7878).

L'Espalier Time-tested European cooking techniques with fresh New England ingredients characterize the fare at this polished Back Bay restaurant. The three-course meals are prix fixe (and a bit expensive). Among devotees' favorites are the salad of Maine lobster with corn fritters, tempura soft-shelled crab, grilled Atlantic salmon, morels and minted peas, and maple cheesecake. During the weekdays, a sampler menu is available. Chef Frank McClelland now features simpler dishes and larger portions, but he has not tampered with the impressive 150-item wine list. Set in a restored 19th-century townhouse, this elegant eatery has three lovely dining rooms: The salon and the parlor, both on the first floor, are light and airy, thanks to their large windows; the library, on the second floor, has a clubby atmosphere, enhanced by deep peach walls and lots of mahogany. Each has a marble fireplace and dazzling displays of flowers. Closed Sundays. Reservations advised. Major credit cards accepted. 30 Gloucester St. (phone: 262-3023).

Hamersley's Bistro A bustling little place in the chic South End, it offers all the atmosphere and inexpensive delights of a French country bistro. A favorite is the roast chicken (marinated in garlic, lemon, and parsley) and old-fashioned mashed potatoes. Also featured are veal chops, bouillabaisse, and, as an appetizer, grilled shiitake mushrooms with garlic on toast. The extensive wine list is prepared and explained by one of the best stewards in town, and you can order excellent wine by the glass. The main dining room has a window on the kitchen; the redhead in a red baseball cap working over the grill is none other than proprietor Gordon Hamersley. On Sunday nights, he hands the kitchen over to his sous-chef. Prices drop slightly and the experimental factor rises, but it's worth the risk: One sous-chef, Jody Adams, went on to get rave reviews as head chef at *Michela's* restaurant (below). Reservations advised. MasterCard and Visa accepted. 578 Tremont St. (phone: 267-6068).

Jasper's Owner/chef Jasper White attracts local seafood aficionados by featuring Yankee classics with a twist including an elegant version of a New England boiled dinner with johnnycakes and caviar, pan-roasted lobster with chervil, and a mixed grill of marinated quail and duck sausage. But the menu changes often to take advantage of local produce and seafood, so you're likely to find other surprises. In deference to the recession of the early 1990s, Jasper lowered his prices, at least to the point where it is possible for two to enjoy an excellent meal here for under $100 (including wine). *Jasper's* has three intimate dining areas, one with booths. The decor, with its exposed brick, red lacquer chairs, and blown-glass sculptures, shows the same artful blend of rusticity and elegance as the menu. Open Tuesdays through Saturdays for dinner only; last seatings at 9:45 PM. Reservations advised. Major credit cards accepted. 240 Commercial St. (phone: 523-1126).

Locke-Ober Café This is an authentic Boston institution, and a crucial link in the proverbial old boys' network. Tucked into an unassuming side street near *Filene's Basement,* this restaurant has more mahogany, Victorian stained glass, and blue serge suits than you can shake a croquet mallet at. About the only thing that has changed since the restaurant opened in 1875 is that women are now allowed in the *Men's Grill.* This Brahmin stronghold has probably hosted more business deals and political arrangements than most of the office towers in the nearby financial district. The menu seems to be immune from change, still heavy on seafood dishes and such traditional dishes as steak tartare and Indian pudding; try the lobster bisque or the chicken Richmond under glass. The gray-haired staff, in black ties and long white aprons, is almost as venerable as the restaurant itself. On the wall behind the dark-mahogany L-shaped bar is a painting of a reclining nude; she is draped in black when *Harvard* loses to *Yale.* There's a private club, *Yvonne's,* in the rear. Don't enter without a fat wallet and (for men) a jacket and tie. Reservations advised. Major credit cards accepted. 3 Winter Pl. (phone: 542-1340).

Anago Bistro An understated, tranquil space enlivened by bouquets of fresh flowers, it serves some of the city's best continental fare from a menu that changes constantly. Specialties include crab and scallop casserole, braised venison, maple barbecued chicken, and wild mushroom stew. Closed Sundays and Mondays. Reservations advised. Major credit cards accepted. 798 Main St., Kendall Sq., Cambridge (phone: 492-9500 or 876-8444).

Anthony's Pier 4 Sometimes overrun with tourists, this Boston institution has a dramatic location on the harbor, plus a commodious waterfront deck where you can have drinks and enjoy the view while you wait for your table. Good seafood and generous servings are its stock in trade. Reservations advised. Major credit cards accepted. 140 Northern Ave. (phone: 423-6363).

Armani Express This upscale dining emporium offers dishes as finely tailored as the suits in the adjacent *Armani* boutique: Try chef Roberto Saracino's *pansoti* (triangular ravioli) *al funghi porcini* sautéed in a butter and sage sauce, or any of the consistently wonderful seasoned rice dishes such as the *risotto al pescatore,* with seafood and a light tomato broth. There is a trattoria downstairs, with a busy oak bar, and the refined, Italianate upstairs dining room was designed by Armani himself. Major credit cards accepted. Reservations advised. 214 Newbury St. (phone: 437-0909).

Aujourd'hui The lovely, second-story centerpiece of the *Four Seasons,* this hotel dining room has few peers for ambience, food, or wine. The American-cum-continental menu, which changes seasonally, features appetizing "alternative cuisine" specials, the creation of chef Jamie Mammano, that are both good and good for you. Excellent service. Open daily for all three meals. Reservations advised. Major credit cards accepted. 200 Boylston St. (phone: 451-1392).

Bay Tower Room Featuring a breathtaking view of Boston Harbor from 33 stories up, this restfully elegant dining room is the perfect setting for special-occasion suppers and banquets. The American and continental specialties change seasonally. Piano music is featured during early evening hours, with a live combo taking over later on Fridays and Saturdays. Open Mondays through Saturdays for dinner only; open on Sundays for private functions. Reservations necessary. Major credit cards accepted. 60 State St. (phone: 723-1666).

Le Bocage Some of the most consistently delectable French food available in New England is served in this elegant establishment, located in a suburb west of Boston. Both Gallic regional and classic entrées grace the menu, which changes to suit the season. A bright, efficient staff and a fine wine cellar add to the pleasurable dining. Closed Sundays. Reservations advised. Major credit cards accepted. 72 Bigelow Ave., Watertown (phone: 923-1210).

Café Budapest Decorated in the lavish Eastern European tradition, it is renowned for fine continental and Hungarian cooking. This is a wonderful place to linger over superb strudel and some of the best coffee anywhere. Reservations advised. Major credit cards accepted. 90 Exeter St. (phone: 266-1979).

Chez Nous Sophisticated French fare is served in a luxurious, yet intimate, setting. The service is truly accommodating and, in the tradition of quiet, elegant establishments, nearly invisible. Daily fresh fish, rack of lamb Provençal, beef tenderloin spiced with thyme and port, and roast duck garnished with green peppercorns and cognac are all menu standouts. Closed Sundays. Reservations advised. Major credit cards accepted. 147 Huron Ave., Cambridge (phone: 864-6670).

Davide Though on the edge of the North End, it's far from the typical neighborhood red-checked tablecloth and red sauce place. Specialties include rack of lamb *valdostana,* a lightly breaded veal chop stuffed with prosciutto and fontina cheese, and pasta, which is hand-rolled by Davide himself. Closed at lunchtime on weekends. Reservations advised. Major credit cards accepted. 326 Commercial Ave. (phone: 227-5745).

Davio's This northern Italian eatery has developed into a local chain. Regional and continental entrées are consistently well prepared, highlighted by veal chops, homemade pasta, and "upscale" pizza combinations. Good wines, good service, elegant surroundings. Reservations advised. Major credit cards accepted. Three locations: 269 Newbury St. (phone: 262-4810); 204 Washington St. in Brookline Village (phone: 738-4810); and in the *Royal Sonesta,* 5 Cambridge Pkwy., Cambridge (phone: 661-4810).

Hampshire House Thoroughly evocative of 19th-century Boston is this former mansion turned tavern, restaurant—and tourist trap. The *Oak Room Lounge* is a paneled, clubby café-bar with moose heads on the wall and a fire blazing in the winter. It offers a simple continental menu and a range of lighter fare. In the eminently Victorian dining room overlooking the *Public Garden,* more elegant American offerings, such as New York strip steaks and chicken Divan, are served. The *Bull & Finch* pub was the inspiration for (but not the actual setting of) the television series "Cheers" (see *Nightclubs and Nightlife*). Reservations necessary. Major credit cards accepted. 84 Beacon St. (phone: 227-9600).

Harvest Look for the neon sign marking this colorful eatery. Sandwiches and generous drinks are served in its cordially cramped bar; there's also a café and a secluded outdoor patio. Although inconspicuously tucked into a back corner of the former Design Research complex in Harvard Square, the dining room menu here features nicely executed international dishes in its nouvelle cuisine repertoire as well as fine salads, wines, and desserts. The café and bar offer bistro fare, and excellent service. Reservations advised. Major credit cards accepted. 44 Brattle St., Cambridge (phone: 492-1115).

Julien The grandeur of the decor, with its high ceilings, gilded walls, and graceful Queen Anne chairs, creates a wonderful dining atmosphere. Situated in the old Members Court of the former *Federal Reserve Bank Building* (now the *Meridien* hotel), this dining spot produces Alsatian-inspired creations such as homemade terrine of foie gras, a ragout of sea scallops and sea urchins, and breast of squab with cabbage and truffles, under the attentive eye of consulting chef Marc Haeberlin, whose *L'Auberge de L'Ill* in Alsace has earned three Michelin stars. Reservations advised. Major credit cards accepted. 250 Franklin St. (phone: 451-1900).

Maison Robert Among the finest French restaurants in the city, with first-rate food, drink, ambience, and service. Owner-chef Lucien Robert, one of the founding fathers of Boston's culinary revolution, has taught many of the city's chefs and continues to prepare unusual sauces for his fish, fowl, and meat dishes. Two dining areas, *Ben's Café* downstairs (on the patio in summer) and the elegant *Bonhomme Richard* upstairs, are open for lunch and dinner. Closed Sundays. Reservations necessary. Major credit cards accepted. 45 School St., in the *Old City Hall* (phone: 227-3370).

Marais The latest hot spot in Boston's theater district, it resembles an intimate Paris bistro from the 1920s, with dark wood furniture, yellow walls, and authentic posters from the period. The menu features a wide array of Mediterranean dishes. Open for dinner only. Closed Sundays. Reservations advised. Major credit cards accepted. 116 Boylston St. (phone: 482-7799).

Mr. Leung's Linen napery, artful flower arrangements, lavish service, and a subdued, elegant setting dispel the myth that Chinese restaurants have to mean Formica tables and noisy dining. The flavors of the dishes are as subtle as the decor. Specialties include Peking duck and lobster with ginger and scallions. Closed for lunch on weekends. Reservations advised. Major credit cards accepted. 545 Boylston St. (phone: 236-4040).

Plaza The space and decor are the height of Victorian splendor, the menu is classic continental, and the service is exquisitely correct. A great place to go when you want to impress someone. Open for dinner Tuesdays through Saturdays. Reservations advised. Major credit cards accepted. *Copley Plaza Hotel,* 138 St. James St. (phone: 267-5300, ext. 1048).

Rarities This elegant hotel dining spot features a creative nouvelle American menu, impeccable service, and a quality wine list. The seasonal menus highlight fresh local products, prepared with an international touch; the chefs take inspiration from Asian and South American cooking styles. Open for dinner Mondays through Saturdays. Reservations advised. Major credit cards accepted. *Charles Hotel,* 1 Bennett St., Cambridge (phone: 864-1200, ext. 1214).

Ritz-Carlton Large, lovely, and serenely elegant, this is one of only two places in town where you can enjoy a view of the *Public Garden* while dining with old-fashioned formality. The cuisine is continental, very good, and served by an expert staff. Men must wear jackets and ties at dinner. Reservations advised. Major credit cards accepted. *Ritz Carlton Hotel,* 15 Arlington St. (phone: 536-5700).

St. Cloud One of the first culinary outposts in the now-trendy South End, it's still one of the best. The menu changes monthly, but you'll always find dishes such as rack of lamb with grilled vegetables and roasted salmon served with artichoke risotto. They serve the city's best hamburgers, too: A recent incarnation was accompanied by avocado salsa and a Maine crab fritter. A light, café-style menu is also available. Reservations advised. Major credit cards accepted. 557 Tremont St. (phone: 353-0202).

Upstairs at the Pudding Set in the old upstairs dining room of Harvard's famous *Hasty Pudding Club* (the walls are lined with original, hand-painted show bills from the club's productions of years past), this elegant place is truly Old Ivy, but the food is decidedly contemporary—and first-rate. Subtle northern Italian fare is featured. The veal scaloppine is excellent. Order from the à la carte menu, or choose the prix fixe tasting menu, which allows you to choose one dish from each of the four courses offered. The outdoor terrace, situated in the herb garden, offers a savory dining experience on warm summer nights. *Harvard* singing groups frequently perform at Sunday brunch. Reservations advised. Major credit cards accepted. 10 Holyoke St., Cambridge (phone: 864-1933).

MODERATE

Another Season An intimate spot on Beacon Hill with murals evoking turn-of-the-century Paris, its menu changes monthly and features inventive continental cooking. Fresh seafood, a vegetarian entrée, and a marvelous array of desserts always are available. There's also an inexpensive prix fixe menu that has a weekly culinary theme. Dinner only; closed Sundays. Reservations advised. Major credit cards accepted. 97 Mt. Vernon St. (phone: 367-0880).

Art Zone Among the city's trendiest dining spots, it features delicious barbecued meat, served in a funky former warehouse. The tables are especially interesting—dioramas under glass, they were created by local artists especially for this place, and each one is different. Reservations advised. Major credit cards accepted. 150 Kneeland St. (phone: 695-0087).

Blue Diner This is authentic American food in a refurbished downtown diner—despite its wine list, fancy neon lights, and designer label clientele. Though there are items on the menu that lean toward the nouvelle, there is enough hearty meat loaf, mashed potatoes, gravy, cranberry sauce, and coconut pie to make up for it. Since there aren't many tables, this is a cozy dining experience. Open 24 hours Tuesdays through Saturdays, and until late on Sundays and Mondays. No reservations. Major credit cards accepted. 178 Kneeland St. (phone: 338-4639).

The Blue Room Despite the name, the latest inspiration of local restaurateurs Chris Schlesinger and Stan Frankenheimer feels as warm and cozy as a red brick oven, thanks to the open kitchen, glowing grills, and exposed brick walls. The house specialties are grilled and roasted meat and seafood, such as rabbit mole, black-and-blue T-bone steaks, Persian spiced duck, and peanut-crusted tuna steaks. Their pupu platter—an assortment of exotic salads, pickles, and noodles—is a real treat. Closed at lunchtime on weekends. Reservations necessary. Major credit cards accepted. 1 Kendall Sq. (phone: 494-9034).

Broadway Deli The Boston–New York "deli wars" have found a savory, satisfying harmony in this bright, bustling little eatery in the theater district. From corned beef and chopped liver to authentic egg creams and ultra-rich cheesecake, all the required deli delights are available at tables and for takeout. No reservations. Major credit cards accepted. 275 Tremont St. (phone: 426-1344).

Café Lampara The Italian-cuisine cousin to *Skipjack's* (see below) in terms of the creativity of the menu, this is the place to get excellent and unusual pizza and pasta. The café's popular roasted half chicken, however, is the item many favor. Reservations advised. Major credit cards accepted. 916 Commonwealth Ave. (phone: 566-0300).

Cajun Yankee The original gathering place of the New England crawdaddy crowd, this down-home, creole spot is perpetually packed. All the Cajun staples are here—blackened fish, jambalaya, sweet potato pie—in spicy, pungent abundance, and the beverages are correspondingly "down South." Closed Sundays and Mondays. Reservations advised. Major credit cards accepted. 1193 Cambridge St., Inman Sq., Cambridge (phone: 576-1971).

Changsho The food served in the recently relocated home of this Cambridge institution is still the best Chinese cooking you'll find outside New York's Chinatown. The restaurant has moved from its tiny, crowded storefront into a strikingly elegant—and much larger—space a block away. No reservations. Major credit cards accepted. 1712 Massachusetts Ave., Cambridge (phone: 547-6565).

Chart House In the oldest building on Boston's waterfront, its interior is a strikingly handsome arrangement of lofty spaces, natural wood, exposed red brick, and comfortable captain's chairs. The menu consists of abundant portions of steaks and seafood, with all the salad you can eat included in the reasonable prices. The award-winning clam chowder is superb. Reservations advised on weekend nights. Major credit cards accepted. 60 Long Wharf (phone: 227-1576).

Cottonwood At this very popular café, both food and decor are done in a modern Southwestern style. Look for such imaginative dishes as Rocky Mountain lamb chops, served over cilantro with raspberry *chipotle* chili sauce. Snack on deep-fried jalapeños stuffed with cheese and shrimp at the bar, or sip fresh fruit margaritas on the tiny terrace on a Cambridge summer evening. Reservations advised. Major credit cards accepted. Two locations: 1815 Massachusetts Ave., Cambridge (phone: 661-7440); and 222 Berkeley St. (phone: 247-2225).

Dali Garlic braids hanging from the ceiling, white plaster walls daubed with kitschy swirls, and waiters in red jackets and black cummerbunds are not the only things that make this *tapas* bar not far from *Harvard* seem authentic: The kitchen turns out Spanish specialties seldom seen outside Iberia. From the marinated olives served with drinks to the changing list of *tapas* (hors d'oeuvres) and entrées such as *pescado al sal* (whole snapper baked in a salt crust) or *conejo escabechado* (rabbit braised in red wine with juniper berries), dining here is a delicious adventure. There's usually a wait for a table, but if you're not in a hurry, order a pitcher of sangria and have another dish of olives. Closed Sundays. No reservations. Major credit cards accepted. 415 Washington St., Somerville (phone: 661-3254).

David's This new restaurant, which took over the space previously occupied by the popular *Bnu* trattoria, is busy establishing its own dedicated following. Its decor reflects the restaurant's theater district location, as does its pre- and post-theater dinner service. The menu is heavily influenced by the flavors of the Mediterranean, with an imaginative pasta selection and entrées such as lamb kebabs with couscous and minted chutney. In fine weather, there is limited outdoor seating as well. Closed Sundays. Reservations advised. Major credit cards accepted. 123 Stuart St. (phone: 367-8405).

Dover Sea Grille This understated, relaxed, beautifully appointed seafood restaurant and lounge in Brookline is just a clamshell's throw from both *Fenway Park* and the *Harvard Medical School*. Marvelous grilled entrées, especially salmon and swordfish, are specialties, as are bountiful salads and superb desserts. A lighter café menu is also served. "Early Catch" specials are available weeknights from 5:30 to 6:30 PM. Reservations advised. Major credit cards accepted. 1223 Beacon St. (phone: 566-7000).

Durgin-Park Though famed for generous servings of roast beef, pot roast, prime ribs, oyster stew, Boston baked beans, and Indian pudding, the kitchen now is way below par. However, its long, communal tables are still crowded with convivial diners attended by sharp-witted waitresses who like to give patrons a rough time (it's partly an act). No reservations. No credit cards accepted. 340 *Faneuil Hall Marketplace* (phone: 227-2038).

East Coast Grill You might not expect great Southern barbecue around Beantown, but this coolly stylish Inman Square grill repeatedly wins national praise and prizes—and the crowds waiting to be seated testify to the attitude of the locals. In addition to authentic North Carolina shredded pork barbecue, Texas brisket barbecue, and Memphis-style dry-rub ribs, you can get a great spit-roasted chicken, imaginative duck and lamb dishes, and delectable grilled swordfish paired with something spicy—ginger-scallion relish or a mayonnaise of smoked *chipotle* chilies. And if the food isn't hot enough for you, the owners thoughtfully leave a bottle of their Inner Beauty Hot Sauce on every table. No reservations (and there's usually a good wait). Major credit cards accepted. 1271 Cambridge St., Cambridge (phone: 491-6568).

Icarus For some reason, this respected restaurant is never crowded, making it a great place for a quiet, intimate meal. The room resembles a Brahmin's drawing room with dark wood, green walls, and oversize sculptures. The contemporary American food is always imaginative and well prepared. The menu, which is predominantly seafood, changes every six weeks. On Sunday nights, the wine café offers *tapa*-size portions and wine by the glass. Open daily for dinner; there is also brunch on Sundays. Reservations advised. Major credit cards accepted. 3 Appleton St. (phone: 426-1790).

Jimmy's Harborside Located about a whale's tail from the Fish Pier, this is an incredibly popular seafood spot with a solid reputation. Every seat in the main dining room has an excellent view of Boston Harbor. The traditional seafood menu has been expanded to include some Italian dishes, veal, and tenderloin. The wine list is replete with fine American wines. Don't mistake *Jimmy's* for *Jimbo's,* a less engaging place across the street. Reservations advised. Most major credit cards accepted. 242 Northern Ave. (phone: 423-1000).

Legal Sea Foods If you don't mind waiting in line, you'll find fresh and well-prepared seafood. No reservations. Major credit cards accepted. Several locations: *Park Plaza Hotel,* corner of Columbus Ave. and Arlington St. (phone: 426-4444); in the *Chestnut Hill Shopping Mall,* 43 Boylston St. (phone: 277-7300); 5 Cambridge Center, Kendall Sq., Cambridge (phone: 864-3400); and *Copley Place* (phone: 266-7775).

Michela's Housed in a huge, converted building in the Kendall Square area of Cambridge, this chic eatery draws the cognoscenti from all around Boston to sample American food with a distinct northern Italian accent. Choose either the dining room proper or the café (which doesn't take reservations). The two menus are completely different, but not the panache with which the food is prepared. Closed Sundays. Reservations advised for the dining room, especially Friday and Saturday nights. Major credit cards accepted. 1 Athenaeum St., Cambridge (phone: 225-2121).

Milk Street Café Its original home sandwiched into a sparkling niche of the financial district (there's now a second location), this bustling vegetarian and fish cafeteria presents superb breakfasts and lunches. The muffins, smoked salmon platter, flavorful soup, and generous, artful quiche are perennial pleasers. Open weekdays until 3 PM. Reservations advised. No credit cards accepted. Two locations: 50 Milk St. (phone: 542-2433) and 101 Main St., Kendall Sq., Cambridge, near *MIT* (phone: 491-8286).

Mirabelle Beautifully adorned with murals and warms woods, this place is the pride of catering wizard Stephen Elmont. Chefs are adept at many cuisines. Open daily for breakfast, lunch, and dinner. Reservations advised. Major credit cards accepted. 85 Newbury St. (phone: 859-4848).

Olives Superb Tuscany-influenced Italian food is served here in a soothing dove-colored dining room with comfortable banquettes. Try the grilled lobster with white bean *raviolone* and artichoke sauce or the *tortelli* of butternut squash with brown butter and sage. Open Tuesdays through Saturdays. Reservations advised for groups of six or more. MasterCard and Visa accepted. 67 Main St., Charlestown (phone: 242-1999).

Paolo This sophisticated place is piles of pasta above every other Hanover Street eatery, offering elegant northern Italian fare in intimate subterranean rooms. You can choose from unusually shaped homemade pasta—the lasagna is a delicate roulade—and delicious meat dishes, such as a veal chop with wild mushrooms in cognac. Ray Santisi and other local pianists make the most of the 1917 Steinway grand. Open for dinner Tuesdays through Sundays. Reservations advised. Major credit cards accepted. 216 Hanover St. (phone: 227-5550).

Rebecca's In this comfortable, modern place, the walls are decorated with hand-painted flowers and accented by exposed brick and works by local artists. The menu, described as "new American," borrows from French, Greek, Indian, and Italian cuisines. No reservations. Major credit cards accepted. 21 Charles St. (phone: 742-9747).

Rocco's The decor in this theater district dining place is as dramatic as the neighborhood's atmosphere, with stage-scale curtains, murals on the ceiling, and two-story picture windows overlooking the street. The menu offers an eclectic choice of Italian fare. Closed Sunday dinner. Reservations advised. Major credit cards accepted. 5 S. Charles St. (phone: 723-6800).

St. Botolph Actually a restored 19th-century brick townhouse, this two-story eatery sports a contemporary interior with exposed brick walls and a continental menu with good, fresh seafood. Lunch served weekdays; dinner nightly; brunch on Sundays. Reservations advised. Major credit cards accepted. 99 St. Botolph St. (phone: 266-3030).

Skipjack's With a dazzling aquarium-like decor, this mariner's delight features an extensive array of innovative seafood dishes (it claims to serve the widest variety of seafood in New England). Snapper Veracruz, ginger calamari, grilled cilantro shrimp, and blackened redfish are just a few of the outstanding choices. For dieters, a spa menu offers 10 items of 400 calories or less. The wine list is extensive and carefully assembled, and the Sunday jazz brunch is a treat. Reservations advised. Major credit cards accepted. Several locations: 500 Boylston St., Copley Sq., Back Bay (phone: 536-3500); 2 Brookline Pl., Brookline (phone: 232-8887); and 5 Bennett St., Charles Sq. (phone: 876-9900).

Small Planet Formerly the *Back Bay Bistro,* this casual place just across Boylston Street from the majestic *Trinity Church* is one of Boston's best modestly priced eateries. The various awards displayed in the bay window tell the story. The duck, venison, and roasted hen dishes are all excellent. Perhaps the best single item is an interesting preparation of catfish in cornmeal with black beans. The wine list is extensive and the decor inviting. Open 11:30 AM until midnight Tuesdays through Saturdays (with a scaled-down menu between main meal hours); opens at 5 PM on Sundays and Mondays. Reservations advised for large parties. Major credit cards accepted. 565 Boylston St. (phone: 536-4477).

Sonsie Owner Patrick Lyons has made a splash with his new restaurant on this busy shopping thoroughfare by offering a menu as inviting as the atmosphere. Doors open into the café in front, and just beyond is a salon filled daily with international newspapers and overstuffed Parisian 1930s chairs. Then there is the dining room, with spacious booths (total dining room capacity is 90), Oriental rugs, and bird's-eye maple paneling; the paintings on the walls were commissioned for the restaurant. Some of the menu choices are grilled pork loin, salmon cooked in sake, and pizza with lime guacamole chicken and jack cheese. Open for breakfast, lunch, and dinner. Reservations strongly advised. Major credit cards accepted. 327 Newbury St. (phone: 351-2500).

Toscano Authentic northern Italian food is served in this elegant room with brick walls and red tiles. The menu changes daily, but you'll always find excellent risotto, homemade pasta, and fresh truffles in season. Closed Sunday lunch. Reservations necessary. American Express accepted. 41 Charles St. (phone: 723-4090).

West Street Grill Off the beaten track, between the *Common* and *Lafayette Place,* this trendy meeting place is the historic home of the Peabody family. Here Nathaniel Hawthorne married Sophia, and Elizabeth opened the bookstore that became the meeting place for such literati as Emerson and Thoreau. Today, it has been renovated to accommodate a striking restaurant (formerly *Cornucopia*) and bar. The menu changes seasonally, but always relies heavily on pasta and grilled dishes. Closed Sundays; dinner only Thursdays through Saturdays. Reservations advised. Major credit cards accepted. 15 West St. (phone: 423-0300).

Ye Olde Union Oyster House It's the real thing: Boston's oldest restaurant. Daniel Webster himself used to guzzle oysters at the wonderful mahogany bar, where skilled shuckers still pry them open before your eyes. Full seafood lunches and dinners are served upstairs, amid well-worn colonial ambience. (One booth is dedicated to John F. Kennedy, once a frequent diner.) Don't miss the seafood chowder. Reservations advised. Major credit cards accepted. 41 Union St. (phone: 227-2750).

INEXPENSIVE

Addis Red Sea Boston's best Ethiopian restaurant (it doesn't have a lot of competition). Patrons sit on tiny, handwoven benches and (the fulfillment of everybody's secret dream) eat only with fingers without social demerit. You just scoop up piles of *watts* (stew) with *injera,* the spongy Ethiopian pancake. Portions are large, the music and ambience are quietly mesmerizing, and the Ethiopian red wine is a delight. Open daily for dinner and for lunch on weekends. Reservations advised. Major credit cards accepted. 544 Tremont St. (phone: 426-8727).

The Barking Crab At the city's only urban clam shack, customers sit at picnic tables under a tent, look out over a none-too-scenic channel of water, and order fresh seafood—fried clams, grilled fish, and boiled lobsters—from a takeout window. Don't miss the homemade clam chowder (New England, natch) and coleslaw. It's rustic, but that doesn't stop legions of suited businesspeople from the nearby financial district from stopping in for a summertime lunch. Closed October through April; closed Monday dinnertime during the first two weeks of May; open until 1 AM nightly the rest of the season. No reservations or credit cards accepted. 88 Sleeper St. (phone: 426-2722).

Bob the Chef Located in the South End is Boston's best soul food restaurant. If you're looking to get downright stuffed, this is the place. All the favorites are served here in generous portions: chitterlings (just say chitlin'), barbecued spareribs, black-eyed peas, collard greens, and grits with breakfast. The sweet potato pie is excellent. All meals come with biscuits and corn bread. Reservations advised for large parties. No credit cards accepted. 604 Columbus Ave. (phone: 536-6204).

Boca Grande If Tex-Mex is what you crave, this eatery is one of the best food values in Boston. Black bean tostadas, generous handmade tamales, and burritos are the favored fare. Reservations unnecessary. Major credit cards accepted. Two locations: 1728 Massachusetts Ave. (phone: 354-5550) and 149 First St., Cambridge (phone: 354-7400).

Casa Romero Though most people don't link Boston with Mexican food, there are indeed a couple of good Mexican eateries. The food here is authentic—

marinated tenderloin of pork, *enchiladas verdes,* garlic soup, and *mole poblano.* The tile tables and wrought iron give this place enough of a Latin American feel to let you forget for a moment that when Bostonians think of south of the border, they're thinking Rhode Island. Open daily for dinner. Reservations advised. Major credit cards accepted. 30 Gloucester St. (phone: 536-4341).

Chau Chow Delicious and inexpensive Cantonese food is served in this plain, crowded little diner in Chinatown. Critics rave over the soup and seafood, particularly the salt-baked shrimp and oysters with black bean sauce. Open weekdays 10 AM to 2 AM, and until 4 AM on weekends. No reservations or credit cards accepted. 52 Beach St. (phone: 426-6266).

Elsie's Lunch This storefront shop, a block from Harvard Yard, has been serving food and drink to famished Harvard students for longer than anyone can remember. A great place to go when your feet are tired, or when you just want to fill up with a basic sandwich or salad. No reservations or credit cards accepted. 71 Mt. Auburn St., Cambridge (phone: 354-8781 or 354-8362).

Goeman The best noodle/tempura shop you'll find outside Tokyo, this is Japan's version of fast food. Big hearty bowls of flavorful broth, *udon, soba,* or *ramen* noodles, and artfully arranged meat or vegetables. Order a classic combination or create your own by choosing ingredients from their list. Open daily for lunch and dinner. Reservations accepted for parties of six or more. Major credit cards accepted. 267 Huntington Ave. (phone: 859-8669) and 1 Kendall Sq., Building 100, Cambridge (phone: 577-9595).

La Groceria Northern Italian cooking in an old house with several dining rooms, each with a distinct character (the intimate top floor is recommended). The pasta is homemade, as are the cheesecake and cannoli. The veal dishes and antipasto, hot and cold, are excellent. Extensive wine list. Open daily for dinner. Reservations advised for large parties. Major credit cards accepted. 853 Main St., Cambridge (phone: 547-9258 or 876-4162).

Jae's Café The food is Korean in inspiration and healthy in preparation. You can find *yukhai* (Korean raw beef), pan-fried dumplings stuffed with shrimp, and several light, mild curries. Every dish has lots of fresh vegetables and little oil. There's also a sushi bar downstairs. Reservations advised. Major credit cards accepted. 520 Columbus Ave. (phone: 421-9405).

Jake and Earl's Dixie BBQ If you feel more like jumping in a taxi, grabbing some great takeout, and heading back to your hotel, aim for this place next door to the *East Coast Grill* (above). It's owned by the same duo, and it's equally passionate about authenticity in barbecue. In addition to doing all the smoking for its sibling next door, this spot offers its own list of spicy specialties. The half-jerk chicken is hot and juicy, and the daily specials, such as a barbecued bologna sandwich, are always original and surprisingly good. And for $3.95, the pulled-pork sandwich (it comes with a moist hunk of corn bread, fresh coleslaw, rich, spicy beans, and a slice of watermelon) is a bargain hunter's delight. The Elvis memorabilia (from license plates to an assortment of plastic and plaster busts) will keep you entertained while you're waiting, which is never very long. Reservations unnecessary. Major credit cards accepted. 1273 Cambridge St., Cambridge (phone: 491-7427).

Massimino's This lovely little spot serves fresh, delicious Italian food at incredibly low prices. Specialties include hot seafood antipasto, saltimbocca, veal marsala, pork chops with vinegar peppers and potatoes, and homemade *tiramisù.* Closed Sundays. No reservations. MasterCard and Visa accepted. 207 Endicott St. (phone: 523-5959).

No-Name Restaurant The name was not a conscious decision. Beginning as a ramshackle joint that counted only the local fishermen as its clientele, this has become a Boston institution serving the freshest seafood in the city (though the folks at *Jimmy's* might dispute this point) to tourists, businesspeople, and the ancient mariners who still frequent the place. With a view of the harbor, this nameless place is also frill-less: Expect Formica tables, paper napkins, and plastic cups. But that's its charm. Though the waitresses are a tad surly, they will fetch some of the finest fried seafood, boiled lobster, and broiled scallops on record. (Also see *Quintessential Boston* in DIVERSIONS.) No reservations. No credit cards accepted. 15½ Fish Pier, just off Northern Ave. (phone: 338-7539).

Rubin's Kosher Delicatessen One of only a few kosher restaurants in the Boston area. Its chopped liver, potato *latkes* (pancakes), and lean pastrami (hot or cold) are the genuine articles. Closed Saturdays, and on Fridays after 2 PM. Reservations unnecessary. Major credit cards accepted. 500 Harvard St., Brookline (phone: 566-8761).

S&M New York Deli This large, bright, and bustling delicatessen is filled with the financial district crowd at lunchtime. The food is authentically New York-style, and the sandwiches (try the Reuben) rival the Big Apple's best. There are about 10 stools along a front counter and 20 tables in the back, or take your order out and have a picnic on *Boston Common,* a short walk up Beacon Street. Closed Sundays. No reservations or credit cards accepted. 12 Beacon St. (phone: 523-8776).

NORTH END RESTAURANTS

This Old World, predominantly Italian district boasts dozens of restaurants crowded into a few square blocks, ranging in quality and price. For cozy, homemade meals, try *Mother Anna's* (211 Hanover St.; phone: 523-8496; reservations only on weekdays; American Express accepted). For great seafood Italian-style, try the *Daily Catch,* which specializes in calamari (squid) dishes, cooked in an open kitchen (323 Hanover St.; phone: 523-8567; reservations advised; major credit cards accepted). Similar in spirit but less well known is *Giacomo's* (355 Hanover St.; phone: 523-9026; no reservations; American Express accepted). Many locals swear by the crunchy, crusty pizzas at *Circle Pizza* (361 Hanover St.; phone: 523-8787; reservations accepted for large groups only; no credit cards accepted). Don't leave the North End without experiencing *la dolce vita*—that's short for how sweet life seems when you're sitting at a sidewalk café, sipping espresso, savoring a cannoli or gelati, watching the world go by. The best espresso and sweets are at *Caffè Dello Sport* (307 Hanover St.; phone: 523-5063) and *Caffè Roma* (241 Hanover St.; phone: 723-1760). Neither accepts reservations or credit cards.

Diversions

Exceptional Pleasures and Treasures

Quintessential Boston

Whether savoring a hot dog at a *Red Sox* game, gutting fish on a harbor pier, participating in a heated political discussion, or sipping tea at the *Ritz,* lowbrows, highbrows, and all sorts in between make up Boston's soul—and they all come together at around 5 PM on Fridays, in the 12-lane mayhem of weekend rush-hour traffic known as the Kenmore Krush. If there is anything at all quintessential about Boston, it is trying to merge in this mess. Other unique—and more enjoyable—Boston experiences are described below.

SPORTS SPOTS Sports are as close to Boston's soul as colonial history or the Democratic Party.

Fenway Park In summer, this sports-obsessed town focuses on the usually unspectacular (though cocky-to-the-bitter-end) hometown baseball team, the *Red Sox.* On home game evenings, Kenmore Square clogs with mad packs of *Sox* fans clamoring to reach one of Boston's main sports shrines, *Fenway Park.* Any summer visit to Boston should include a *Red Sox* game, even if you aren't a fan. Enjoy the smell of freshly mown grass while munching on a Fenway frank (hot dog) and sipping a "beah" (beer) in this, one of the last great urban ballparks. Built in 1912, *Fenway* is home of the Green Monster (the 37-foot-high left-field wall that has driven many a pitcher into early retirement) and many precious memories—for *Red Sox* fans, that is. The *Red Sox* generally beat up on their opponents at home, setting the stage for their annual plummet. (The team hasn't won a *World Series* since 1918, but has come agonizingly close several times.) 4 Yawkey Way (phone: 617-267-1700).

Shawmut Center The dingy but beloved *Boston Garden* (locally pronounced "*gah-*den") will be no more by this autumn, but the glory of the *Celtics,* many-time NBA champions, will blaze just as brightly at the new *Shawmut Center,* next door to the old arena at 150 Causeway Street. The new arena will continue the tradition of festooning the court with championship banners won by the *Celtic* dynasty, with the help of such legends as Bill Russell, Bob Cousy, John Havlicek, and Larry Bird. Meanwhile, the big, bad *Bruins,* who have captured many a *Stanley Cup* thanks to the charismatic Bobby Orr and other hockey greats, will count *Shawmut Center* as their home arena at the start of the 1995–96 season. (Also see *Sports and Fitness* in THE CITY, and *Walk 1: The Fens* in DIRECTIONS.)

Sports Bars When tickets are impossible to get or the teams are playing out of town, it's almost as much fun to join the cheering crowds watching the game at one of Boston's many sports bars (almost any bar in Boston is a sports bar). Since contemporary Bostonians take their sports every bit as seriously as the Puritans took their religion, the sports bar has become the latter-day temple for local team boosters; probably the holiest of shrines is the *Sports Depot* (353 Cambridge St., Allston; phone: 617-783-2300), which bills itself as "the ultimate in casual dining." It's actually the ultimate in casual viewing, with 38 color television sets trained to as many sporting events around the world as its two mammoth satellite dishes can track at any one time (there even are TV sets in the men's and women's rooms, so that not a single play need be missed). Two other spots have unbeatable locations—the *Cask and Flagon* (corner of Lansdowne St. and Brookline Ave.; phone: 617-536-4840), a foul ball away from *Fenway Park;* and the *Sports Café* (120 Causeway St.; phone: 617-723-6664), near the *Shawmut Center,* which is a favorite of the pre- and post-*Celtics* game revelers.

CAMBRIDGE COFFEEHOUSE CONVERSATIONS In Cambridge, home of the country's oldest university, the connoisseur of the fading art of conversation may still hear witty references to Kierkegaard, Kandinsky, and Roger Clemens—all in the same breath. Cantabrigians love to converse, and never more than on Sundays, in their wonderfully cramped coffeehouses. Armed with the Sunday papers, a good dose of Viennese coffee, a piece of linzertorte or a croissant, they settle down for hours of leisurely exchange. There are coffeehouses to suit every temperament. More reserved residents cherish *Café Pamplona* (on Bow St.; no phone or restroom), a little dungeon with a black-and-white tile floor covering its meager square footage. The *Coffee Connection* (36 JFK St.; phone: 617-492-1881) is a favorite of the *Harvard* crowd, and *Passim* (47 Palmer St.; phone: 617-492-7679), which hosts folk music in the evenings and on Sunday afternoons, attracts an earthy, musical clientele. An alert eavesdropper in one of Cambridge's coffeehouses might overhear anything from the pedantic disputations of tweedy, professorial types to the moving confessions of a lovestruck coed; it's almost as much fun to listen as it is to hold one's own in the discourse. This river of conversation must be fed by steady streams of print, and a huge variety of reading materials is sold at *Out of Town News,* a kiosk with the arresting address of Zero Harvard Square. An international temple to the written word, it is the axis around which all Cambridge revolves: Newspapers and magazines from around the world, from the *London Times* to *Pravda,* can be purchased here.

CONCERTS AT THE GARDNER Among the scores of places where you can take in a classical concert in Boston, the most outstanding is one built by a bon vivant

New Yorker who liked to shock Bostonians by wearing a headband at performances of the *Boston Symphony Orchestra* that read, "Oh, you *Red Sox.*" The *Isabella Stewart Gardner Museum* is among the most splendid spaces with four walls and a roof in all of Boston. Gardner, who married John Lowell Gardner, a wealthy Brahmin industrialist, in 1860, built this marble Venetian palazzo with its magnificent courtyard to house the art that she had collected during her worldwide travels. As is stipulated in her will, all the objects in the museum are arranged in the same quirky and crowded way as they were when Mrs. Jack (as she was called) lived on the top floor. Every Sunday afternoon and Tuesday evening (except during the summer), the museum's *Tapestry Room* hosts performances by anyone from grand masters to talented young locals. The large room, with its dark tile floor and subdued lighting, has the quiet serenity of an ancient chapel. Mrs. Gardner's "knickknacks" include an iron pulpit from 16th-century Spain, a Gothic stone fireplace that dates from the early 1500s, and three oaken choir stalls from the late 16th century. The 16th-century Belgian tapestries shimmer in the indirect light that streams in from the mansion's astounding courtyard, while the great mahogany beams in the ceiling—the secret behind the room's excellent acoustics—reverberate with the sound of violin sonatas, piano concertos, or string quartets. The stillness of the room and the richness of its treasures somehow make the experience of the music all the more complete. Though Mrs. Gardner preferred champagne and doughnuts, wine and hors d'oeuvres are served in the *Spanish Cloister* area after each performance. (Also see *Special Places* in THE CITY and *Walk 1: The Fens* in DIRECTIONS.) 280 The Fenway (phone: 617-734-1359).

A RIDE IN THE SWAN BOATS The graceful circling of the swan in the *Public Garden*'s Lagoon is as sure a sign of summer in Boston as the disappearance of ski racks from the tops of automobiles. A 10-minute ride in the Swan Boats, pedaled by student athletes earning next year's tuition under what is billed as the world's smallest suspension bridge, is an experience longer on tradition than on adventure. Nineteenth-century Bostonian Robert Paget originated the rite, inspired by his favorite opera, *Lohengrin,* in which the hero glides to the rescue of his beloved on a boat pulled by a swan. Since most children, however, identify the swan pond with the happy ending of Robert McCloskey's story *Make Way for Ducklings!* (Mr. and Mrs. Mallard and their brood find a safe haven here), the boats are particularly enjoyable for them. Look for the bronze statuettes of the Mallards along the path to the pond—and for the live mallards that skim about the lagoon, keeping a vigilant eye out for bread. (Bring your own bread, especially if you have children with you who might want to join in.) After your ride, be sure to stroll about the painstakingly manicured flower beds, monuments, fountains, and exotic trees of the *Public Garden,* which is adjacent to *Boston Common* and bordered by Beacon, Charles, Boylston, and Arlington Streets. (Also see *Special Places* in THE CITY.)

INTELLECTUAL BOSTON—THE LECTURE CIRCUIT The old adage states that in Washington success is measured by one's influence, in New York by one's wealth, and in Boston by one's knowledge. The city's tradition of serious public lectures dates back to the Puritans, who conducted a "Thursday Lecture" for those assembled near *Faneuil Hall* for market day. Rogues and rapscallions were subjected to fire-and-brimstone excoriations before being hustled out of the meeting hall, the audience fast on their heels, for public punishments and executions. Although those festive times are long past, the tradition of the Thursday Lecture lives—fed by area residents' acute political awareness and varied cultural interests, and by the intellectual ferment provided by more than a dozen local colleges and universities. Consult the Thursday "Calendar" section of the *Boston Globe* or the weekly *Boston Phoenix* for listings. In any given week there may be lectures by distinguished profs, poets, pols, pundits, and policymakers intent on presenting and defending their ideas on topics ranging from "Racism and Science" and "Roots of US Global Policy" to "Women Filmmakers from Québec" and "Urban Gardeners." When lectures end, more is in store. Be sure to wait around for the question-and-answer session that follows nearly every talk—it often leads to a lively exchange of ideas, and occasionally declines into an ugly shouting match. The most respected of the city's ongoing lecture series are the Arco Forum at *Harvard's Kennedy School of Government* (phone: 495-1380), the *Ford Hall Forum* lectures (phone: 617-373-5800), and the midday Thursday lectures at the *Old South Meeting House* (phone: 617-482-6439).

ON AND ALONG THE CHARLES Despite its pollution problem, the Charles River, which flows along the northern edge of Boston and separates it from Cambridge, plays a big role in making Boston livable.

The Charles River Bostonians relish playing both along and on the Charles. During the warm-weather months sailboats lazily tack back and forth, their masts glistening in the sun and mainsails puffing with the steady breeze that sweeps in from the harbor, with the gold dome of the *State House* high atop Beacon Hill shimmering in the background. Thanks to *Community Boating, Inc.,* a sailing club that offers a two-day membership to out-of-towners, visitors with sailing experience can navigate 15-foot Cape Cod Mercuries in the stretch of river between the Longfellow and Memorial Bridges. Even if you can't distinguish a jib from a jibe, or if you think points of sail are *Jordan Marsh* and *Filene's Basement,* you can get your start as a sailor with the assistance of *Community Boating's* seasoned instructors (see *Sports and Fitness* in THE CITY). The savvy seagoer will time a Charles River voyage with one of the occasional summer evening concerts at the *Hatch Shell,* where the *Boston Pops Orchestra* performs its lighthearted repertoire of popular and classical favorites. Only the expert, however, should be on the Charles on *July Fourth,* when the *Independence Day Boston Pops* concert and fireworks display lead to bumper-to-bumper boat traffic. Thousands of people also pack into the Esplanade for the traditional event, which features a sing-along of all-American favorites, a rousing rendition of Tchaikovsky's *1812 Overture,* and a truly spectacular fireworks show. Whether you spectate from land or sea, be advised that your craft must be moored by sundown—and there's usually a tussle for the choice spots of terra firma. You'll want to bring along picnic supplies.

The Esplanade For those who prefer to keep their feet firmly on the ground, the *Esplanade,* a cool strip of parkland along the banks of the Charles, is the perfect place to enjoy the river. The *Esplanade* is Boston's backyard—from this peaceful stretch of greenery, the distant sounds of Boston can be heard in all directions—Cambridge to the right, Back Bay to the left, and *Boston University* straight ahead. It's a favorite spot of cross-country skiers and skaters in the winter; bikers, runners, Frisbee throwers, and sunners in the summer; and walkers, runners, and joggers year-round. If you're feeling especially spirited, take the path that borders the Charles River to Watertown, meandering first through a thin strip of thickets and past the duck-filled lagoon to the west. On the way you'll encounter a number of sprawling parks where there are ample benches, gardens, and green stretches to sit and watch the river flow by.

FILENE'S BASEMENT This subterranean sea of women's and men's clothing, housewares, luggage, shoes, and accessories is the ultimate Boston shopping experience, considered by many Bostonians to be a one-stop clothing shop. There is now a chain of *Filene's Basement* stores that offer the discounts of the flagship, but they can't duplicate its ambience. A visit to the original *Filene's Basement* (*Downtown Crossing,* 426 Washington St.; phone: 617-542-2011) requires grit, assertiveness, endurance, and an indefatigable passion for getting clothes on the cheap. The atmosphere is frenetic, with shoppers pawing through huge racks and tables of merchandise in search of truly stupendous bargains. Don't be surprised if you see women trying on garments in the aisles—for years there was no ladies' dressing room here, so discreet public disrobing became de rigueur. (There is now a small communal dressing room for women.) The diversity of the stock (designer items from such upscale shops as *Neiman Marcus* and *Saks,* more moderate name-brand merchandise, and some goods of questionable quality) makes timing and a little information crucial. The price tags are easy enough to understand: After an item is in the *Basement* for 12 shopping days, the (already low) price goes down 25%; if it's still there after 18 days, the discount is 50%; after 24 days the price is reduced by 75%. When the item has been in the *Basement* a full 30 days, it is donated to charity. There are occasional $60 men's suit sales, $10 dress sales, and $200 wedding gown sales that are advertised in the *Boston Globe.* To some shoppers, *Filene's Basement* is a way of living life on the edge: They gamble that a coveted item will still be around for the next markdown (some shoppers even hide soon-to-be-reduced items—under an ugly coat on the other side of the store, say—in the hopes that they will remain there, undetected, until the next discount kicks in). With the fast-paced turnover, however, there are frequent disappointments. The store is restocked on Sunday nights, so Monday morning is the best time to strike.

TEA AT THE RITZ From the wing-back chairs and ornate gilded ceiling to the Earl Grey tea and delicate watercress sandwiches, afternoon tea at the *Ritz-Carlton* hotel is an experience simply dripping with Bostoniana—which is to say, ossified Anglophilia. A prim musician strums soothing melodies on the harp while doting waiters and waitresses bring delicate, crustless sandwiches, scones with Devonshire cream and strawberry preserves, assorted pastries, and the obligatory teas and coffees. The daily ritual in the second-floor *Tea Lounge* has been a favorite of Boston society since the *Ritz-Carlton,* the grande dame of Boston hotels, opened in 1927 on the corner of Commonwealth and Arlington. This cherished Boston tradition affords visitors temporary entry into a Brahmin stronghold; to avoid ejection, gentlemen should don a jacket first. But don't be intimidated by the aura of tradition. Slide right into that gilded chair, exchange bons mots with your cultivated brethren, and daintily sip and nibble the afternoon away. If you're not sure of protocol, just follow the lead of the punctilious ladies whose poise seems to indicate that they've spent the better parts of their lives here. Tea is served daily from 3 to 5:30 PM. (Also see "Grand Hotels" in *Checking In,* THE CITY.)

AN ARNOLD ARBORETUM PICNIC Bostonians are irrepressible in the zeal with which they reacquaint themselves with nature after the seemingly never-ending winter. Heavy togs are shed and people burst outdoors in a frenzy, and one of their most popular destinations is the *Arnold Arboretum.* Located in the city's Jamaica Plain neighborhood, this link in the *Emerald Necklace* (an 8-mile chain of parkland designed by famed landscape architect Frederick Law Olmsted) is a living laboratory of flowers and foliage. A network of paths weaves among the lilacs, azaleas, rhododendrons, magnolia trees, cherry blossoms, and about 14,000 other species of flowers, fruit trees, and shrubs. The *Arboretum* is an ideal place for a picnic—these 265 acres provide an ample selection of vine-veiled nooks in which to throw the perfect spread, including tablecloth, wicker basket, drumsticks, a loaf of bread, a glass of wine . . . Don't be surprised if a wedding party passes through—this is a favorite place of June brides and grooms. If you're really feeling chipper, you might consider working up an appetite by walking the 3½ miles of parkland from the *Fens Park* west to the *Arboretum,* passing over footbridges and around lakes, streams, and woodland.

FISH PIER Every morning as the sun inches out of the Atlantic to the east, fishing boats carrying salty crews creep back into Boston Harbor to market their catch on the renovated Fish Pier, just off Northern Avenue. A spirited gang of restaurateurs, fish brokers, wholesalers, and assorted fish hucksters shuffle, slurp coffee, and banter like brothers as they await the anglers. But all is business when the boats arrive. The ruddy fishermen in their hip-high boots scramble to get heaping crates of cod, haddock, flounder, and monkfish onto refrigerated trucks without losing a moment's freshness. The buyers move in for a closer look, as do the scavenging gulls overhead, who squawk their approval. Everybody seems to know everybody, and the haggling continues until everyone seems satisfied. The brokers, after poking and prodding and inspecting the finny fare with a keen eye for firmness, shine, and color, snatch it up by the boatload, forcing shop and restaurant owners to buy their fish from them. You can try your own hand at bidding from the brokers if you make the 6:30 AM curtain call. If you prefer to buy the freshest already prepared for a moderate price, go to the *No-Name* restaurant (15$\frac{1}{2}$ Fish Pier; phone: 617-338-7539), right on the pier, which packs in the fishermen, tourists, and locals like sardines. *No-Name* is strictly no frills—no credit cards, no fancy sauces, no discernible decor—but the seafood, simply broiled or fried, is excellent, and wine and beer are available. There's also no sign, so ask at the Fish Pier—or look for the line at the door; for more details, see *Eating Out* in THE CITY.

A Few of Our Favorite Things

Boston has small, intimate hotels, and large, gracious ones, plus bustling dockside and ethnic food restaurants and European-style haute cuisine. Below is a selection of our favorites. Follow our lead; we promise you won't be disappointed.

Each place listed below is described in detail in THE CITY.

GRAND HOTELS

The following are our accommodation favorites. Each offers the highest caliber of service, food, and ambience. Complete information about our choices can be found on pages 68 to 70 of THE CITY.

Boston Harbor
Copley Plaza
Four Seasons
Meridien
Omni Parker House
Ritz-Carlton

INCREDIBLE EDIBLES

The establishments listed on the following page are sure to provide some of the finest eating experiences you can have in Boston. Complete information about our choices can be found on pages 76 to 77 of THE CITY.

Biba
L'Espalier
Hamersley's Bistro
Jasper's
Locke-Ober Café

Antiques: Boston's Best Hunting Grounds

One of the by-products of Boston's venerable history is its antiques, though "proper" Bostonians won't admit to actually shopping for them. (An oft-told story tells of a 19th-century Boston woman asked by a visitor from New York where she buys her hats. The Boston matron replies, "My dear, in Boston we don't buy our hats. We already have them.") But those of us not fortunate enough to be descendants of the Endicotts or Cabots or Lowells must make do with what has made its way from Back Bay and Beacon Hill attics to the city's many antiques shops. With two great antiques avenues—Charles Street, at the base of Beacon Hill, is known by locals as "Antiques Row," and Newbury Street is the site of a number of upscale antiques proprietors—Boston is an ideal place for "antiquing." But be aware that there are some new dynamics at work. American antiques, which are so much in vogue of late, have filtered into the suburbs, while Boston shops are strong on European antiques. And what actually constitutes an antique in Boston? Though Art Deco may seem nostalgic in California, here nothing made after the Civil War is considered really broken in. For some of the better antiques shops in the area, see *Shopping* in THE CITY.

RULES OF THE ROAD FOR AN ODYSSEY OF THE OLD

Buy for sheer pleasure, not for investment. Forget about the carrot of supposed retail values that dealers habitually dangle in front of amateur clients. If you love something, it will probably grace your home for a lifetime, or more.

Buy the finest example you can afford of any item, in as close to mint condition as possible. Chipped or broken "bargains" will haunt you later with their shabbiness. They also don't increase in value the way the mint stuff does.

Train your eye in museums and/or collections of things in the period that interests you. These are the best schools for the acquisitive senses, particularly as you begin to develop special passions.

Get advice from specialists when contemplating major acquisitions. Much antique and collectible furniture and many paintings have been restored several times. If you want to be absolutely certain that what you're buying is what you've been told it is, stick with the larger dealers.

Don't be afraid to haggle—a little. Most dealers don't have fixed prices, so sharpen your negotiating skills and make an offer they can't refuse. Note: Most larger dealers take credit cards, but smaller shops may not.

When pricing an object, don't forget to figure in the cost of shipping. Shipping home a large piece—furniture, sculpture, antique garden paraphernalia—can cost a hefty sum. Figure this in before you make your purchase.

Inside Boston's Theaters

Boston is a city that loves theater. Thanks in part to a steady stream of productions that come here for final polishing and refinement on the way to Broadway, a section of Boston between downtown and the South End has evolved into a real theater district, with a number of grand old stages. Since Bostonians are such avid theatergoers, however, getting impromptu tickets to performances can be a scramble. Before you shell out a premium price for last-minute tickets in the nose-bleed section with a view obstructed by a Doric column, you should explore two options. First, concierges in many downtown hotels have mysterious methods for quickly securing theater tickets for their guests. Second, check with *Bostix,* the city's largest ticket agency. From its booth just to the south of *Faneuil Hall Marketplace, Bostix* sells tickets at half price for same-day performances. *Bostix* is open Tuesdays through Sundays from 11 AM to 6 PM; closed major holidays (phone: 617-723-5181). Arrive early to beat the line. For a pre- or post-theater repast, stop in at the *Broadway Deli* (275 Tremont St.; phone: 617-426-1344), located in the heart of the theater district. It rates close to a real New York delicatessen, with kosher pickles and some of the best corned beef sandwiches and blintzes in town. The following is a list of Boston's most outstanding theaters.

COLONIAL Even if the performance stinks, it's worth the ticket price to see the exquisitely restored interior of this Victorian theater, with its marble, mirrors, brass, and bas-reliefs. Situated within an office building, this lavish theater, built in 1900, was one of the 11 Boston theaters designed by renowned architect Clarence Blackhall. The oldest Boston theater to survive intact under the same name, it has been the setting for many theatrical debuts, from Irving Berlin and the *Ziegfeld Follies* to Rodgers and Hammerstein, and such luminaries as Fred Astaire, George M. Cohan, and Noël Coward have graced its stage. Today, the *Colonial* often hosts major productions en route to Broadway. Information: *Colonial Theatre,* 106 Boylston St. (phone: 617-426-9366).

HUNTINGTON Under the auspices of *Boston University,* this has become the home of Boston's largest resident professional theater company. Built in 1925, it is nondescript on the outside but has a handsome interior with lots of dark wood and brass. Its location—on Huntington Avenue near *Northeastern*

University, bordering on the rough edges of the South End—is a bit inconvenient, but the company's five annual productions are standouts. Each season's line-up usually includes established classics and 20th-century plays; a typical mix might include the works of Harold Pinter, George Bernard Shaw, Henrik Ibsen, Tom Stoppard, and Shakespeare. Information: *Huntington Theatre,* 264 Huntington Ave. (phone: 617-266-0800 or 617-266-3913).

WANG CENTER This is one of the world's largest theaters, with seating for 4,400 patrons and a stage that is 60 feet wide, 30 feet high, and 60 feet deep. Home to the *Boston Ballet* and to other major dance, opera, and theater events, the large stage is particularly suited for the *Boston Ballet*'s elaborate annual production of "The Nutcracker Suite." The theater opened as a "movie palace" in 1925 and began hosting live performances in the 1940s. Originally called the *Metropolitan,* it was renamed the *Wang Center for the Performing Arts* in 1983 after large gifts from An Wang and the Wang computer corporation saved the theater from going under. A $10-million restoration turned the dilapidated giant into the city's most sumptuous theater: Brightly colored murals adorn the walls, a huge chandelier hangs from the central dome, gilt trim sparkles everywhere, and seraphim and cherubim float around the great arch over a huge stage. Information: *Wang Center for the Performing Arts,* 270 Tremont St. (phone: 617-482-9393).

WILBUR Another Blackhall creation, this Boston favorite, built in 1914, has been restored to its original splendor. Like the *Colonial,* the *Wilbur* hosts many productions that are either on their way to Broadway or fresh from a stint in Manhattan, but it is considerably smaller, and makes for an intimate theatrical experience. The theater's portals are modeled after the Thomas Bailey Aldrich home on Beacon Hill. Information: *Wilbur Theater,* 246 Tremont St. (phone: 617-423-4008).

Historic Churches

One of the lasting vestiges of Boston's Puritan past (aside from the fact that you can't buy alcohol in stores on Sundays) is its rich array of churches. The city's most outstanding churches were built at a time when the place of worship was the focal point of the community, whose artistic and architectural energy was devoted to constructing soaring spires, painstakingly crafted woodwork, and grand altars to foster a sense of permanence and awe. The activities within these early churches, however, were not limited to the spiritual. A church figured prominently in the midnight ride of Paul Revere, and it was in a church that the Sons of Liberty worked themselves into a frenzy before withdrawing to the harbor for a spot of tea. All of the following are operating churches; services are open to the public.

KING'S CHAPEL This stately church at the corner of Tremont and School Streets, reminiscent of an English cathedral, was originally a modest wooden building. It was established in 1686 as the Massachusetts Bay Colony's Anglican church for British officers and the royal governor—much to the dismay of the colony's Puritans, who had left their homeland to escape the Anglican Church. In 1785, after the Revolution and the demise of the area's Anglican congregation, the building became the first Unitarian church in America. The present structure of Quincy granite was erected in 1799, literally constructed around the original church. The church within the church was then dismantled and thrown out the windows of the new structure, board by board. The brownish, rough-hewn exterior of the building makes the freshly painted white walls and woodwork of the interior seem even brighter. The chapel's bell is Paul Revere's largest and, according to Revere, the sweetest-sounding one he ever cast. The centerpiece of the interior, which has been restored to its earlier Georgian elegance, is the Governor's Pew, a gilded reminder of a bygone era. The best time to visit the chapel is around noon on Tuesdays, when free classical music concerts are presented in its quiet interior, a sanctuary amid the jungle of skyscrapers in the surrounding financial district. Services are held Sundays at 11 AM and Wednesdays at 12:15 PM; Tuesday concerts begin at 12:15 PM. Information: *King's Chapel,* 64 Beacon St. (phone: 617-227-2155).

OLD NORTH CHURCH Built in 1723, this is Boston's oldest church structure. But the "Old North," as it is affectionately called (its official name is *Christ Church*), is better known for its contribution to the American Revolution. It was from this steeple on the night of April 18, 1775, that church sexton Robert Newman, at the request of Paul Revere, hung two lanterns—"one if by land, two if by sea"—to warn the good people of Charlestown of British troop movements. (Actually, the current steeple is a replica; the most famous steeple in the American Revolution toppled over in a gale in 1804.) Revere's ride and Newman's bravery—he was later jailed by the British for hanging the lanterns—were immortalized by poet Henry Wadsworth Longfellow with more than a little embellishment. Newman, the generally unsung hero of the incident, is also remembered with a plaque in the quiet garden on the church's north side.

To be inside the *Old North* is, well, a religious experience. The ancient wooden floor creaks beneath your feet. The church bells, bearing the inscription "We are the first ring of bells cast for the British empire in North America," sound as sweet as they must have when Paul Revere rang them as a boy. (It's easy to understand why he went on to cast bells for a living.) Members of the Revere family still worship here occasionally. As you advance down the center aisle, look for a niche near the altar that contains the nation's first memorial to George Washington. Also of note are brass chandeliers made in England in the 1700s, the oldest clock still running in a public building in the US, and pews still bearing the brass nameplates of the colonial families that once rented them. The pews are arranged like the box seats at *Fenway Park;* each box was bought by a colonial family (40 British pounds sterling for the center aisle, 20 pounds for the side aisles), which retained the box for life. After the owner died, the church would get to sell it again. All this is according to the church's guide, who is a fount of information. (Ask him to tell the tale of the burial of Major John Pitcairn.) Though several pews near the rear are labeled "Strangers," visitors attending the Episcopalian services held each Sunday may sit anywhere they like. Open daily; Sunday services at 9 AM, 11 AM, and 4 PM. Information: *Christ Church,* 193 Salem St. (phone: 617-523-6676).

PARK STREET CHURCH AND OLD GRANARY BURYING GROUND This early-19th-century Congregational church sits at perhaps the busiest corner in all of Boston, the intersection of Park and Tremont. It was once called *Brimstone Corner,* though no one is sure why: Some say it is was named for the gunpowder that used to be kept in the church basement during the War of 1812 (a major ingredient of gunpowder is sulfur, or brimstone); others claim it was for the demonstrative speechifying that used to spew from the pulpit. The *Park Street Church* was designed by Peter Banner and completed in 1810. It was here that abolitionist William Lloyd Garrison delivered the first of his famous anti-slavery addresses, one of the earliest such attacks on slavery, in 1829. It was also here that the patriotic song "America" ("My country, 'tis of thee . . . ") was first sung, on July 4, 1832. Baptist clergyman Samuel Smith, who wrote the lyrics, borrowed the tune from an old German hymn, which also happened to have been borrowed for the British national anthem. The cemetery, which is next door, dates to 1660. It's the final resting place of such Revolutionaries as John Hancock, Paul Revere, and Samuel Adams. Look for the grave of Mary Goose, popularly believed to be Mother Goose. Although a large memorial to the parents of Benjamin Franklin dominates the burial ground, most of the tombstones are small and stark. Unfortunately, few of the markers are actually assigned to their correct graves, as tidy gravekeepers have uprooted gravestones, using them to edge new paths throughout the cemetery. Sunday services are at 9 and 10:45 AM and 6:30 PM; outside of services, the church is open to the public Tuesdays through Saturdays in July and August; otherwise by appointment. The church bells play such old-time favorites as "Ragged Old Cross" and "Rock of Ages" daily at 9 AM, noon, and 4:45 PM; try to time your visits around one of these mini-concerts. The cemetery is open daily year-round. Information: *Park Street Church,* 1 Park St. (phone: 617-523-3383); *Old Granary Burying Ground* (phone: 635-4505, ext. 6516).

TRINITY CHURCH Visitors to this masterpiece by architect H. H. Richardson invariably describe it, in reverential tones, as "magnificent." Located in Copley Square in Back Bay, *Trinity Church* is certainly one of the most impressive churches in the US. Built in 1877, the exterior is deep red sandstone in the

Italian Romanesque style (it reflects well in the mirro[...]
modern *John Hancock Building* across the street[...]
glass windows scatter jewels of colored light thro[...]
upon entering, is startling in its sheer enormity. [...]
conies are sumptuously carved. To appreciate [...]
ture—the tower itself weighs 12.5 million po[...]
stand the difficulties of building in this area. Since u[...]
from filled-in wetlands, the church was built on 4,500 wo[...]
must be kept constantly wet to avoid dry rot. The water leve[...]
periodically from a hatch in the church's basement. Richardson emp[...]
some of the greatest artistic talent of the day to adorn the church's interioi
walls and vaulted ceilings with paintings and murals. Open daily; Episcopalian
Sunday services at 11 AM and Communion at 8 AM and 6 PM; free organ
recitals Friday at noon from September through mid-June. Guided tours
are available by appointment. Information: *Trinity Church,* Copley Sq.
(phone: 617-536-0944).

Salem: More Than a Witch Hunt

About 18 miles north of Boston on Route 107 is the town of Salem. It was
the capital of the Massachusetts Bay Colony from 1626 to 1630, and again,
briefly, in 1774, when the British closed Boston Harbor after the Boston
Tea Party. However, Salem earned a bitter name in American history as
the scene of the witch trials, in which a group of more than 100 villagers
were accused of witchcraft. The hysterical allegations resulted in the deaths
of 25 of the accused. Salem is also the site of Nathaniel Hawthorne's *House
of the Seven Gables* (54 Turner St.; phone: 508-744-0991). Open daily.
Admission charge. Hawthorne worked in the *Salem Custom House* and
wrote his masterpiece, *The Scarlet Letter,* at 14 Mall Street. Like Boston,
Salem has a history trail winding through its streets and port. Visit the *Salem
Maritime National Historic Site* (174 Derby St.; phone: 508-744-4323 or 508-
745-1470), run by the *National Park Service,* for information, maps, and a
variety of seasonal tours. It's open daily.

While you're in the neighborhood, stop at the *Witch Museum* (19½
Washington Sq. N.; phone: 508-744-1692). It's closed *Thanksgiving,
Christmas,* and *New Year's Day;* there's an admission charge. The *Witch
House* (310½ Essex St.; phone: 508-744-0180), site of some of the interro-
gations, radiates a claustrophobic, spooky feeling when you pass it at night.
It's open daily mid-March through December 1; there's an admission charge.
You can get in the mood for this tour by picking up a copy of Arthur Miller's
play *The Crucible.*

The *Peabody Museum* (E. India Sq.; phone: 508-745-1876) has fascinating scrimshaw carvings and nautical regalia from the early days of shipping and from far-off ports. It's closed *Thanksgiving, Christmas,* and *New
Year's Day;* there's an admission charge. *Pier Transit Cruises* offers harbor

s that leave from *Salem Willows Pier* (phone: 508-744-6311 or 800-696-
11).

A few miles east of Salem, the sailboating town of Marblehead has myr-
iad colonial houses, places to sit and look at the harbor, boats, and shops
selling New England seascapes and elegant, old-fashioned furnishings.
Toward evening, you can watch fishermen unloading the day's catch.

Great Golf Outside the City

Golf is beloved in and around Boston for several reasons: the clubby atmosphere of the grand old game; the love of a challenge; and, perhaps foremost, the escape it offers from the urban jungle. A round of golf provides
the perfect opportunity to stride through the green spaces, draw deep
breaths of clean air, and enjoy nature while testing your skills against its
wily ways. There are a number of surprisingly well-manicured, challenging,
and scenic public golf courses throughout the greater Boston area that can
be reached in a short drive (with a car, not a club).

COLONIAL COUNTRY CLUB Located just outside the *Colonial Hilton* hotel in
Wakefield, north of Boston, this club has an excellent 18-hole course that
is open to the public. A benign front nine will stroke a golfer's ego, and the
feeling of elation will last until the dreaded hole 13, the front end of a trio
of holes (a par 4, par 3, and par 5, respectively) that are so daunting they
are known in these parts as "Amen Corner." Since the back nine is located
along the Saugus River, water figures prominently in the experience. Eleven
of the course's 18 holes are encroached by marshland. Tee times for weekend play should be made on Thursday mornings. Information: *Colonial
Country Club,* Exit 43 off Rte. 128, Wakefield, MA 01880 (phone: 617-245-
9300).

GEORGE WRIGHT GOLF COURSE This hilly course, thick with pine and sassafras
trees, was designed by Donald Ross, the great American golf course architect. It is of medium length (6,166 yards) and must be the only course in
the country with a brick wall around it. (The hopelessly erratic golfer can
thank the New Deal government, which erected the wall a year before the
course was built.) Though there is no water to speak of, there are plenty of
other impediments on these links to test your mettle. Greens fees are reasonable. Weekend tee times should be made by 11 AM on Thursdays. There
is a restaurant and bar. Information: *George Wright Golf Course,* 420 West
St. (near Rte. 28), Hyde Park, MA 02136 (phone: 617-361-8313).

NEWTON COMMONWEALTH GOLF COURSE Built in 1895, this old course is known
for its small targets, its fast greens, and its premium on hitting the ball
straight. It was a country club until it filed for bankruptcy in the late 1970s,
when it was converted into a public course. Very accessible by public trans-

portation, it is located about a tee shot from the *MBTA* station at the end of the *Boston College* branch of the *Green Line.* There is not much water and not many trees, but it is tight and challenging. Make tee times a week in advance for weekend play. Information: *Newton Commonwealth Golf Course,* 212 Kerrick St., Chestnut Hill, MA 02158 (phone: 617-630-1971).

STOW ACRES Several years ago, this was rated by *Golf Digest* magazine as one of the top 50 public courses in the country. The verdant pine trees make a round on either of the two 18-hole courses here seem like a trek into an enchanted forest, especially after making repeated rescue missions into its treacherous roughs for lost balls. There are hills and dales, cleverly crafted ponds, fairway traps, nettlesome streams, and even a craggy old rock wall, a vestige of the farm that formerly occupied this land. All of these combine to create a course of uncommon beauty or unrelenting obstacles, depending on your skill and state of mind. Also here are a driving range, a putting green, and a good crowd on weekends (golfers are juggled about on the roster to create foursomes). Open daily; make reservations at least five days in advance. About 15 miles northeast of Boston. Information: *Stow Acres Country Club,* 58 Randall Rd., Stow, MA 01775 (phone: 508-568-8690).

Gone Fishing

A trip to see the nearly 2,000 species of aquatic life at the *New England Aquarium* on Boston's Central Wharf may inspire visitors to partake in some angling. Several bodies of fresh water in and around Boston are stocked with everything from bass and crappie to trout and perch. Freshwater fishing in Boston requires a license from the *Division of Fisheries and Wildlife* (phone: 617-727-3151). Non-residents may purchase a special seven-day license for $16.50. Since ten questions about whether fish caught in Boston are safe to eat would yield ten different answers, it's best to be cautious— if fellow fishermen seem doubtful, don't do it. There is ample saltwater fishing in the Atlantic as well, but since this is a metropolitan area with a notorious pollution problem, don't expect to just throw a line off any city pier and come up with anything other than spare tires or shopping carts. A better bet would be to take a commercial fishing tour of the harbor, or to rent a boat and equipment for deep-sea fishing. The following places are some of the favorite spots of local anglers and are open year-round.

CASTLE ISLAND A landfill project attached this island to South Boston in 1930. The pier, which juts out into the harbor from Day Boulevard in South Boston, is one of the best saltwater fishing spots in the city. The causeway is so long that the angler feels far removed from the surrounding industrial blight, making it a favorite among locals, who have reported landing good-sized striped bass, bluefish, and flounder here. No permit is required.

CHARLES RIVER The muddy water of the Charles carries a surprising array of freshwater fish, including largemouth bass, catfish, crappie, and sunfish. Many local fishermen recommend the Charles—though not very loudly, since they consider it a well-kept secret. The farther upstream you go, the better the fishing: The Watertown area is a particularly good place to sink a hook.

JAMAICA POND This 68-acre freshwater pond (and the surrounding park area and bicycle paths) on Jamaica Way in Jamaica Plain is part of Frederick Law Olmsted's *Emerald Necklace* of parkland that stretches west for 8 miles from the *Boston Common*. Jamaica Pond is stocked primarily with trout and bass. A number of woodsy spots near the water's edge shelter you from the thunder of joggers huffing and puffing around the pond. Whether or not you catch anything, this is a serene place to try. Fishing here may require an additional license from the city of Boston. Information: *Boston Park Rangers,* Franklin Park, Dorchester (phone: 617-635-7383).

WALDEN POND This will require a pilgrimage from Boston à la Henry David Thoreau, who adopted this pond as his home for two years of solitary living in the mid-1800s. The pond is stocked heavily with brook and rainbow trout. Be sure you have enough fishing line—at 102 feet, this is one of the deepest ponds on the eastern seaboard. If you wish, you may take one of many rarely trodden paths to escape the crush of people sunning themselves or playing games on the beach. Take the Fitchburg or South Acton train from *North Station* to Concord. Information: *Walden Pond State Reservation,* 915 Walden St., Concord, MA 01742 (phone: 508-369-3254).

A Shutterbug's Boston

If you can get it to hold still long enough, Boston is an exceptionally photogenic city. There is architectural variety: old juxtaposed with new, ornate with ordinary, and a skyline bristling with the temples of modern commerce that's also graced with an 18th-century church spire—a humble reminder of when God was the only game in town. There is natural variety: A column of magnolias embroiders a park footpath, ivy inches up a colonial red brick building, and a summer sunset sparks the river ablaze. And there is human variety as well: Immigrants exchange the latest news from the Old Country in rapid-fire Sicilian, ruddy fishermen return with their catch, and stocky sports fans sit cheek by jowl, dressed in their team's full regalia. With raw material like this, even a novice shutterbug can achieve remarkable results with a basic set of lenses and filters. Equipment is, in fact, only as valuable as the imagination that puts it to use.

LANDSCAPES, SEASCAPES, AND CITYSCAPES Boston's bustling byways and historic buildings are most visiting photographers' favorite subjects. But the city's green spaces and waterways provide numerous photo possibilities as well. In addition to the *State House, Hancock Building,* and *Trinity Church,* be sure to look for natural beauty. The magnolia trees that line the Commonwealth Avenue Mall, the well-manicured plots of flowers in the *Public Garden,* the marshy ponds of the *Fens Park,* and the sailboats that skim along the Charles River are just a few examples.

Although a standard 50mm to 55mm lens may work well in some landscape situations, most will benefit from a 20mm to 28mm wide-angle. The *Common,* with city skyscrapers looming in the distance, for example, is the type of panorama that fits beautifully into a wide-angle format, allowing not only the overview but the opportunity to include people or other points of interest in the foreground. A flower, for instance, may be used to set off a view of the *Public Garden;* or people can provide a sense of perspective in a shot of Copley Square.

To isolate specific elements of any scene—a particular carving in a historic church, perhaps, or the interplay of light and shadow on a cobblestone Beacon Hill street—use your telephoto lens. The successful use of a telephoto means developing your eye for detail.

PEOPLE As when taking pictures of people anywhere, there are going to be times in Boston when a camera is an intrusion. Consider your own reaction under similar circumstances, and you have an idea as to what would make others comfortable enough to be willing subjects. People are often sensitive to having a camera suddenly pointed at them, but a polite request, while getting you a share of refusals, will provide a chance to shoot some wonderful portraits that capture the spirit of the city as surely as the scenery does.

For candids, an excellent lens is a zoom telephoto in the 70mm to 210mm range; it allows you to remain unobtrusive while the telephoto lens draws the subject closer. And for portraits, a telephoto can be used effectively from as little as two or three feet away.

For authenticity and variety, select a place likely to produce interesting subjects. The *Faneuil Hall Marketplace* is an obvious spot for visitors, but if it's local color you're after, visit Chinatown or one of the North End's Italian street festivals, sit at a Newbury Street café and watch the fashion parade, or walk around the *Common,* where everyone from elderly Brahmins to college students to street people flock to enjoy a sunny day. Aim for shots that tell what's different about Boston. In portraiture, there are several factors to keep in mind. Morning or afternoon light will add richness to skin tones, emphasizing tans. To avoid the harsh facial shadows cast by direct sunlight, shoot in the shade or in an area where the light is diffused.

SUNSETS When shooting sunsets, keep in mind that the brightness distorts meter readings. When composing a shot directly into the sun, frame the picture in the viewfinder so that only half of the sun is included. Read the meter, set, and then reframe and shoot. Whenever there is this kind of unusual lighting, shoot a few frames in half-step increments, both over and under the meter reading. Bracketing, as this is called, can provide a range of images, the best of which may not have been shot at the meter's recommended setting.

Use any lens for sunsets. A wide-angle is good when the sky is filled with color-streaked clouds, when the sun is partially hidden, or when you're close to an object that silhouettes dramatically against the sky. Telephotos also produce wonderful silhouettes, either with the sun as a backdrop or against the palette of a brilliant sunset sky. Bracket again here. For the best silhouettes, wait 10 to 15 minutes after sunset. Unless you are using a very fast film, a tripod is recommended.

Red and orange filters are often used to accentuate a sunset's picture potential. Orange helps turn even a gray sky into something approaching a photogenic finale to the day, and can provide particularly beautiful shots linking the sky with the sun reflected on the ocean. If the sunset is already bold in hue, however, the orange will overwhelm the natural colors. A red filter will produce dramatic, highly unrealistic results.

NIGHT If you think that picture possibilities end at sunset, you're presuming that night photography is the exclusive domain of the professional. If you've got a tripod, all you'll need is a cable release to attach to your camera to assure a steady exposure (which is often timed in minutes rather than fractions of a second).

For situations such as evening concerts on the Esplanade or nighttime harbor cruises, a strobe does the trick, but beware: Flash units are often used improperly. You can't take a view of the skyline with a flash; it may reach out as far as 30 feet, but that's it. On the other hand, a flash used too close to a subject may result in overexposure, resulting in a "blown out" effect. With most cameras, strobes work with a maximum shutter speed of 1/125 or 1/250 of a second. If you set the exposure properly and shoot within range, you should come up with pretty sharp results.

CLOSE-UPS Whether of people or of objects such as antique door knockers, close-ups can add another dimension to your photography. There are a number of shooting options, one of which is to use a 70mm or a 210mm lens at its closest focusable distance. Unless you're working in bright sunlight, a tripod will be worthwhile. If you are very near your subject and there is a good deal of reflective light, it may pay to underexpose a bit in relation to the meter reading.

If you do not have a telephoto lens, you can still shoot close-ups using a set of magnification filters. Filter packs of one-, two-, and three-times magnification are available, converting your lens into a close-up lens. Even better is a special macro lens designed for close-up photography.

A SHORT PHOTOGRAPHIC TOUR

Following are some of Boston's great pictorial perspectives.

PUBLIC GARDEN Stand at the head of the Commonwealth Avenue Mall (the center park area on Commonwealth Avenue), with the *Ritz-Carlton* hotel to your right and the tricolor flying from the *French Consulate* to your left. The view east to the *Public Garden* is, perhaps, the city's best photo op. Picture this: Sitting high atop his steed and checking troop movements to the south is the robust, yet graceful, equestrian statue of General George Washington. At his feet (in the spring) are circular beds of tulips. Behind the good general is the *Public Garden*'s suspension bridge, fringed by elms and gas lamps, which gives way to the upward, verdant slopes of the *Boston Common.* The trees of the *Common* enshroud all but the tops of a jungle of financial district high-rises. Their aircraft warning lights flicker just above the treetops. The pure white steeple of the *Park Street Church* reaches for the heavens to the left. From this angle, Boston seems an Emerald City in spring and summer. Snap one with the focus on the background and one with the focus on General Washington.

FIRST BAPTIST CHURCH/JOHN HANCOCK TOWER Stand again on the Commonwealth Avenue Mall, this time just past the corner of Clarendon Street and Commonwealth Avenue. Face south to gaze upon the *First Baptist Church.* Completed in 1872, the building quickly earned the nickname the "Church of the Holy Bean Blowers" because of the trumpeting angels sculpted into the church's soaring tower, which was created by Auguste Bartholdi, the French sculptor also responsible for the *Statue of Liberty.* With your lens pointed toward the upper reaches of the church (you may want to go vertical on this one), capture the ivy climbing between the rounded windows of the church's pudding-stone façade, the intricate detail of the trumpeting angels (on which you may want to focus), and the stark contrast of the glistening *Hancock Tower* in the background.

TRINITY CHURCH/HANCOCK TOWER From Copley Square on a sunny day, the sight of the deep red sandstone of the *Trinity Church* reflected in the light blue panes of mirror window of the gargantuan *Hancock Tower* seems to exemplify all that Boston is about—from solid old spirituality to the towering heights of the modern high-tech world. Find the right angle and the entire history of Boston can be told in the click of a shutter.

STATE HOUSE Probably the best view of the golden dome of the *State House,* which Oliver Wendell Holmes called "the hub of the solar system," is from the *Brewer Fountain,* a bronze replica of a Parisian fountain next to the *Park Street T* stop in *Boston Common.* Standing on the sidewalk that runs along Tremont Street you can get the fountain, one of the *Common*'s most beautiful ornaments, in the picture's foreground. Beyond the fountain is a plush strip of turf, resembling a bowling green, which rises higher and higher until it tucks into Beacon Street at the foot of the *State House.* The dome is most picturesque when it glistens in the midday sun. If one of the park's mounted police are in the area, they are usually game for a pose.

ACORN STREET This is Beacon Hill's most photographed street. Steep and narrow, charming, and petite (it's really more an alley than a street), it was once home to coach drivers, servants, craftsmen, and a couple of stables. Grass can be seen sprouting in the cobblestone street, and its gas lights at dusk set the jet black shutters aglow. Whatever the angle, this shot's bound to be a keeper.

Directions

Introduction

There are many reasons why walking is the best means of transportation for seeing Boston. Most of them, however, have less to do with sightseeing than with the total impracticability of driving a car in Boston proper, where parking spots are an endangered species, the chance of getting your car stolen is eclipsed only by the likelihood of its being ticketed, and driving is an anarchic battle of wills largely ungoverned by any higher authority. (Boston's police force has a full bag of problems that prevent it from being overly picky about most moving violations.)

Happily, Boston is (for the most part) a pedestrian-friendly city. The Freedom Trail, the Heritage Trail, the Emerald Necklace, and the South End's Southwest Corridor are examples of how walkers have figured prominently in city planning. Confusion does arise, however, when visitors learn that there is both a South End and a South Boston, a West End that no longer exists (when it did it was actually north), a North End but no North Boston, and an East Boston but no East End. Visitors (and locals) are also baffled by the haphazard placement of the city's streets. In fact, Boston may have the most illogical avenue layout of any major US metropolis: Manhattan has numbered streets, after all; finding a location in Los Angeles is as easy as working the card catalogue in a library; and Washington, the American city that comes closest to Boston's well-shuffled deck of asymmetrical streets, was at least the intentional chaos of a French planner.

But what the city lacks in order, it makes up for in intimacy. Boston is remarkably condensed; one can get from the southernmost brownstone in the South End to the northernmost pier in the North End in a brisk, 25-minute walk, and with some fancy footwork, the entire city can be traversed in a day.

Just because the locals are flitting about at breakneck speed, however, doesn't mean you have to keep up; in fact, you're better off not even trying. (A recent study deemed Boston the fastest-paced city in America, with Manhattan—home of the fabled New York minute—downright sluggish by comparison.) While traipsing along the routes outlined in the following seven walking tours and one driving tour to Cambridge, Lexington, Concord, and Lincoln, linger amid the blooming magnolia trees and stalwart statues of the Commonwealth Avenue Mall, ruminate over cannoli and cappuccino in the North End, poke around the shops of the *Faneuil Hall Marketplace,* dawdle about the 18th-century homes of Beacon Hill, and loll under the midday sun in *Boston Common.*

The seven walking routes and one drive, which are presented in geographical order (roughly west to east), have been designed to guide visitors past the lion's share of historic Boston landmarks, into intriguing shops, around common traffic quandaries, and away from questionable areas (assuming you don't travel heavily armed), all the while considering appetite and the primal American lust for occasionally wandering off the beaten path. This is not to say you should take leave of your street smarts, however. Boston is a big city, and like any big city, it's hopelessly congested with more people, places, and (potentially dangerous) things than should be situated on such a small chunk of real estate, so stay alert.

One more thing to consider before stepping out into a Boston intersection: A taxi cab was spotted recently with a bumper sticker reading, "So many pedestrians. So little time."

Note: Throughout this section, all telephone numbers are in the 617 area code unless otherwise indicated.

Walk 1: The Fens

In the 19th-century frenzy to fill in the putrid marshes of the Back Bay and turn them into a posh residential area, it is remarkable that Boston city planners had the foresight to realize that enough was enough. Deciding that some of the original marshland should remain undeveloped, they hired the renowned landscape architect Frederick Law Olmsted to work his magic on a marshy area in the southwest of the city. Olmsted, romancing nature as only he could do, created a park that retains the feel of the salt marshes and tidal flats that it replaced—clusters of reeds rise above still ponds, irregular pools lie scattered amid meadows and flower gardens—while it also serves as a pleasant, green space where the city's residents may enjoy the outdoors.

Today, *Fens Park* is the centerpiece of an area of Boston that includes Kenmore Square and *Fenway Park* to the north, *Symphony Hall* and *Northeastern University* to the east, the *Museum of Fine Arts* and the *Isabella Stewart Gardner Museum* to the south, and the *Longwood Medical Area* to the west. Though portions of the Fens have given way to crime and urban blight of late (don't wander its paths after dark), it remains a godsend to neighborhood residents seeking a natural oasis, and a crucial link in what is known as the *Emerald Necklace,* 8 miles of Olmsted-designed parkland that stretches from *Boston Common* to Roxbury's *Franklin Park Zoo.*

Our walking tour of the Fens area (allow about two hours) begins at *Symphony Hall,* at the corner of Massachusetts and Huntington Avenues. (Also see *Quintessential Boston* in DIVERSIONS.) This grand hall of Boston music, built in 1900, is considered one of the world's best; the acoustics are so fine that there's not a bad seat in the house. Just loitering about the foyer watching the crunch of Brahmins bedecked in furs, sequins, and black-tie formal wear rushing to take their seats is a memorable experience. *Symphony Hall* is home to the venerable *Boston Symphony Orchestra* and the *Boston Pops,* and it frequently hosts guest performances. Tours are offered by appointment; ask for the volunteer office (phone: 266-1492).

Music permeates the area surrounding the Symphony stop on the *MBTA's Green Line.* Two blocks down Huntington Avenue to the west is the *New England Conservatory* (*NEC;* 30 Gainsborough St.), the training ground for many of the musicians who have taken their seats down the street with either the *Boston Pops* or the *Boston Symphony Orchestra.* The *NEC's Jordan Hall* is the venue of many acclaimed local musical groups. Walk up Massachusetts Avenue to the north to see musicians of a different ilk. Here a trendier crowd sits on stoops drumming their knees, grooving to Walkmans, and perfecting their existential looks. This is the *Berklee College of Music* (138 Massachusetts Ave.), the *Juilliard* of jazz and rock music education (though jazz purists claim the latter has been holding sway of late).

Walk back down Massachusetts Avenue ("Mass. Ave." in local parlance) in the direction of *Symphony Hall.* On the right is *Bangkok Cuisine* (177A Massachusetts Ave.; phone: 262-5377), an excellent restaurant with some of the tastiest, most moderately priced Thai food in Boston. Try the extra spicy *tom yum kong* soup—if you dare.

Continue down Mass. Ave. past the *Christian Science Church* headquarters and reflecting pool on the left (see *Walk 2: South End*). Make a sharp right on Westland Avenue. From here the *Fens Park* is straight ahead. The lights of *Fenway Park* (also see *Quintessential Boston* in DIVERSIONS) are visible, peeking over the treetops. Nearby is Kenmore Square, this tour's ultimate destination; should you lose your bearings, just head for the neon *Citgo* sign that hovers over this busy square (more on this unlikely landmark later).

First cross Hemenway Street—primarily the site of student housing for *Northeastern University*—and proceed between the two columns that offer a stately entrance to the Fens. Walk diagonally across the grassy area to The Fenway, the road that traces the east boundary of the Fens Park. Be sure to look both ways several times before negotiating this street, as you're crossing at a bend and every other car is likely to be driven by a college student who considers the roadway surrounding the park a convenient racetrack. Once safely across, walk left along the lower path under the magnolia trees. If it's a nice day, an artist may be adjusting the position of his easel, trying to find just the right angle to capture the glint of sunlight on the water, the frolicking ducks, or one of the miniature bridges that span the still pond. From this vantage point, it's easy to appreciate what Olmsted had in mind when he chose to simply enhance the marsh rather than radically transform it.

Across The Fenway are a handful of the buildings that house dorms, classrooms, and administrative offices of the sprawling *Northeastern University,* which, with a student body of 35,000, is one of the largest cooperative-plan schools in the country (students alternate classroom instruction with paid employment in their chosen profession). As The Fenway bends, the ornate building on the left is *Forsyth Dental Center,* which sits across Forsyth Way from the *Museum of Fine Arts* (*MFA;* 465 Huntington Ave.; phone: 267-9300).

The *MFA,* housed in this magnificent building since 1909 (it first opened in Copley Square in 1870), has developed into one of America's finest cultural institutions. To enter the museum, follow The Fenway along the back of the building, then turn left on Museum Road, which leads to the main entrance in the newer west wing, designed by architect I. M. Pei. Be sure to follow Huntington Avenue around to the front of the building to see Cyrus Dallin's statue *Appeal to the Great Spirit.* In the *MFA*'s grand halls is a vast array of American works, an impressive number of paintings by the French Impressionists (including 38 Monets), some of the Western world's best Oriental art, and possibly the largest collection of Egyptian art outside Egypt. The museum merits at least a half-day visit, so you may want to skip it for now and return when time allows. It's closed Mondays; open late on Wednesdays; there's an admission charge. (Also see *Special Places* in THE CITY.)

Leaving the museum, be sure to stop in the *Tenshin Garden,* where Japanese design fused with New England flora elevates gardening to an art form. Just past the garden is the *Japanese Temple Bell,* given to Boston by the Mayor of Kyoto, Japan, as a symbol of friendship. From here, take a left on The Fenway and follow it around. At the bend is the *School of the Museum of Fine Arts;* directly ahead and to the left is the former home of the flamboyant "Mrs. Jack," the *Isabella Stewart Gardner Museum* (280 The Fenway). This four-story yellow brick Venetian palazzo may not look spectacular from the outside, but inside is one of the best private galleries in the country, including works by Titian, Matisse, Botticelli, and Rubens. It's easy to spend several hours perusing the art and antiques (make sure to purchase a museum guide upon entering) and enjoying the blooms in the serene courtyard. There's also a pleasant café that serves light bistro fare during lunch hours. The museum is closed Mondays. There's an admission charge for the upper galleries, but you can stroll through the spectacular courtyard free of charge. 280 The Fenway (phone: 566-1401). (For more information, see *Special Places* in THE CITY and *Quintessential Boston* in DIVERSIONS.)

Continue left along The Fenway to *Simmons College* (300 The Fenway). Take a short detour, continuing on The Fenway to Louis Pasteur Avenue and then turning left on Longwood Avenue, to visit the majestic *Harvard Medical School* building located in the *Longwood Medical Area,* one of the world's foremost medical complexes. Or cross back to the park side of The Fenway, and follow the path to the right over a stone bridge to the road that borders the other side of the Fens. This part of the Fens, site of several baseball diamonds, basketball courts, and a running track, is admittedly unattractive, but forge ahead. A bit farther along the path, in an enclosed area on the right, is the *Rose Garden,* which blooms in the summer months with thousands of wild and cultivated varieties of roses. There are also monuments in this area to local soldiers who died in World War II, the Korean conflict, and Vietnam.

Continuing along the edge of the park, just beyond the *Rose Garden* are the *Victory Gardens,* where city dwellers can be found cultivating small plots of vegetables and flowers. When World War II sent food prices soaring, four and a half acres of the Fens Park were cleared so that city residents could grow their own vegetables. Though the area since has been reduced, 100 plots now are maintained by the *Fenway Garden Society,* which parcels them out to soil-starved urbanites.

From here the tour leads to *Fenway Park,* the home of the *Red Sox.* Walk past the *Victory Gardens* and cut across the grassy triangle, heading north from the *Texaco* station. Cross Boylston Street and take a quick right onto Ipswich Street. Directly ahead is *Fenway Park,* built in 1912. Make a left on Van Ness Street; walk along the side of the stadium for one block, then turn right on Yawkey Way, where autograph seekers lurk after games, trying to get the signatures of players leaving the *Red Sox* parking lot. This street was named after Tom Yawkey, the late owner of the *Red Sox,* who bought the team in 1933 as a 30th-birthday present for himself and, until his death in 1976, tried unsuccessfully to win the *World Series* (the *Red Sox* haven't won a *World Series* since 1918). On the left are *Red Sox* souvenir shops and a candlepin bowling alley, a strange form of the game that's indigenous to New England and uses down-scaled pins and balls. If the *Sox* are in town, it's worth trying to get tickets (4 Yawkey Way; phone: 267-1700). Even if you don't like the game (or if you're a *Yankees* fan), there's nothing like the ambience of this grand old ball field. (Also see *Quintessential Boston* in DIVERSIONS.)

From Yawkey Way, turn right on Brookline Avenue. At the corner of Brookline Avenue and Lansdowne Street is the nerve center of game days, the *Cask and Flagon* (phone: 536-4840). For many years a smoke-filled, low-key watering hole with pool tables, the *Cask* has become downright flashy since catching the sports bar bug several years ago. Along with some solidly American food, there's an original team photo of the 1948 *Red Sox* and the blueprints for *Fenway Park* on the wall. When emerging from the *Cask,* look left down Lansdowne Street. On the right looms the Green Monster, *Fenway*'s inordinately tall left-field wall, which has contributed to so much baseball lore. Lansdowne Street could also be called "Nightclub Row." It's here that the city's young and hip come to dance at places such as *Axis* (No. 15) and, the latest, *Alley Cat* (1 Boylston Pl.).

Follow Brookline Avenue toward the *Citgo* sign into Kenmore Square. This big lug of a neon sign, an unusually ambitious example of self-promotion even for a large corporation, has been saved several times from destruction by preservationists. It's there to stay, it seems, a landmark as much identified with Kenmore Square as its horrendous evening traffic jams. (In the spirit of Rome, Kenmore Square consists of a harrowing convergence of five streets.)

Though Kenmore Square is largely a collection of fast-food joints, music stores, and quick-cash machines (*Boston University* is a block down Commonwealth Avenue to the west), it also contains a few places of note. The *Boston University Bookstore* (660 Beacon St.; phone: 267-8484), a five-story building on the other side of Kenmore Square, is one of the largest bookstores in New England. And if you're hungry or parched, *Souper Salad* (524 Commonwealth Ave.; phone: 536-7662) has a bounteous salad bar; *Cornwall's* (510 Commonwealth Ave.; phone: 262-3749) is a handsome pub and restaurant with a wide variety of ales and a dart board atop a wooden stand in front of the kitchen; and *Pizzeria Uno* (1 Brookline Ave.; phone: 262-2373) serves up a formidable deep-dish pizza and good pasta dishes and salads. Any of the three will provide a pleasant epilogue to your walking tour of the Fens.

South End

Start

BOYLSTON ST.

Hynes Convention Center

PRUDENTIAL CENTER

Prudential Tower

Colonnade Hotel

West Newton St.

Boylston St.

Clearway

Reflecting Pool

Mother Church

CHRISTIAN SCIENCE CTR

Publishing Bldg.

Christian Science Basilica

Symphony Hall

MASSACHUSETTS AV.

HUNTINGTON AV.

HUNTINGTON AV.

COPLEY PLACE

Neiman Marcus

Back Bay Station

COPLEY SQ.

John Hancock Tower

ARLINGTON ST.

STUART

BERKELEY ST.

AVENUE

COLUMBUS ST.

DARTMOUTH ST.

DARTMOUTH

Dartmouth Pl.

W. Canton St.

Braddock Pk.

W. Newton St.

Rutland Sq.

Pembroke St.

W. NEWTON

MASSACHUSETTS AV.

COLUMBUS AV.

TREMONT ST.

TREMONT ST.

Warren Av.

Tremont St.

Dartmouth St.

Berkeley St.

Appleton St.

Cyclorama Building

WARREN AV.

Boston Center for the Arts

TREMONT ST.

Union Park

W. DEDHAM ST.

SHAWMUT ST.

SHAWMUT AV.

E. BERKELEY ST.

WASHINGTON ST.

HARRISON AV.

Holy Cross Cathedral

0   350
yards

Walk 2: South End

During the warm months, stoop sitting is a common weekend pastime in Boston's South End. Walk down any of several South End streets on a balmy day and you'll see a rainbow coalition of residents gathered on the steps of their Victorian brownstones and red brick townhouses, taking in the sun, snapping photos of their kids, swapping recipes and tales of urban life. Blacks still live next to Hispanics here, gentiles next to Jews, and Irish alongside Armenians, creating a sense of tolerance unmatched in any other part of Boston. This synthesis of colors and creeds gives the South End its identity.

Boston's South End has been many things to many people since 1855, when it was claimed from the marsh along a narrow neck of land connecting the Boston peninsula to the mainland. In the intervening years it has been first nouveau riche, then lower middle class, then skid row; it started to rally back to respectability again beginning in the 1970s, and today it is a partially gentrified neighborhood that is home to an interesting mix of people.

The South End makes for an attractive and interesting walk, offering visitors a look at a side of the city that many tourists never see. The neighborhood has neither downtown Boston's concentration of historic sites nor the Back Bay's homes of famous old families. Rather, the South End offers a living testament to Boston's ethnic diversity, to the wave after wave of immigrants that have kept the city vibrant. And then there is the architecture. Even during the worst of times, it was said that the South End was the "most beautiful slum in the world."

This walk should take about two and a half hours. Begin on the Boylston Street side of the *Prudential Center* (the *"Pru"*). The *Pru* and Copley Square Plaza separate the South End from the rest of Boston, with the *Pru* serving as the boundary between the Back Bay and the South End. To cross over from the Back Bay, ascend the escalator just beyond (and slightly to the left of) the outstretched arms of the statue *Quest Eternal* in front of the *Pru*. Walk the length of the plaza (there is an *Au Bon Pain* here, in case you need coffee or a croissant for sustenance) and descend the escalator on the other side. Voilà! The South End is before you.

Before crossing Huntington Avenue and plunging in, first visit the life's work of Mary Baker Eddy, founder of the *Church of Christ, Scientist* (better known as the *Christian Science Church*). The vast *Christian Science World Headquarters* complex, on the corner of Massachusetts and Huntington Avenues, sits at the juncture of the South End, the Fens, and the Back Bay.

Just across Belvidere Street is the complex's fountain and reflecting pool, a popular spot on steamy summer days, when local youth take turns maneuvering their skateboards and bicycles through the spouting water (it's better than opening a fire hydrant on a busy street). Take a stroll around the 670-foot rectangular pool, where continually circulating water gently rolls over the pool's rounded inner edge, so that someone walking on the outer ledge of the opposite side of the pool appears to be walking on water. (Before giving in to the impulse to convert or to try it yourself, be fore-warned—it's just an illusion.)

The original church, built in 1894, is on the right at the end of the pool. Today, the granite building is enveloped by an immense structure that is best viewed from the sidewalk on Massachusetts Avenue. It's even more dazzling at night. All the other contemporary buildings in the area are administrative offices for the church and were designed by architect I. M. Pei.

Turn right after reaching the main structure. Straight ahead is the *Christian Science Publishing Society Building,* which houses the offices of the venerable newspaper the *Christian Science Monitor,* which is read in 147 nations. The offices of *Monitor Radio* are located in the *Christian Science Broadcast Building.*

The most interesting aspect of the *Christian Science Publishing Society Building,* however, is the *Mapparium* (no need to run to *Webster's*; the word was coined here). A stained glass globe you can walk through, the *Mapparium* was built in 1935, when Sri Lanka was still known as Ceylon, and Laos and Vietnam were part of French Indochina. Another notable feature of this domed room is its acoustics; a whisper at one end can be heard loud and clear on the opposite side. The *Mapparium* is closed Sundays and Mondays June through mid-October and Saturdays through Mondays mid-October through May. Remember to pick up a free issue of the *Christian Science Monitor* on the way out.

Once outside on Mass. Ave., follow the sidewalk to Clearway (the first street), a charming little tree-lined thoroughfare with narrow, red brick buildings and gas lamps. Follow this street to the rear of the church complex, then veer left onto Belvidere Street and turn right. The hotel on the left is the *Sheraton,* where the doormen dress, inexplicably, like British military officers during the Boer War. The *Hilton* is across the street. When Belvidere crosses Huntington Avenue, it becomes West Newton Street. The *Colonnade* hotel, on the left, is known for its Old World European luxury. (For details on hotels, see *Checking In* in THE CITY.) At the end of this first block on West Newton (which becomes a veritable wind tunnel and umbrella graveyard when the weather is foul) is *St. Botolph* restaurant, on the corner of West Newton and St. Botolph Streets (see *Eating Out* in THE CITY).

Just past St. Botolph Street is a wide, well-manicured corridor with shrubs, trees, and wrought-iron gates. This is the Southwest Corridor, a pleasant pedestrian avenue that stretches from the Back Bay *T* stop on the *Orange Line* (behind *Neiman Marcus* near Copley Square) all the way to the *Forest Hills* station. The fact that one can stroll casually down this mall is a tribute to the civic activism of local residents, who successfully agitated against plans to build the Southwest Expressway through this space. (A highway here would have been as damaging to the character of the South End as the Southeast Expressway proved to be for the North End.)

Past the Southwest Corridor, at the corner of West Newton and Columbus, is the *Union United Methodist Church,* its exterior paved in mossy pudding stone. The church's leader, Rev. Charles Smith, is an influential voice in Boston's African-American community. Built in 1872, it originally served the Universalist congregation that migrated to the South End. Across Columbus Avenue and to the right is Rutland Square, a quiet block with a small fenced-in mall—little more than a tiny sliver of grass adorned with pink-and-white magnolia trees. The Italian bowfront houses in this block, which date from the 1860s, are more modest than in larger South End squares like Union Square (see below). Rutland Square remains much more ethnically diverse than Union Square, but the whole area continues to be in a state of flux. Some residences house lower-income families, others belong to former suburbanites who moved here as part of the re-gentrification of the 1970s, while still others are being gutted.

Walk along Rutland Square to Tremont Street, noting the twin-towered *New Hope Baptist Church* across the way. On Sundays, cars sometimes are parked three deep at the curb. Sermons are frequently interrupted by distressed car owners who are hemmed in and late for brunch. As the church doors open, the sweet sound of the gospel choir floods the street.

Turn left on Tremont, the South End's spinal column. There is an astonishing array of ethnic restaurants on or near Tremont Street. Between them, they offer continental, soul, West Indian, Puerto Rican, Brazilian, Irish, Cajun, Italian, Ethiopian, Greek, Lebanese, Korean, and Chinese fare. These aren't just catering to yuppies, either; each place has a sizable ethnic clientele.

One block south down Tremont Street is West Newton, where residents exult in painting their doors bold reds, deep greens, or stately blues. One can quickly determine if a building has been restored or gentrified by the condition of its front door. Street fairs are frequently held here, community events during which the whole block is closed to automobile traffic and members of the South End's large artistic community display their craftwork and their art.

Along with the hodgepodge of ethnic groups and wealthy, socially aware liberals, many gays live in this area of the South End. They staked their claim long ago, as part of the first wave of renovators here in the early 1970s. Politically, South End gays are a very cohesive bunch. They have their own newspaper, *Bay Windows,* and are a force to be reckoned with on local issues.

The next block south is Pembroke Street; turn left. If it's a nice day, you may see a portly fellow squatting on his stoop in his undershirt, bantering with a neighbor in a jackhammer voice that can be heard for blocks. His name is Al, but he is known throughout the block as the "Mayor of Pembroke Street," one of the area's old guard. The "mayor" bought his four-story townhouse for $25,000 in 1957 and has been running it as a boardinghouse ever since. With the South End's brilliant comeback and decades of soaring property values, he is sitting in a very good place.

Follow Pembroke Street to its intersection with Columbus Avenue. *Braddock Park* is on the left. At the end of the block on the opposite side of the street is *Charlie's Sandwich Shop* (429 Columbus Ave.; phone: 536-7669). *Charlie's,* a family-run operation for more than 50 years, is a South End institution. Open for breakfast and lunch every day except Sundays, it is beloved for its cranberry pancakes, western omelettes, home fries, and sweet potato pie.

Backtrack to *Braddock Park.* On most days there are a few people hanging out in front of *Braddock Drug* (437 Columbus Ave.; phone: 266-6445), since it is one of the few pharmacies here—or anywhere—that sells beer.

Make a sharp left onto Warren Avenue, an attractive residential street that passes several typical, small South End squares along its unhurried route to Tremont Street. On the right is the *Concord Baptist Church,* built in 1869. While townhouses in the Back Bay are influenced by French design, those in the South End reflect English architectural styles. When these buildings were single-family homes, the kitchens and dining rooms were tucked under the stoops on the buildings' first floors (called English basements), while the steps rose a full story to the second floors. This design made them easy to convert into multiple-family dwellings when, in the 1930s, the South End began its decline and Mayor Jerome Smith concluded that the neighborhood "should be opened to mechanics of limited means."

At Dartmouth Street, a short walk to the left leads to Dartmouth Place, a charming cul-de-sac. These brick row houses all have second-story bay windows that face the rear gardens of the Appleton Street houses.

Backtrack down Dartmouth Street to Tremont. The residents of the section to the right, beyond Tremont Street, are predominantly Hispanic. Across this intersection, in the first block of West Dedham Street, is *Villa Victoria,* an award-winning experiment in low-income housing. The complex consists of nearly 200 three-family units with private entrances that don't smack of public housing. Once in fear of displacement, this community now has housing it can be proud of. Across the street is the *Buteco II* restaurant (57 W. Dedham St.; phone: 247-9249), which serves authentic Brazilian food.

Two blocks to the right off Tremont is *Union Park,* a real South End treasure. The first square to be completed in the neighborhood, this is some city residents' favorite spot in the Hub (though Bostonians are prone to fall in love with anything that isn't too common). Its plush green spaces, fountains, and ample foliage make for a resplendent foreground to the large Victorian brick row houses. At the end of the street on the left is *On the Park* (315 Shawmut Ave.; phone: 426-0862), an intimate café that serves some of the finest shepherd's pie in town. The turkey pot pie is another good choice—and inexpensive, too. The restaurant's owner is also one of the city's best-known caterers, whose *East Meets West to Go* sandwich shop and bakery across the street (314 Shawmut Ave.; phone: 482-1015 or 426-3806) is rife with unusual entrées, salads, and cookies.

On the corner of *Union Park* and Washington Street, a block past Shawmut, is the *Cathedral of the Holy Cross.* As the largest Catholic church in the country at the time, it was the reason that many Irish immigrants crowded into this area in the late 1870s. The cathedral is located on the site of the old town gallows, on what was formerly the neck of land connecting Boston to the mainland.

For decades, Washington Street lay in the shadow of the unsightly *"El"* (elevated train track), which was built at the turn of the century and hastened the South End's rapid early decline. Dirty and noisy, the *El* created blight along its path, and its underside became a shadowy refuge for the city's street-dwelling alcoholics. The *El* was put out of its misery when the new *Orange Line* was built in 1987; the last remaining sections of the old elevated line were finally taken down in 1990.

Cut back through *Union Park* to return to Tremont Street. In the several blocks in both directions along Tremont are a number of establishments worthy of attention. Dining spots are dense here. *Azita's* (560 Tremont St.; phone: 338-8070), a petite subterranean restaurant with slick, black tables and indirect lighting, serves a delicious Cornish game hen with rosemary. Farther up the street are *Hamersley's Bistro* and the glass-walled *St. Cloud;* for more on these two restaurants, see *Eating Out* in THE CITY. Next is *Botolph's on Tremont* (569 Tremont St.; phone: 424-8577), the more moderately priced cousin of the *St. Botolph* restaurant. (The word "Boston," by the way, is derived from the saint's name.)

Across the street from *St. Cloud* is the *Boston Center for the Arts* (539 Tremont St.; phone: 426-5000 or 426-7700), the highlight of which is the *Cyclorama Building,* which is listed as a national landmark. The structure was built in 1884 to house a 400-foot-long circular painting of the *Battle of Gettysburg* by Paul Philippoteaux, a famed chronicler of the Civil War. After the painting was sent to Philadelphia, the *Cyclorama Building* became, in succession, a bicycle riding academy, a wholesale flower market, a garage (in which Alfred Champion invented the spark plug), and, finally, art exhibition space. During warm-weather months, the *St. Cloud* uses the plaza area for outdoor dining; it's always festive in the summer. The arts complex also has the *Millis* gallery, three theater spaces, and artists' studios.

Turn left on Berkeley. At the corner of Berkeley and Appleton Streets is a grand old building that houses the *Franklin Institute.* Founded with money from Benjamin Franklin, whose will grants funds to "the city of Boston's needy youth," it offers associate degrees in industrial and engineering technology.

Turn left onto Appleton, the South End's most prestigious residential address. After three blocks, cross Columbus to West Canton, a small thoroughfare that leads to the Southwest Corridor. Turn left at the corridor and walk three blocks to West Newton Street; turn right to the *Prudential Center* area. The *Skywalk* at the top of the Prudential Tower, which offers an excellent overview of the city, is a fitting place to conclude this walking tour of Boston's South End.

Walk 3: Back Bay

In the first half of the 19th century, the Back Bay section of Boston was a reservoir of trapped tidal backwater crisscrossed with railroad beds and a mill dam. It reeked of sewage and dumped refuse and was considered an eyesore and a health menace. By the turn of the century, however, many elite Boston families called Back Bay home.

Today, Boston's Back Bay is a posh area that is a living museum of residential Victorian architecture. With wide Commonwealth Avenue—reminiscent of a Parisian boulevard—and a gridwork street layout with alphabetized cross streets, this section of the city couldn't be more different from downtown's random jumble of narrow, crooked byways.

The filling in of Boston's Back Bay was a remarkable achievement for its time. In roughly 30 years, beginning in the 1850s, Boston nearly doubled in size, growing from a crowded, pear-shape peninsula to a bustling Victorian city with easy access to new parks and expanding suburbs. Almost as soon as land emerged in the Back Bay, upper crust Bostonians began their migration from Beacon Hill, the North End, and downtown. Churches, social clubs, and other institutions were soon to follow.

The process of creating a neighborhood from a marsh, however, was not without its headaches, some of which persist today (the area's rat problem is notorious, and at least one block of Back Bay is thought to be sinking). But Back Bay was and is worth the trouble. An afternoon spent walking along its magnolia-lined streets can be surprisingly relaxing for a big-city excursion.

The starting place for our Back Bay walk is the head of Commonwealth Avenue, where it meets the *Public Garden.* The tour—which will take about three hours if done at a leisurely pace—begins with a stroll around the *Public Garden.* Since the Back Bay area is roughly rectangular, the rest of this walk weaves back and forth over Commonwealth Avenue and residential Marlborough and Beacon Streets to the north, then explores Newbury and Boylston Streets to the south, winding up at the *John Hancock Tower* near Copley Square.

Bostonians tend to think of the *Public Garden* and *Boston Common* as one, but the two have vastly different histories. The *Common* has been a green for time immemorial, while the *Public Garden* was a muddy salt marsh before it was transformed by the Back Bay landfill project into one of the nation's first botanical gardens, a small enclave of nature in the heart of the city. (Also see *Special Places* in THE CITY.) The two parks are separated by Charles Street, just over and beyond a bridge that spans the pond.

On the Arlington Street (west) side of the *Public Garden* is Thomas Ball's statue of General George Washington atop his spirited horse (the sculptor's model was the steed ridden by the Prince of Wales during a visit

to Boston in 1860). To the north is the red marble and granite *Ether Monument* and fountain commemorating the first successful use of ether as a painkiller during surgery at nearby *Massachusetts General Hospital* in 1846. Other historic statuary includes the likeness on Charles Street of Edward Everett Hale, author of the disturbing novel *The Man Without a Country*; the sculpture depicting Unitarian preacher William Ellery Channing, which faces his *Arlington Street Church;* the one of abolitionist Senator Charles Sumner, which stands on Charles Street; and the statue of Civil War hero Colonel Thomas Cass, located on the Boylston Street side of the park. If you visit during the spring or summer, you may want to take a ride on one of the park's famous Swan Boats. Cold-weather visitors needn't be disappointed, however; even when the Swan Boats are put to bed, the *Public Garden* retains its magical charm. Skaters swirl across the frozen lagoon, and the icy trees give the snowy scene a fairyland feel.

Cross Arlington Street at the southern foot of the *Public Garden.* Here is the grande dame of Boston hotels, the *Ritz-Carlton,* where afternoon tea is a Boston institution—and one that requires a certain code of dress (also see *Quintessential Boston* in DIVERSIONS). With jazz performances nightly, this Boston institution may even be loosening up a bit. While the blue blood is still coursing through your veins, have a peek inside *Firestone and Parsons* (phone: 266-1858) in the *Ritz* building entrance around the corner on Newbury Street. The ultimate old-guard jewelry store, it is known for its antique tea services (try not to knock anything over). Farther up Newbury Street is a row of sumptuous fur and jewelry shops—but don't stray too far, since the route heads in the other direction. After browsing (or buying), return to Commonwealth Avenue.

Cross Commonwealth Avenue (the locals just say "Comm. Ave.") to the center mall area near the statue of Alexander Hamilton. Look back in the direction of the Washington statue for one of Boston's most attractive views. The general sits high upon his mount just beyond the wrought-iron fence of the *Public Garden.* The white tower of the *Park Street Church* can be seen beyond the general, and the skyscrapers of the financial district are beyond that.

Across the street are a pair of venerable buildings. On the corner of Commonwealth Avenue and Arlington Street is the *Harbridge House.* Built in 1860 by Arthur Gilman, who also designed the *Arlington Street Church,* it is the grandest of the surviving houses on Arlington, but is now subdivided into office space at 8-11 Arlington Street. *Atlantic Monthly* magazine, one of the nation's oldest periodicals, was published in here until 1989, when it moved to 745 Boylston St.

Walk straight ahead to where Arlington intersects Beacon Street. If the year were 1830, you would now be standing on the old *Mill Dam,* built across Back Bay in 1814 to harness energy from the tides for mill power. The dam extended westward along what is now Beacon Street to what today is Kenmore Square, home of the mammoth *Citgo* sign and *Fenway Park.*

Bostonians used the 50-foot-wide dam for winter sleigh rides and summer evening strolls until it was filled in, along with the rest of Back Bay, during the second half of the 19th century.

Ahead is a brown ramp leading over Storrow Drive to the *Esplanade,* an elongated park along the Charles River. This ramp is the *Fiedler Footbridge.* Named after the late, legendary *Boston Pops* conductor Arthur Fiedler, it is the best route from Back Bay to the *Hatch Shell,* site of summer concerts and the enormously popular *Independence Day* performance of the *Boston Pops* (see *Special Events* in THE CITY).

Return to Commonwealth Avenue and turn right. The building with the billowing tricolor flag in front is the French consulate. Beyond that, at No. 5, is the *Boston Center for Adult Education (BCAE),* an organization that offers evening courses in more than 500 subjects, including beginning Russian, stand-up comedy, fly-fishing, and Brazilian cooking. Visitors are welcome to poke around the *BCAE* building (phone: 267-2465), originally a mansion built by cotton broker Walter Baylies in 1904. Baylies demolished a house identical to the French consulate building on this site, erecting in its place the present, more fashionable structure. He built the lavish Louis XIV ballroom on the building's west side in 1912 for his daughter's debut into Boston society.

Turn right on Berkeley Street. When you round the corner, the *Hooper Mansion* (25-27 Berkeley St.) will be over your right shoulder. Once the home of congressman and merchant Samuel Hooper, it has a huge (by Back Bay standards) corner yard. On the left is the *First and Second Unitarian Church* (66 Marlborough St.; phone: 267-6730), built by former Puritans in 1867. All that remains of the original structure are the tower and arcade (fire ravaged the building in 1968). A statue of John Winthrop, the Massachusetts Bay Colony's first governor, stands around the corner on the Marlborough Street side of the building. Across Marlborough Street is the *French Library* (53 Marlborough St.; phone: 266-4351). Films and lectures about France and French culture are frequently held at this handsome 19th-century Victorian mansion, which is surrounded by a tall iron fence.

Continue one more block down Berkeley to Beacon Street. This section of Beacon Street has been Back Bay's most blue-blooded since the neighborhood was created. In earlier times, a Beacon Street address meant an old family with money; old families without much money resided on Marlborough Street; and the nouveau riche lived on Commonwealth Avenue.

For a more in-depth look into Victorian Boston, tour the *Gibson House Museum* at 137 Beacon, a preserved 19th-century Back Bay row house filled with six floors of the Gibson family's original furnishings. It is shown by guided tour several afternoons a week; for details, see *Museums* in THE CITY. Then walk west on Beacon to the *French Library*'s Saxon counterpart, the *Goethe Institute* (170 Beacon St.; phone: 262-6050). This German cultural center for New England, a branch of the *Goethe Institute* in Munich, offers language and other cultural programs.

The stark metal-and-glass monstrosity at the corner of Beacon and Clarendon Streets is a housing complex completed in the 1970s. Its institutional feel scared the daylights out of local supporters of historical preservation, who have since redoubled their efforts to regulate construction in the area; they now seem to have the upper hand in Back Bay development.

On Clarendon Street, turn left and walk down to the central mall on Commonwealth. Designed by landscape architect Frederick Law Olmsted, the mall is a link in Boston's 8-mile *Emerald Necklace,* which includes the *Common* and the *Public Garden.*

Ahead, on the corner of Commonwealth and Clarendon, is another landmark that merits at least one photograph. The *First Baptist Church* (phone: 267-3148), designed by architect H. H. Richardson (who also designed *Trinity Church*—see below), is especially photogenic when contrasted with the ultramodern Hancock Tower in the background. (See also *A Shutterbug's Boston* in DIVERSIONS.)

Notice the sturdy building at the end of the block to the left (152 Commonwealth Ave.). This is the home of the *Chilton Club,* the female counterpart to Boston's gentlemen's club culture. At one time it had three separate entrances—one for members, one for members with guests, and one for the help.

Two more noteworthy buildings face each other from different sides of Commonwealth Avenue at the beginning of the next block to the right. On the south side is the *Vendome,* a former hotel of some grandeur that once boasted General Ulysses S. Grant, President Grover Cleveland, P. T. Barnum, Mark Twain, Oscar Wilde, and Sarah Bernhardt as guests. It has been converted into an office condominium complex with a high-tech interior. In the basement is *Spasso* (phone: 536-8656), a charming Italian bistro with an outdoor dining area just below street level.

Across Commonwealth Avenue is the *Ames-Webster Mansion* (306 Dartmouth St.), at one time among the most spectacular residences in Back Bay. Members of Boston society once would clatter up to the wrought-iron gate on the Dartmouth Street side in carriages. Men would debark and enter through the doorway to the left; ladies would be driven through the porte cochère to a rear door where they would ascend to a second-floor powder room via elevator. Once properly powdered, they could make their grand entrance to the first floor down an elaborately carved staircase. The mansion is now an office building, although it almost became student housing in 1969. Much of its inner grandeur has been revived.

Proceed north (right) on Dartmouth to Marlborough Street. At the northeast corner is the noteworthy *Cushing-Endicott House.* Built in 1873, it's named after two Boston families that were the house's only residents until 1953. The great American painter John Singer Sargent used one of its bedrooms as his studio in the early 1900s. It was subdivided into six condominiums in the mid-1980s; the largest sold for more than $1 million.

Head west (left) down Marlborough. At the corner of Marlborough and Exeter, turn right and walk two short blocks for a panoramic view of the Charles River. Across the river, the granite building with the rotunda is the main administration building of the *Massachusetts Institute of Technology (MIT)*.

Return to Commonwealth Avenue via Exeter and turn right. This block is home to two of Boston's most elite social clubs. On the right is the *St. Botolph Club* (199 Commonwealth Ave.), an august establishment of "men of letters." It is so proper that, according to legend, a member sat dead in his club chair for two days before his death was noticed: The gentleman was thought to be asleep, and no employee was so brash as to speak to him before being spoken to first. From the street, the balding heads of club members may be visible above their leather, high-back chairs through the first-floor bay window. The statue on the Commonwealth Avenue Mall of a pensive man dressed in a raincoat and seated on a bluff overlooking the sea is of the noted American historian Samuel Eliot Morison, a member of the *St. Botolph Club.* His casual appearance and posture contrast markedly with the other formal statues on the mall.

Farther down the block on the right is the *Algonquin Club* (217 Commonwealth Ave.), another stockyard for Boston Brahmins, identified by its blue-and-white banner and limestone façade. Business types can be seen through the second-floor windows nursing their brandies and exchanging the news of the day. The townhouse known as *267 Commonwealth* (see also *Checking In* in THE CITY) offers intimate Victorian lodging; try to convince the manager to give you a tour of the hotel's suites, which feature working fireplaces, ornate woodwork, and floral print papers similar to the original Victorian patterns.

On the next block, on the northeast corner of Commonwealth and Hereford, is the *Andrew Mansion,* an Italianate renaissance revival structure with a wrought-iron balcony on the third floor that comes from the *Tuileries Palace* in Paris. Today, passersby may see somebody hanging by his feet from that balcony, since the mansion is now an *MIT* fraternity house. (The fraternity, to be fair, maintains this building proudly.)

At this point, architecture buffs may want to take a small side trip to see an outstanding example of a church gone condo. Turn right on Hereford and cut over to Beacon Street, then turn left. *Church Court,* a complex of condominiums on the corner of Beacon Street and Massachusetts Avenue, was the *Mount Vernon Church* before it was ravaged in a spectacular fire in 1978. Portions of the church are brilliantly blended into an L-shape building that now houses 42 condominium units. Turn left on Massachusetts Avenue to rejoin the route.

If you prefer to pass up the detour, simply follow Commonwealth Avenue to Massachusetts Avenue, noting the *Burrage Mansion* (314 Commonwealth

Ave.) to the right. It is one example of New York architectural flamboyance that managed to infiltrate conventional Back Bay. The limestone palace seems to have been inspired by the Vanderbilts' mansion in New York. Today, it is the *Boston Evening Clinic,* which provides health care during "off" hours for working people and has become the workhorse in Massachusetts's attempt to ensure quality health care for all, regardless of whether they have health insurance.

Turn left on Massachusetts Avenue. *Newbury's Steak House* (94 Massachusetts Ave.; phone: 536-0184), located about mid-block, is an excellent choice for a hearty New York strip steak or prime ribs in an old Boston atmosphere at a reasonable price. Around the corner is the newer *Capital Grille* (359 Newbury St.; phone: 262-8900), a steakhouse that ages its own meat. Across Mass. Ave. and roaring below is the "Mass. Pike" (Massachusetts Turnpike), running from downtown Boston across the state to the New York border.

Turn left at the next corner onto Newbury Street, where antiques shops, record stores, hair salons, art galleries, trendy restaurants, designer boutiques, jewelry stores, fur salons, bridal shops, bookstores, sidewalk cafés, vintage clothing shops, imported gift emporiums, florists, and purveyors of countercultural comic books stand side by side in the basement and first-floor retail spaces of attractive brownstone buildings. Boston's most fashion-conscious byway, Newbury Street features an endless parade of people with personal styles ranging from Bohemian to preppy and from Euro-chic to yuppie.

Of particular interest in the first block of Newbury Street is *Trident Booksellers & Café* (338 Newbury St.; phone: 267-8688), on the right, one of two such hybrid establishments on Newbury Street. After browsing through the books, including an extensive selection of works on Eastern religions, relax with a cup of herbal tea and a muffin, coffee and pastries, or a light meal of nouvelle (or is that novel?) American cuisine. You may want to stop into *Sonsie,* a restaurant incorporating a cozy, newspaper-strewn reading salon across the street at No. 327 (see *Eating Out* in THE CITY).

Back on the other side of the street, you will find the offices of the *Hellenic Chronicle* (324 Newbury St.; phone: 262-4500), a newspaper that serves Boston's sizable Greek population. Appropriately, *Steve's* (62 Hereford St.; phone: 267-1817), an informal, authentic Greek restaurant, is on the northeast corner of Newbury and Hereford. It serves first-rate Greek salads and *spanikopita* (pastry filled with spinach and cheese).

Turn right on Hereford Street. The colossal building ahead is the *Hynes Convention Center,* a state-owned complex that hosts conventions for groups ranging from wood-siding manufacturers to members of the clergy.

Head right on Boylston Street, which was named after Dr. Zabdiel Boylston, who fearlessly began smallpox inoculation in America in the early 1720s. Past a fire station is the *Institute of Contemporary Art* (see also *Special*

Places in Back Bay in THE CITY), once a police station and now one of Boston's primary exhibit venues. Next door is *Division Sixteen* (phone: 353-0870), an informal, trendy restaurant named after the building's former occupant, a fire station.

Turn around and head back down Boylston Street. On the corner of Boylston and Hereford is the *Cactus Club* (phone: 236-0200), a restaurant with reasonably good Santa Fe–style food, considering that it's in the home of the baked, not the refried, bean. The decor features a real stuffed buffalo over the bar. The tall building across the street is the *Prudential Center* (the Pru, among locals), a 52-story tower built in the 1960s to replace unsightly railroad yards; many feel the Pru isn't any more sightly. It houses stores and offices as well as some hotels and apartments. Donald DeLue's statue of a man reaching for the heavens in front of the Pru, titled *The Quest Eternal,* was the old finish line for the *Boston Marathon.* When the John Hancock company became the primary sponsor of the grueling 26.2-mile April race, it moved the finish line closer to its own building, several blocks from here. A must on any itinerary is the *Top of the Hub,* a forgettable restaurant with a breathtaking view of the city from the Pru's highest floor. The *Skywalk* (50th floor) offers the best view of the *Christian Science Center* and its reflecting pool.

At 777 Boylston is the *Atlantic Fish Co.* (phone: 267-4000), a restaurant that serves an array of fish and shellfish rivaled in scope only by the *New England Aquarium,* where they are not for consumption. The restaurant—not the aquarium—offers outdoor dining in summer. *Lord & Taylor* (phone: 262-6000), a fine department store, is across the street.

Now turn left on Fairfield and then take a right to head down Newbury Street again for a short stretch. This block features a number of acclaimed art galleries, such as the *Randall Beck Gallery* (263 Newbury St.; phone: 266-2475), which is highly regarded for its contemporary prints.

Stroll to *Waterstone's Booksellers* (181 Newbury St.; phone: 859-7300), the only US link in this British-based bookstore chain. Housed in an ornate former theater sporting a bright red awning, this huge shop stocks about 150,000 titles—one of the largest collection of books in the city. It's a must for confirmed bookworms.

Two notable galleries on this block are the *Pucker-Safrai* (171 Newbury St.; phone: 267-9473), with a permanent collection of works by New England, European, Israeli, and other artists, and the *Nielsen Gallery* (179 Newbury St.; phone: 266-4835), which shows the work of a stable of talented young artists. If the weather is good, you may find another type of art exhibit beneath your feet. Sidewalk Sam, an irrepressible Boston-based artist, has created more than 1,000 perishable works—elaborate chalk murals, often copies of well-known masterpieces—on Boston walkways. You may even be lucky enough to run across Sam Guillemin himself laboring over a work in progress.

Turn right on Dartmouth, and walk to the *"New" Old South Church* at the corner of Dartmouth and Boylston Streets. This northern Italian Gothic–style church was built in 1877, and was the successor to the *Old South Meeting House* of Boston Tea Party fame downtown. Open daily.

Directly ahead is Copley Square. Cross Boylston Street at this point (the current *Boston Marathon* finish line) to come to the *Boston Public Library* (666 Boylston St.; phone: 536-5400), commonly known as the *BPL*. This grandiose renaissance revival structure was built in 1895, but the oldest section is under renovation (scheduled to continue until the end of the century), so visitors must enter through the blocky new addition, designed by Philip Johnson and built in 1972. Once inside, turn left and go up a few stairs. Turn left and quickly right and you'll find yourself in a beautiful courtyard. Rest a while or continue across the courtyard to the older section, which is decorated with work by some of the greatest painters of the day. Murals by Puvis de Chavannes, Edwin Abbey, and John Singer Sargent adorn the walls of the second and third floors. The barrel-vaulted *Bates Hall* reading room is simply breathtaking. It looks and smells like everything a library should be. As Robert Parker, Boston-based author of the once-popular "Spenser" detective series, remarked, "Even when I went in to look up Duke Snider's lifetime batting average, I felt like a scholar." Open daily (phone: 536-5400).

Down Dartmouth Street past the library's main entrance is *Copley Place,* a shopping magnet. The first indoor mall erected inside Boston's city limits, it was a controversial project. Development critics suggested it would cheapen the surrounding architecture of Copley Square. Yankee shoppers, who are quite content to wear the proverbial old hat passed down from generation to generation, complained it would be too expensive. Nonetheless, *Copley Place* has gotten along just fine with upscale names such as *Tiffany* and *Neiman Marcus.* There's even *Le Chapeau,* which carries a staggering variety of hats (perhaps the Yankee stereotype itself is becoming old hat).

Across Dartmouth Street from the shopping center is the *Copley Plaza* hotel (also see *Checking In* in THE CITY), a stately structure that has hosted presidents, royalty, and numerous gala social events in its venerable career. Afternoon tea is served from 3 to 5 PM among the potted palms in the hotel's lobby.

Cross St. James Avenue in front of the hotel. At the end of the wide plaza is *Trinity Church,* one of the most impressive churches in America. With its beautiful medieval decorations and its awe-inspiring sense of enormity, *Trinity Church* deserves an extended visit. Guidebooks and brochures are available inside. Open daily (phone: 536-0944). (Also see *Historic Churches* in DIVERSIONS.) Across St. James Avenue from *Trinity Church* is the entrance to the *Observatory* of the 62-story *John Hancock Tower,* a spectacular place from which to view the city and learn about the development of Boston, see a scale model of the city as it was in 1775, and get an aerial view of your tour of Boston's Back Bay.

To return to the *Public Garden,* just walk one block north to Boylston Street or two blocks to Newbury Street, and head right. These remaining blocks feature many lavish clothing boutiques and furriers.

Walk 4: Boston Common

All kinds of people have long enjoyed *Boston Common,* America's oldest public park. Those who do—Beacon Hill socialites, Frisbee-hurling college students, street people, soapbox pontificators, hand-holding couples, families on picnics, tourists, skateboarding adolescents, Christian proselytizers, political rally participants—all owe this calming stretch of greenery to an eccentric Anglican clergyman who loved books, madeira wine, and the anger these two passions incited in the uptight Puritans of the 17th century.

The clergyman, William Blaxton (pronounced, and sometimes spelled, *Blackstone*), was Boston's first settler, having put down stakes on the land that would become *Boston Common* in 1630. But when the Puritans tried to convert him, he headed south to the more permissive Rhode Island. He could easily afford the move, since he had sold the 50-acre *Common* to Royal Governor John Winthrop and his band of Puritans at the then-exorbitant price of 30 pounds. Winthrop thought it was a great deal, however, because it provided plenty of space for cattle grazing and military training. For all the good that Bostonians over several centuries have gotten out of their park (even after cattle were banned from the *Common* in 1830 to avoid the nuisance to pedestrians), it was a steal.

The best place to begin a tour of the *Common* (this one will take about an hour and a half) is the visitors' information center along Tremont Street. The attendants in this big blue booth, halfway between the Park Street and Boylston *T* stops, can accurately answer almost any Boston-related question (except when the *Red Sox* will end their *World Series* drought). Trolley tours offered by several companies originate here. Across the street is the *Boston Welcome Center* (phone: 451-2227), which has every conceivable Boston souvenir, book, postcard, or gift. Free maps are available.

Adjacent to the visitors' center is Parkman Plaza, a lovely place to sit, though it tends to be a gathering spot for the down-and-out. The plaza's namesake, George Parkman, lived up to his surname: He bequeathed $5 million to the *Common* and other city parks, no small chunk of change in 1908. Parkman's house still stands on Beacon Street (see *Walk 5: Beacon Hill*).

Cut through the middle of the plaza and walk to the *Parkman Bandstand,* a neo-classical structure tucked in the shade of the surrounding elm trees that can be reached by any one of a number of paths. No longer used for concerts, the bandstand, which has reasonably good acoustics, is now the venue for the raspy singing and late-night howls of the crowd who call the *Common* home. (It's safe here by day, but don't get caught in this area after sundown.)

Boston Common

Concerts on the Common, performances occasionally held on summer evenings, take place in a big, wooden pen erected just to the north of the bandstand. Many Bostonians to whom sound is more important than visuals enjoy the music of topnotch performers while picnicking outside the concert area. There are usually more listeners outside than in, since it's free and there is more legroom (50 acres). The music can be heard for blocks (which is why area neighbors have fought—successfully—to reduce the number of concerts presented each year).

Work your way through the intricate web of paths to the extreme south section of the *Common,* the location of the *Central Burying Ground.* This is best done via a path called Railroad Mall, which runs parallel to Tremont Street about 50 to 100 feet inside the *Common.* Along the way is a monument commemorating the Boston Massacre, which occurred at the *Old State House* not far from here (see *Walk 6: Downtown*). At the burial ground, the baseball field and tennis courts will be on the right.

A burial ground in a public park and at a busy intersection seems at best poorly planned, at worst disrespectful, but this was not part of the original *Common* grounds. The area was an obscure piece of real estate when it was purchased in 1756, after gravediggers complained that the downtown cemeteries (the *Old Granary* and *King's Chapel*) were so crowded that bodies had to be buried four deep. The burial ground's most famous occupant (in an unknown grave site) is Gilbert Stuart, portraitist of George and Martha Washington, Paul Revere, and other early American patriots.

Across Boylston Street is the *Colonial Theatre* (106 Boylston St.; phone: 426-9366), which marks the northern edge of Boston's theater district. If time allows, round the corner to Tremont Street, where a number of old theaters and the *Broadway Deli* (275 Tremont St.; phone: 426-1344), Boston's best delicatessen, are located. (Also see *Inside Boston's Theaters* in DIVERSIONS.) Here also are a number of music stores, including *Carl Fischer Music* (156 Boylston St.; phone: 426-0740), *M. Steinert & Sons* (162 Boylston St.; phone: 426-1900), and around the corner, the *Boston Music Co.* (172 Tremont St.; phone: 426-5100), all wonderful places for browsing. At the end of the block in a former bank building is *Remington's* (124 Boylston St.; phone: 574-9676), a restaurant and pub that has excellent burgers and ale.

A plaque on the building at 176 Boylston Street, at the corner of Carver Street, marks the birthplace in 1809 of Edgar Allan Poe (the actual house at 62 Carver no longer stands). The writer, who seemed to be miserable everywhere, made no bones about disliking Boston. Perhaps his only kind comment about the city was when he remarked that *Boston Common* was "no common thing." Nonetheless, Poe always said he was "heartily ashamed" to have been born here.

Farther down is Park Square, where Boylston meets Charles Street. Follow the path around the bend and walk parallel to Charles Street. This is MacArthur Mall, which was a seawall before Back Bay was filled in. Below the seawall was the site of many gallows executions; instead of being given a decent burial, the bodies of the executed were allowed to wash out to sea.

This area, with its greenery cleared to accommodate a baseball field, bleachers, and a chain-link fence, is the *Common*'s least attractive. Street vendors usually peddle pretzels, fried dough, and Italian sausages along here. Across Charles Street is the lovely *Public Garden* (see *Walk 3: Back Bay*). After rounding the next bend, you're plunged into the heart of the *Common*.

There is a plaque along MacArthur Mall, about halfway to Beacon Street ahead, which commemorates the place where in April 1775 the redcoats embarked on their fateful voyage across the Charles River and on to Lexington and Concord. Though their "oars were muffled to prevent noise," as the plaque says, the attack was no surprise to the colonists.

Past the plaque on the right are the *Parade Grounds,* the former site of military training, which was one of the *Common*'s original purposes. In fact, MacArthur Mall was built large enough to hold a full column of soldiers. America's oldest military order, the *Ancient and Honorable Artillery Company,* founded in 1638, sometimes holds elaborate ceremonies in full regalia here. (The company has a museum on the top floor of *Faneuil Hall.*) In 1979, thousands gathered on the *Parade Grounds* for an outdoor mass conducted by Pope John Paul II. A granite marker commemorates the event.

At the corner, Charles Street intersects with Beacon Street, the southern boundary of Beacon Hill. Turn right on the Beacon Street Mall. A short jaunt uphill opposite Spruce Street leads to a monument to William Blaxton. The statue depicts an ebullient Blaxton—who must have been desperate for companionship, since he didn't like the Puritans any more than the English Lord Bishops from whom he fled—inviting Governor John Winthrop onto the Boston peninsula to share its beauties and ample springs.

Take a path on the right leading up to Flagstaff Hill, the highest point on the *Common.* At the top is the *Soldiers and Sailors Monument,* which honors those who fought in the Civil War. While graffiti artists have since added some of their own commentary to the monument, the hilltop is still a wonderful place to view a panorama of the *Common* or to enjoy a picnic on one of the benches.

Downhill to the north is the Frog Pond, which has no frogs and is scarcely even a pond, since it is lined with concrete. Formerly a watering place for cattle, the pond is now a children's wading pool in the summer. During the early spring, when there is no water, the empty pool is the domain of skateboarders and roller skaters.

A shade-drenched walkway skirts the edges of the Frog Pond, then intersects with a path that leads back to Beacon Street. Head down this walk—called the Long Path because it stretches diagonally across the *Common* from Beacon to Tremont Street—away from Beacon Street. At the intersection of three paths, in the "V" that opens up to Flagstaff Hill, the Great Elm once stood. A mammoth tree (over 70 feet tall, with branches that spread out 100 feet), the Great Elm was the site of many executions, including that of Mary Dyer, a Quaker who was hanged here in 1660 for her religious beliefs. Though the tree died in 1876, it lives on as a symbol of stern Puritan justice.

Backtrack to the Beacon Street Mall along the Long Path, which is also called Oliver Wendell Holmes Walk, after the author, doctor, and father of the Supreme Court Justice who so loved to stroll along this route (the Long Path was the site of a famous romantic scene in Holmes's celebrated *Autocrat of the Breakfast Table*). The 19th-century British author William Makepeace Thackeray likened this elm-studded portion of the *Common* to the promenades of *Windsor Castle.*

Turn right on the Beacon Street Mall. Several yards ahead is the *Robert Gould Shaw Memorial,* designed by Augustus Saint-Gaudens. Shaw, the 26-year-old son of a prominent Boston family, died while leading the 54th Regiment—the first regiment of free blacks—into battle during the Civil War. Shaw and the regiment are the subjects of the 1989 film *Glory.* (Also see *Special Places* in Beacon Hill in THE CITY.)

Now turn right and head downhill along the red strip in the middle of the pavement, which indicates the Freedom Trail. This path is usually busy with *State House* employees walking to and from *Park Street Station,* the site of the country's first underground trolley (a.k.a. "subway"). At the top of the hill, on the corner across from the *State House,* is the *Ticknor Mansion,* built in 1804 but heavily rebuilt to accommodate offices and an excellent antiques shop on the corner. Farther down Park Street are the exclusive *Union Club* and the Roman Catholic *Paulist Center.* Walk downhill, with Park Street on your left. The trees along this walk and those in the rest of the *Common* are resplendent with sparkling lights at *Christmastime.* It is wise not to get too engrossed in the natural beauty or the architecture, however; keep a lookout for stray Frisbees and boomerangs in this most boisterous area of an otherwise peaceful *Common.*

The corner of Tremont and Park Streets is one of Boston's busiest intersections. Heavy traffic merges with rabid shoppers jaywalking across Tremont Street in droves, their eyes fixed on the shops of Winter Street and the Downtown Crossing retail district beyond. Complicating matters are the usual array of protesters, sidewalk evangelists, pretzel vendors, and street people. Overseeing this jumble of humanity is the *Park Street Church,* across Park Street, with chimes that thrice daily attempt to calm the madding crowd.

Just behind the granite Park Street *T* stop entrance and exit is the *Brewer Fountain.* Clear a path through the pigeons and pause to enjoy this beautiful monument, a bronze replica of a Parisian fountain that was quite the rage at the *Paris Exposition* of 1855. The view beyond the fountain up the lawn to the gold dome of the State House is arresting.

Jaywalk (carefully) across Tremont Street with the shoppers to the rather gloomy, seemingly unfinished *St. Paul's Cathedral. St. Paul's* has a generic feel from the outside because the pediment over the porch is blank. It was supposed to be graced with rich ornamentation, but lack of funds prevented any further work. Colorful—and slightly incongruous—banners are hung from the outside columns to jazz the place up. But don't be fooled by the plain façade; inside, this Episcopalian church, built 10 years after the *Park Street Church,* is sumptuously decorated. Cross the street once more to return to the visitors' information booth, the last stop on the *Boston Common* walking tour.

Walk 5: Beacon Hill

The hub of activity in the Hub is the corner of Park and Tremont Streets on *Boston Common*'s east boundary, a bustling area that revolves around the *Park Street* subway station. The country's oldest subway station, where in 1897 a trolley car first operated underground, today it is the intersection of the *Red* and *Green Lines* of Boston's famed (some residents say infamous) *Massachusetts Bay Transit Authority,* commonly known as "the *T.*" The walking tour of the Beacon Hill historic district, which takes approximately four hours at a leisurely pace, begins here.

Take a few moments to enjoy the panoramic view from this spot. As you look up toward the gold dome of the *State House,* the seat of Massachusetts government, you'll also see the *Boston Common,* the nation's oldest park, stretching out before you and to the left. The road at the right, Park Street, runs down from the foot of the *State House* to Tremont Street. Turn to the right to view the historic *Park Street Church* at the intersection of the two streets, then turn farther to face Tremont. To the right is Winter Street, which leads downtown to the city's financial and retail districts.

The spot where you are now standing was once known as *Brimstone Corner.* As on nearly every issue, other city residents beg to differ on the source of the corner's colorful name, but some say it was the "fire and brimstone" speechifying that used to sally forth from the church's pulpit. At 9 AM, noon, and 4:45 PM, the church's chimes ring out familiar hymns. The church is closed Mondays (phone: 523-3383). See also *Historic Churches* in DIVERSIONS and *Special Places* in THE CITY.

The plaza area near the entrance to the Park Street *T* stop is reminiscent of London's *Hyde Park.* Though free speech is never in short supply here, your patience may be. If you haven't been handed a pamphlet, asked to sign a petition, urged to boycott a product, or coaxed to write to your congressman, it's probably raining. And even rain doesn't dampen the zeal of a group of Quakers who regularly bear witness to sinful acts and exhort passersby to mend their ways. Panhandlers also work this area with aplomb, congregating on the steps down to the *T* where hurried commuters fumble for subway change. Here a scruffy fellow once delivered one of the greatest lines in the business: "Hey buddy, can you spare a thousand dollars? Well, no problem. If you've got a quarter, I can make up the rest." This corner is also home to a number of vendors, who peddle everything from hot pretzels to jewelry. Try a monster pretzel, slathered with a generous dose of mustard. Many a relationship has been saved by the resident flower vendor, whose business blooms during rush hour.

Following the Freedom Trail, which is marked by a painted red line on the sidewalk, start up the hill toward the *State House.* On the right is Park Street, which began as a pathway through the *Common* to the beacon, a

signal lantern atop a pole that warned townspeople of any danger, and gave this hill its name. The row of 19th-century, Federal-style buildings on Park Street was once called *Bulfinch Row* because most were designed by the famous architect Charles Bulfinch. The only Bulfinch building still standing on Park Street is the *Amory-Ticknor House,* on the corner of Park and Beacon. The house was built for Thomas Amory, a merchant who went broke before he got a chance to move in.

Follow the Freedom Trail up the walkway to the steps that climb to Beacon Street. In between the two sets of steps is the *Robert Gould Shaw Memorial.* (See *Walk 4: Boston Common.*) Clamber up the steps to see the crowning glory of Bulfinch's many Boston landmarks, the Massachusetts *State House,* completed in 1798. The governor's office is on the third floor, just left of the columns and behind the statue of Horace Mann, the great advocate of public education. The location has its pros and cons for Massachusetts governor William Weld, the first Republican to occupy the office in 18 years. Although it's far removed from the offices of the state legislators (mostly Democrats), it overlooks an area commonly used for political demonstrations.

There is a closer look at the *State House* and its inside attractions later in the walk. For now, cross the intersection and turn left. A small park of statues on the right features likenesses of statesman Henry Cabot Lodge, who lived not far from here; Anne Hutchinson, who was banished from the Massachusetts Bay Colony for her 82 heretical opinions, "some blasphemous, others erroneous, and all unsafe"; and President John F. Kennedy, who is captured in his familiar, confident stride.

Begin down Beacon Street, an old thoroughfare steeped in history. Though it was called "Poor House Lane" in the 17th century because of an almshouse nearby, by the end of the 19th century Oliver Wendell Holmes had dubbed it "the sunny street that holds the sifted few."

By now some of the high-rises of the Back Bay should be visible ahead in the distance. Next to the blue glass *Hancock Tower* is an older building with a vertical row of colored lights on its spire. This is the old *Hancock Building;* its lights forecast the weather. This epigram tells it all: "Steady blue, clear view. Flashing blue, clouds are due. Steady red, rain ahead. Flashing red, snow instead." (Flashing red lights in the summer indicate that the *Red Sox* game has been canceled, but no one yet has been able to fit that into the rhyme.)

Stroll down Beacon Street and note the purple glass in some of the windows. These purple panes, of which their owners are very proud, were originally a mistake: The violet hue is the result of imperfections in a type of glass shipped from Hamburg, Germany, around 1820. Brought out by the sunlight, this flaw must have caused quite a row among proper Bostonians when it was detected. Today, however, purple means a pane of glass is old, which is synonymous with "status" in Beacon Hill parlance.

Nearly every building along Beacon Street figured prominently in the history of Boston. Two of the most interesting are the *Appleton-Parker* homes (39-40 Beacon St.), a stately pair of early Greek Revival bowfront houses. Nearby is the *Somerset Club* (42 Beacon St.), a three-story granite house that was Daniel Webster's favorite haunt. Now a social club, it's strictly private—and profoundly conservative. Also note the former home of the Cabot family (34 Beacon St.) and the *Third Harrison Gray Otis House* (45 Beacon St.), built for the patriot and Mayor of Boston. At 55 Beacon Street is the *William Prescott House,* former home (from 1845 to 1849) of the grandson of Colonel William Prescott, who commanded the colonial troops at the Battle of Bunker Hill. The younger Prescott, who was blinded in an accident while he was a student at Harvard, was a historian who also devised a system of reading and writing for the blind that preceded Braille. The building is now headquarters for the *National Society of Colonial Dames.*

Children may be best qualified to recount what happened at the intersection of Beacon and Charles. This is the spot where, in Robert McCloskey's *Make Way for Ducklings!,* Officer Clancy and four fellow Boston policemen held up traffic so Mrs. Mallard could escort her eight ducklings to the *Public Garden* to reunite with Mr. Mallard. On the path to the *Public Garden* pond are bronze statuettes of Mrs. Mallard and her offspring.

Most visitors to Boston want to see *Cheers,* the bar made famous by the long-running television series (now in reruns)—and most people are disappointed with what they find. The one on TV used only the façade of a pub on Beacon Hill whose real name is the *Bull & Finch* (84 Beacon St.; phone: 227-9605); the interior is altogether different. Nonetheless, scads of tourists swarm the place to lap up overpriced beer and buy $20 sweatshirts with the "Cheers" logo. If this sounds appealing, cross the intersection and continue down to where Beacon Street levels out. (The place is so popular that it has expanded from its original basement location and now also includes part of the first floor.) The *Hampshire House* (phone: 227-9600), located upstairs at 84 Beacon Street, is an entirely different matter. The dining room of this 19th-century mansion overlooking the *Public Garden* is conservative, elegant, refined, reserved, and all those other adjectives that describe things Bostonian.

Head back on Beacon to Charles Street, turn right, then stand for a few moments to let the Old World feel of this beloved Boston street sink in. If you stood in this precise location 180 years ago, charm would not be the only thing sinking in; you would be standing knee-deep in the Back Bay. Before it was filled in during the second half of the 19th century, the area west of *Boston Common* and Charles Street was a bay. The part of Charles Street between the *Common* and the *Public Garden* is where British troops embarked for Charlestown in their fateful voyage to Lexington and Concord on April 18, 1775.

Charles Street was originally a residential area. It now serves residents of Beacon Hill with antiques shops, bookstores, pubs, and markets. Even

Christy's, one link in a ubiquitous New England convenience store chain, seems downright civilized in its elegant Greek Revival building.

Farther down is *Deluca's Market* and an adjacent package store (New England–speak for liquor store), with an excellent wine cask street sign, a Victorian form of advertisement which is now a rarity. At the end of the block is *Rebecca's* (21 Charles St.; phone: 742-9747), a relaxing restaurant with walls decorated with hand-painted flowers and a menu that features fresh salads and excellent pasta dishes. Try the linguine with plum tomatoes, shrimp, and capers. Farther down Charles Street on the opposite side (west) is a building with a clock tower and belfry. This is the *Charles Street Meeting House,* one of the first great forums of anti-slavery activity. Built in 1807, this building, which was in succession a temple of worship for Baptists, Methodists, Episcopalians, and Universalists, is now a temple of commerce. The ground level consists of five retail shops. The upper floors are office space for financiers, attorneys, and other professionals.

Continue down Charles Street to see the antiques shops tucked cheek-to-jowl between Revere Street and Charles Street Circle. Have a look through the *Boston Antique Cooperative* (119 Charles St.; phone: 227-9810), a six-owner shop that reflects each owner's specialty. (Also see *Shopping* in THE CITY and *Antiques: Boston's Best Hunting Grounds* in DIVERSIONS.) Along the way, pop in for a "pop" (Boston jargon for a beer) at the *Seven's Ale House* (77 Charles St.; phone: 523-9074), a typical Boston drinking haunt. But beware of "walking under the influence" in this hilly neighborhood. An imbiber was once witnessed accelerating so fast down a steep Beacon Hill incline—on foot, mind you—that he body-slammed a parked car. The only injury was a small dent—in the car.

Return to the corner of Charles and Chestnut Streets to begin the trek up Beacon Hill.

The townhouses on Chestnut Street, remarkably harmonious in architectural design, are known for their embellishments. Fanciful boot scrapers, ornamental iron balconies, gas lamps, a cast-iron hitching post, and outlandish brass door knockers are just some of the frills that enhance these dwellings. But first, a quick detour. After passing by the *Harvard Musical Association* at 57A Chestnut (whose remarkable music library is the oldest in the nation, and whose occasional evening concerts feature a pre-concert supper of baked beans and beer for its members), turn left onto West Cedar Street and then take an immediate right. This is Acorn Street, Beacon Hill's most precious byway.

Now the showcase of Beacon Hill, Acorn Street has done some social climbing since the days when servants, coachmen, and traders called it home. Be careful when crossing its cobblestone street; some visitors get to gawking at the photogenic buildings and sprain an ankle. At Acorn's crest, go right on Willow Street, then left, to continue up Chestnut Street.

Among the historic houses on Chestnut Street are the home of Edwin Booth, a famous actor and brother of John Wilkes Booth, Abraham Lincoln's assassin (29A Chestnut); the residence of Julia Ward Howe (13 Chestnut), a member of Boston literary circles and author of "The Battle Hymn of the Republic" (inspired by a personal visit with a war-weary President Lincoln in the White House); and the meeting place of the *Radical Club* (17 Chestnut), which claimed Whittier, Emerson, and Longfellow as regular visitors. Former Secretary of State Henry Kissinger lived at 1 Chestnut Street when he was teaching at *Harvard.* Look for the gaslight at the foot of its stone steps.

Turn left at the top of Chestnut and walk along Walnut Street to Mt. Vernon Street, the street of mansions; then turn left again. Two houses, both designed by Charles Bulfinch, stand majestically toward the end of this block. The *Second Harrison Gray Otis House* (85 Mt. Vernon St.) is an exception to Beacon Hill's dense development, reflecting Bulfinch's vision (never realized) of a group of freestanding mansions with landscaped grounds in this area. If the gate is open, walk up the cobblestone drive toward the rear of this private house and see the stable, which is now a separate dwelling (across the street is a whole row of stables converted into homes), and a fountain with water spurting out of a lion's mouth. Also notice the octagonal cupola on the roof. Bulfinch built the house next door (87 Mt. Vernon St.) for himself and his family. Unfortunately, they never got a chance to live in it, because financial woes plunged the architect into bankruptcy.

Past these homes is *Louisburg Square,* the Hope Diamond of Beacon Hill gems. This quiet oval park framed by bowfront dwellings is an exquisite reminder of Boston's British heritage. Statues of Aristides the Just and Christopher Columbus, gifts of a former Turkish consul to Boston, stand on either end of the small fenced park. On the northern side of the park once bubbled a freshwater spring. "Blackstone's Spring" (named after William Blaxton, the first settler, who lived not far from here) still seeps into Pinckney Street basements after unusually heavy rainfall. The serene, pensive aura of the square must have been ideal for Louisa May Alcott, the author of *Little Women,* who lived at No. 10 during her last years. Wander slowly around the park, savoring its ample shade. Unfortunately, this carefully tended swatch of green is for the exclusive use of *Louisburg Square* residents. But if the gate is open . . .

Leave *Louisburg Square* from the other end and continue up Pinckney Street to the right. This street was an endeavor in defensive city planning. Composed mainly of horse stables behind the Mt. Vernon Street mansions, Pinckney Street was designed in 1802 as a buffer zone between the affluent south slope of Beacon Hill and the seedy north slope or "back of the hill," which had become known throughout the great ports of the world as "Mount Whoredom." Accordingly, the only access to the north slope from Pinckney was Anderson Street, just ahead.

But Pinckney Street has made a brilliant comeback. It was swept clean in 1823 by Mayor Josiah Quincy and his police force, who evicted 300 residents, described by a clergyman of the time as "females wholly devoid of shame and modesty." Now home to literary figures, artists, and academics, it offers Beacon Hill's best view of the Charles River. During the late afternoons of summer, sailboats can be seen tacking to and fro on the Charles, as the river blazes with the light of the setting sun.

Several buildings on Pinckney Street have interesting pasts. Louisa May Alcott and family lived in three dwellings here—Numbers 20, 43, and 81—in the family's ongoing pursuit of shelter. Her father, Bronson, though he frequently hobnobbed with Emerson and the other transcendentalists, was a hopeless mystic and terribly irresponsible with the family's funds. And transcendentalist lawyer and publisher George Hillard lived at 62 Pinckney in the 1840s and 1850s. During that time, he became a US commissioner in charge of issuing warrants for the arrest of fugitive slaves, putting him at serious cross-purposes with his abolitionist wife, who hid slaves in the house without her husband knowing.

Head north on Anderson Street (always think of the harbor to get your bearings). *Massachusetts General Hospital,* where the first successful operation with ether was performed in 1846, can be seen down the hill from around 62 Anderson Street.

Ramble down Anderson to the corner of Revere Street. To the right (about half a block down) is Rollins Place, a cozy, little alley illuminated by gaslights. At the end of the block is a wooden Greek Revival façade; resembling a stage set, it was installed by the owner of the property to prevent the absentminded from toppling off the cliff just behind.

Head back down Revere Street (west) to view *Goodwin Place, Sentry Hill Place,* and *Bellingham Place,* private courts and alleys that are among the most sought-after residential areas on Beacon Hill. These cul-de-sacs, built around 1845, are lined with red brick houses and were originally the homes of artisans and traders. If the gates are open, feel free to stroll.

Swing around the block—turn right on the West Cedar Street footpath, then right again onto Phillips Street. The dwelling at 66 Phillips, once the home of Lewis and Harriet Hayden, figured prominently in the abolitionist movement. After the Fugitive Slave Act of 1850 gave slave owners the legal right to recapture escaped slaves, the Haydens became leaders of the *Underground Railroad,* and their house became a "station" on the way to Canada. The couple reportedly kept several kegs of gunpowder in the basement, vowing to blast the whole building sky-high rather than return a single slave. Luckily, the house was never searched.

After all this climbing and snooping about, it may be time to refuel. Turn right on Anderson, then make a left on Myrtle Street, just past Revere. A short stroll from here is *Primos* (28 Myrtle St.; phone: 742-5458), a latter-day Beacon Hill institution and the best (possibly because it's the only) pizza joint on the hill. The Italian and the eggplant hero sandwiches, called grinders in these parts, are quite good, and so is the pizza. All in all, it's a fine place for a snack and a breather.

Farther east, Myrtle Street intersects with Joy Street. Turn left on Joy and make another left on Smith Court. The first black church in the United States, the *African Meeting House,* is here (8 Smith Court). Founded in 1806, it has long been a gathering place for supporters of abolition and civil rights. William Lloyd Garrison founded the *New England Anti-Slavery Society* here in 1832. The *Museum of Afro-American History* (phone: 742-1854) is located on the first floor. It's open weekdays; no admission charge. The home of William Nell, an early black crusader for school integration, is across the street at 3 Smith Court. Built in 1799, this site and others are part of the Black Heritage Trail, a walking tour that explores the history of the black community in Boston. Call the *National Park Service Visitor Center* (phone: 742-5415) for more information on the route. (Also see *Special Places* in THE CITY.)

Return to Joy Street, following it back to Mt. Vernon, then make a right. The *Nichols House Museum* (55 Mt. Vernon St.; phone: 227-6993) is an early Bulfinch mansion. Under the terms of the will of Rose Standish Nichols, the last resident, it remains a private museum that provides visitors with a rare look at the interior of a gracefully furnished home of a Beacon Hill Brahmin. Among its many interesting features are a spiral staircase, portraits of Nichols family ancestors, and a console table that belonged to John Hancock. Closed December through February; open Tuesdays through Saturdays, June through August; open Wednesdays and Saturdays the rest of the year; admission charge.

Now head back to the *State House,* following Mt. Vernon Street to its beginning. Pass under a carport where the governor's limo sometimes waits to whisk its high-ranking passenger to his next official visit. Beyond the carport is an entrance to the right; enter for a tour of Bulfinch's most famous Boston building. Among the more important features of the *State House* interior are the Doric Hall, with its busts, statues, memorials, and paintings of famous Americans (join a guided tour, or pick up information for a self-guided tour); *Memorial Hall* (or the *Hall of Flags*), which displays an impressive collection of regimental flags from the Civil War, the Spanish-American War, and both world wars; the *House of Representatives,* where hangs the historic Sacred Cod (a symbol of the state's economy, donated to the legislature by an early member, and an outstanding example of early American folk art); and the *Senate Chamber* and *Senate Reception Room.* (Also see *Special Places* in THE CITY.)

Exit through the doors on Mt. Vernon Street (where you entered) into the new *Ashburton Park,* which was a parking lot until recently. Here the *Beacon Hill Memorial Column* stands on the former site of the warning beacon, which blew over on a particularly windy night in November 1789. The present column was erected in 1898. Sixty feet were sliced off this hill in 1811 to provide earth to fill in the old Mill Pond, a project that added 50 acres to the northern edge of Beacon Hill.

Pass through the gate and across Bowdoin Street to No. 122, where a wiry young John F. Kennedy established his untidy office and Boston residence after winning a seat to the US Congress in 1946.

Diagonally left from *Ashburton Park* is the *John W. McCormack Building,* home to an alphabet soup of commissions and departments characteristic of Massachusetts state government. Few visitors to Boston (or Bostonians, for that matter) are aware of a series of conference rooms on the building's 21st floor that offer an ideal aerial view of Beacon Hill on one side and the financial district, harbor, and North End on the other. No one will bother you if you act as if you belong there.

Follow Bowdoin Street south to the *Golden Dome Pub* (150 Bowdoin St.; phone: 227-7100) on the left. This boisterous joint always seems to be pushing the maximum capacity limit of the fire code. Known in some circles as the "State House Annex," it is used by press and pols as a news exchange. It's an ideal venue to leak stories to the press and exchange gossip since nobody—sometimes even including your companions—can hear a thing you're saying. If you're looking for a tavern with real Boston ambience, this is it. It serves great ale, too.

The best stop on this Beacon Hill historical walking tour has been saved for last—the *Boston Athenaeum* at 10½ Beacon Street. An independent library, art gallery, and museum, the *Athenaeum* is a legacy of Boston's aspirations to be the "Athens of America." Among other treasures, the *Athenaeum* features a collection of George Washington's books on the top floor, periodic exhibitions by acclaimed artists in the gallery on the second floor, and a scenic view of the *Old Granary Burying Ground* out the rear windows. Tours (no charge) are given on Tuesday and Thursday afternoons; reservations are necessary (phone: 227-0270). Also see *Special Places* in THE CITY.

A final note: Just a block down Beacon Street, on the way back to *Boston Common,* is a great delicatessen. Despite its name, a visit to the *S&M New York Deli* (14 Beacon St.; phone: 523-8776) is a pleasurable experience—the corned beef on rye is the best this side of New York City's *Carnegie Deli.* Also see *Eating Out* in THE CITY.

Walk 6: Downtown

The important thing to remember about Boston is that, according to reliable lore, there was never any attempt to organize the city's downtown streets (Back Bay is a different matter). Instead, they just evolved, as paths trod by cattle wandering about on the Boston peninsula were paved over. But Bostonians have never seemed to mind that their downtown streets are glorified cowpaths. As Ralph Waldo Emerson observed, "We say the cows laid out Boston. Well, there are worse surveyors." The legacy of this bovine school of city planning, however, is that even native Bostonians sometimes get gloriously lost.

The jumble of streets that gives Boston its charm and Old World feel is nowhere more evident than in the city's cradle, the downtown area, which now consists of the *Faneuil Hall Marketplace, Government Center,* and the financial, retail, and waterfront districts. The walking tour of downtown (allow up to five hours) begins at the corner of Park and Tremont Streets, site of the *Park Street Church* and Park Street *MBTA* station, where the *Red* and *Green Lines* intersect (see *Walk 5: Beacon Hill*).

Face Tremont Street, which runs north and south (remember the harbor is directly ahead), and proceed north past the *Park Street Church* to the *Old Granary Burying Ground,* named after the public granary that stood on the church site in the 1700s. Established in 1660, this cemetery is the final resting place of many Boston patriots. Pass through the Egyptian-style granite archway and stroll around the *Old Granary,* enjoying its remarkable tranquillity while Tremont Street bustles just yards away. The burial ground is open daily. (Also see *Special Places* in THE CITY and *Historic Churches* in DIVERSIONS.)

Continue down Tremont Street—formerly a hillside row of the mansions and terraced gardens owned by the colonial aristocracy—to its intersection with School Street, shaded by the skyscrapers of the financial district. Amid this jungle of high-rises, *King's Chapel* (Tremont and School Sts.; phone: 227-2155), one of America's oldest churches, is a welcome sight across the street.

King's Chapel was the colony's most fashionable parish before the American Revolution—though not much liked by the colonists, since it was primarily a place of worship for British officers. The ideal time to visit the chapel is just after noon, when concerts—anything from chamber music recitals to Appalachian dulcimer performances—are presented on Tuesdays. The church has been Unitarian since 1785. Next to the chapel is the *King's Chapel Burying Ground.* Established in 1631, it is the city's oldest cemetery and contains the graves and tombstones of many revered old Bostonians. Along the first path to the right is the grave of Elizabeth Pain, a Puritan who was tried for the murder of her child. Although she was acquitted, she was considered notorious; her story is thought by some to have been the inspiration for Nathaniel Hawthorne's tragic masterpiece, *The Scarlet Letter.*

Backtrack a few yards and turn right, uphill onto Beacon Street. Another right on Somerset Street will bring you to the *Old Courthouse,* also known as the *Suffolk County Courthouse.*

Walk around to the rear of the building, noting its neo-classical design, which is reminiscent of the *Louvre.* Then walk toward the crescent-shape row of office buildings ahead. This is the rear of *Government Center.* The escalator that cuts through this wall of buildings was installed in the late 1960s, in conjunction with the construction of the new *City Hall.* In exchange for allowing developers to build over a little street that had connected Old Scollay Square (where you're going) to Pemberton Square (where you've just been), the city required that the developers provide escalator service "forever" between the two squares. (Anything in Boston is called a square as long as it has a park bench.)

Across Cambridge Street, which is ahead as you step off the escalator, is an endless sea of bricks and concrete, culminating in a top-heavy cement structure that one Boston native justifiably said looks like "the box that *Faneuil Hall* came in." This is *City Hall.*

It wasn't always this way. Completed in 1968, *City Hall* sits smack-dab in the middle of what was Old Scollay Square, the mere mention of which brings a faint smile to the faces of those old enough to remember. In its prime, Old Scollay Square was either rollicking, rowdy, or just plain raunchy, depending on one's point of view. It was a jumble of London-style buildings known in every port on earth for its roaring nightlife, tattoo parlors, short-stay hotels, and pawnshops. In the thick of it was the *Old Howard,* a building that no longer exists but deserves mention here, since the story of its downfall mirrored the demise of the once-respectable district where it stood.

The *Old Howard* was originally a church, built by the Millerites (a religious sect that predicted the exact day the world would end in 1834 and quickly disbanded when that day passed uneventfully). The building subsequently became the *Howard Athenaeum,* a theater featuring classy plays and opera. In the ensuing years, the *Howard* began to decline, playing host to vaudeville, then burlesque, and finally striptease shows. Its last act was being demolished by a wrecking ball to make way for the new *City Hall.* There is a plaque where the *Old Howard*'s stage used to be, near the Sears Crescent building.

Walk across the vast red brick City Hall Plaza, which, when stiff winter winds blow in from the harbor, can seem like the coldest spot in the city. There is no reason to go inside *City Hall,* except to pay one of the parking fines for which this city is notorious. On the right facing *City Hall* is a curving row of buildings known as the Sears Crescent, built in 1816. Next door is the smaller Sears block, built around 1846. This row features Boston's most beloved sign, a large, gold, steam-spewing teakettle, which hangs in front of the coffee shop on the corner of Tremont and Court Streets. The 227-gallon kettle's human capacity—tested in the late 1800s—is eight small boys and a rather tall man.

Another amusing Victorian street sign—a large, smoking pipe—hangs in front of *David P. Ehrlich & Sons* pipe and tobacco shop (32 Tremont St.; phone: 227-1720), a short walk down the street to the right as you face *City Hall*. A brief visit inside this aromatic shop can be an olfactory delight, even for a nonsmoker.

Return to City Hall Plaza, passing just to the left of the teakettle. Continue on to *City Hall*'s south side and down the several flights of steps that lead out onto Congress Street. Across the street is historic *Faneuil Hall*, with *Quincy Market (Faneuil Hall Marketplace)* in tow. A statue of Revolutionary War hero Samuel Adams greets visitors to this popular part of town. But resist the temptation to cross for now. Instead, turn left and follow Congress Street along the east side of *City Hall* to Hanover Street. From here, cross Congress Street for a look at Boston's oldest commercial district.

Turn right onto Union Street, then make an immediate left onto Marshall Street. At 10 Marshall Street is the *Ebenezer Hancock House,* former home of John Hancock's brother. The house is now a law office and is not open to the public. Across from the *Hancock House* is the *Boston Stone,* a millstone imported from England by a colonial painter. (For more information on both, see *Special Places,* North End, in THE CITY.)

Return to Union Street and visit the *Union Oyster House* (41 Union St.; phone: 227-2750), the city's oldest restaurant and a true Boston institution. At night it's impossible to miss the red neon sign atop the building; it's as much a landmark as the beacon atop Beacon Hill was in earlier centuries. If the smell of salt water has piqued your appetite, a plate of oysters on the half shell and a frothy ale may be in order. Think of it as a historical reenactment—it's said that Daniel Webster, the silver-tongued senator himself, often hunkered down at this very establishment to polish off a dozen plates of oysters, accompanied by more than a few pints, in a single sitting.

Passing British troops used to yell for the hanging of the patriot who once lived on the second floor of the *Union Oyster House* building: Isaiah Thomas, publisher of a revolutionary newspaper, the *Massachusetts Spy*. Thomas smuggled his press and type out of Boston three days before the confrontations in Lexington and Concord. From Worcester he published the first official reports of the opening battle of the revolution. About 25 years later, the restaurant's second floor sheltered the exiled and impoverished French King Louis Philippe, who gave French lessons to Boston merchants and their daughters here before he returned to France to claim the throne as the "Citizen King."

Now walk toward *Faneuil Hall Marketplace.* A pleasant little tree-fringed park running parallel to Union Street has several inviting benches, as well as two statues of James Michael Curley, the renowned Boston politician who was accused of everything but bench sitting during his lengthy political career as alderman, mayor, state legislator, governor, and US congressman. The quip "Vote often and early for James Michael Curley" says it all about this scholarly rogue, who had a profound influence on 20th-century Boston politics. (Spencer Tracy played the Curley-based character in the film version of Edwin O'Connor's *The Last Hurrah.*)

This route approaches *Faneuil Hall Marketplace* from the northwest, through Dock Square, the former location of the town dock and site of the colony's first waterfront settlement. Just up North Street is the *Bostonian* (phone: 523-3600), a charming hotel that has been surprisingly well integrated into this ancient block, a cherished remnant of 17th-century Boston. The *Seasons* restaurant and the *Atrium* lounge (beware, drinks have been known to cost as much as $7 at both places) occupy the hotel's first two floors and are fine places to observe the area's robust activity, particularly the "power breakfasts" among the city's movers and shakers for which *Seasons* is famous.

Faneuil Hall was built in 1742 for Peter Faneuil, a French Huguenot merchant prince who donated the building to the city in an early example of American philanthropy. The building became a public meeting place, one that patriot James Otis would call "the cradle of liberty." It was here, on the second floor, that the leaders of the revolution mounted increasingly blistering attacks on King George III and the British *Parliament.* It also was here in 1772 that Samuel Adams proposed that the city form a Committee of Correspondence and invite the other 12 colonies to do the same, a gesture encouraging the disparate colonies to unite in action. Later, this same hall became famous for the oratory heard here, including antislavery speeches and Daniel Webster's 1826 eulogy in honor of John Adams and Thomas Jefferson, both of whom had died on *July Fourth* of that year.

Before continuing on to the *Quincy Market* building, glance up at the grasshopper weather vane proudly perched on the *Faneuil Hall* tower. Nobody is quite sure why it's a grasshopper, but the most plausible explanation is that the grasshopper was part of the family crest of a deceased friend of Charles Bulfinch, who rebuilt the structure in 1806, and that the weather vane is a memorial to him.

Behind *Faneuil Hall* is *Quincy Market,* a long building with an impressive portico fortified by four stout, granite columns. At lunchtime and on weekends, street performers often entertain crowds perched on the market building's wide stone steps. Once Boston's premier meat, poultry, and produce market, *Quincy Market* and the adjacent warehouses were restored and transformed into a bustling, trendy marketplace in 1976, with dozens of shops, restaurants, fast-food concessions, and bars.

A note about terms: Strictly speaking, *Quincy Market* and *Faneuil Hall* are two historic buildings in the renovated marketplace known as the *Faneuil Hall Marketplace.* However, the terms *Faneuil Hall, Faneuil Hall Marketplace, Quincy Market,* and *Quincy Marketplace* are all used—often interchangeably—to refer to the entire marketplace. Also be aware that there's a smoldering controversy about how the word "Faneuil" is actually pronounced, even among Bostonians. Some contend it's pronounced *Fan*'l; others claim it's *Fan*-yool. The merchant's gravestone doesn't offer much insight. It reads "Funel," leading some historians to conclude that the name was pronounced to rhyme with "tunnel." If you don't have a favorite, just call it the "historic meeting house near *Quincy Market.*" You'll be understood.

Take a walk through the center aisle of *Quincy Market,* an alley-like building that has become a runway of fast foods from around the world. There are enchiladas, crêpes, daiquiris, cheese, oysters, bagels, brownies, fresh peanut butter, salads, frozen yogurt, cookies, teriyaki, roast chicken, "designer" coffee, and gyros—and that's just a sampling. Visitors make their purchases at the individual concessions and then search (often in vain) for an open table in the rotunda. Weekday lunch hours are particularly maniacal, as workers pour out of the adjacent office buildings to forage. On the sides of *Quincy Market* are two glassed-in malls, where vendors sell trinkets, souvenirs, and accessories from pushcarts.

The two rows of buildings flanking *Quincy Market,* the *North* and *South Markets,* also have been upgraded considerably from their once lowly status as warehouses. The shops they house now include a mixture of the highbrow and the informal, the traditional and the bizarre. For a list of what's here, see the directory in the *Quincy Market* rotunda. One of the market's more unusual shops is *Boston Scrimshanders* (*South Market*; phone: 367-1552), which specializes in scrimshaw jewelry, a local specialty. New England scrimshaw was originally carved into whale ivory, but since the use of whale tooth has been outlawed, carvings are now done on mammal ivory and fossil walrus.

Durgin-Park (*North Market;* see *Eating Out* in THE CITY), a restaurant featuring traditional, though mediocre, New England food, is so quintessentially Boston that it's in danger of parodying itself. Try as they might, nobody in the history of the place—including Cabots and Lowells, Kissingers and Kennedys—has succeeded in reserving a table, so be prepared for a short wait.

Just down from *Durgin-Park,* at the end of the *North Market* building, is *Lord Bunbury's* (phone: 227-7004), a British pub and restaurant named after a famous 18th-century caricaturist. *Bunbury's* centerpiece is a solid mahogany bar that was once in an English pub; it was disassembled, shipped overseas, and reassembled here (like Arizona's London Bridge). The pub is the ideal place to sip a pint of stout, served, as in bonny old England, at room temperature.

At the end of the marketplace is *Marketplace Center,* a small row of newer buildings that house still more stores and food concessions.

Now take a minute to look back over the marketplace. The view of the city, with the old (*Quincy Market, Faneuil Hall*) juxtaposed against the new (*City Hall* and *Government Center*), is gorgeous. Then turn around and walk out of the market and underneath the behemoth Central Artery overpass, to *Columbus Park* and the waterfront.

The pier directly ahead is Long Wharf, originally built in 1710 to provide Boston Harbor with deep-water mooring. It is considered the greatest construction project of Boston's colonial period. British troops embarked here for the Battle of Bunker Hill. Today, the pier is known as the site of the *Marriott* hotel (phone: 227-0800); the rustic *Chart House* restaurant (phone: 227-1576), which serves award-winning clam chowder; and the offices of F. Lee Bailey (at 66 Long Wharf in the granite Custom House Block), the famous trial attorney. Central Wharf, immediately to the south of Long Wharf, is the home of the *New England Aquarium* (phone: 973-5200), which harbors a spectacular array of fish. Whale watches depart from here April through October; call for schedule information (phone: 973-5277). Open daily; admission charge. (Also see *Special Places* in THE CITY.)

Backtrack to *Faneuil Hall Marketplace.* This time, stroll along the shops of the south side, doffing your cap to the statue of the legendary Red Auerbach, former coach, general manager, and now president of the Boston *Celtics,* whose bronze, cigar-smoking likeness relaxes permanently on one of the benches.

While heading back to Congress Street, notice a tiny kiosk near the entrance to the marketplace. This is the office of *Bostix,* an establishment that sells same-day discount tickets for concerts, theater performances, and other events. (See *Inside Boston's Theaters* in DIVERSIONS.)

Follow Congress Street left a block or two, along the Freedom Trail, then turn right on State Street to the *Old State House* (at the corner of State and Washington Sts.; phone: 720-3290), one of the highlights of this walking tour and a proud reminder of America's colonial past. Before the present building was erected in 1713, this was the location of the *Town House,* Boston's first Town Hall, which was built in 1657; town meetings were held here as early as 1634. Boston's development began at this meeting place—homes and gardens were established nearby and roads struck out, by man and by cow, to connect them.

In front of the east side of this building, the Boston Massacre occurred in March 1770 when a patrol of British troops panicked and fired into a mob of angry colonists, killing five men. A circle of cobblestone under the East Gable of the building marks the spot where the men fell. Reproductions of Paul Revere's lithographs of the incident, which were distributed throughout the colonies, can be purchased across the street at the *Boston National Historical Park Downtown Visitor Center* (15 State St.; phone: 242-5642). Rangers at the center also can answer questions about the city and its history. Completely restored, the *Old State House* is home to the *Bostonian Society,* which has a museum and library with many mementos of Boston history. It's open daily; there's an admission charge.

From here, visitors have the option of embarking on a side trip to the *Boston Tea Party Ship and Museum* and the *Computer Museum,* both located along Fort Point Channel, a brisk 10-to-15-minute walk straight down Congress Street. If you want to skip the side trip, head straight down State Street, toward the water, for a loop through the Custom House District (see below).

The *Brig Beaver II,* a full-size working replica of one of the three original Tea Party ships, is moored just about where the original vessel, owned by the British East India Company, had her heavily taxed cargo jettisoned one fateful evening in December 1773. It was one of the first acts of defiance leading to the American Revolution. Abutting the ship is a museum, where visitors can peruse exhibits that recount the event. As a parting shot, hurl overboard one of the provided crates and pretend it's a bale of tea in belated protest. Don't be too concerned about tainting Boston Harbor: Bostonians mucked up the harbor in 1773 and have been polluting it ever since. Besides, the crate is attached to a rope for easy retrieval. Open daily March through mid-December; admission charge (phone: 338-1773).

Just over the Congress Street Bridge and left at the big milk bottle is the *Computer Museum.* Even non-"techies" usually spend a couple of hours here. Among the hands-on and interactive exhibits are terminals that allow visitors to test a variety of programs, voice-activated computers, robots, and a walk-through computer. Families may want to stop at the *Children's Museum,* also on *Museum Wharf.* (For more information on both museums, see *Special Places* in THE CITY.) Just beyond is the newly outfitted *Barking Crab,* where grilled seafood is served, in season, in a tent (see *Eating Out* in THE CITY).

Turn right onto Atlantic Avenue, then cross Surface Road to State Street and follow it away from the water, for a loop through the Custom House District. For a spectacular aerial view of Boston from a sophisticated setting, locals and visitors alike go to the *Bay Tower Room* (phone: 723-1666), at the top of the 60 State Street building just across from the *Old State House.* The elegant restaurant and piano bar on the top floor are open to the general public after 4:30 PM. (See *Seeing the City* in THE CITY.)

The monstrous building at 53 State Street is the home of Boston's stock exchange. It stands on the site of the historic *Bunch of Grapes* tavern, a favorite meeting place of patriots prior to the revolution that reputedly served up the best bowl of punch in town. The plans for the present structure originally called for a replica of the old exchange building to replace the real McCoy. In response to vocal protests by preservationists, a compromise was reached whereby an L-shaped façade of the original structure was spared and incorporated into the new design. There are many projects like this in Boston, the result of ongoing combat between developers and preservationists; opinions are mixed as to who will ultimately triumph. The aptly named *Stocks and Bonds* restaurant (53 State St.; phone: 723-8505), located in the basement, is a favorite of Boston's financial crowd.

Farther down State Street—called King Street before the Revolution—is an imposing tower, which poet Walt Whitman once called "one of the noblest pieces of commercial architecture in the world." It is the *Custom House Tower,* built between 1912 and 1917, which for decades was New England's tallest structure (the older building at the base of the tower was completed in 1847). Before Atlantic Avenue was built, the building was so close to the waterfront that the bows of boats would bump the windows facing the harbor. The *Custom House's* 22-foot-wide clock was repaired and refurbished recently, and for the first time in years all four faces tell the same time. At night the building is awash in colored light. Customs officials have decamped for more modern offices, and the city of Boston, which bought the building, is planning to convert this property into a luxury hotel by leasing the land to developers. It is hoped that the tower's 25th-floor observation deck, which offers a panoramic view of the city and the harbor, will be reopened one day.

Turn right just beyond the *Custom House,* then follow India Street just as it begins to dogleg left. On the left is the *Flour and Grain Exchange,* a distinctively handsome Romanesque building that houses the offices of a number of architectural firms.

Make a right on Milk Street and another right on Batterymarch Street, then walk straight ahead to Liberty Square. From the square, turn left onto Water Street heading west, back to its intersection with Congress Street. In a building on the northeast corner, in 1831, William Lloyd Garrison began publishing *The Liberator,* an abolitionist newspaper dedicated to the end of slavery. Stay on Water Street one more block until you reach Washington Street, in the middle of Boston's most historic block.

Make a left on Washington Street, an ancient thoroughfare that linked the *Old State House* with the town gate on the neck of the peninsula, when Boston was a peninsula (the *Old State House* is two blocks to the right). The Indians who used to inhabit this area called the road Shawmut, which is why Boston-area banks, streets, and businesses bear that name. At the end of the block, on the right, is the *Old Corner Bookstore,* now called the *Globe Corner Bookstore* (phone: 523-6658). Constructed in 1718, it was long the office of Jamie Fields, a luminary in early American publishing. Today, the building houses an excellent bookstore with volumes and guidebooks about New England on the first floor and travel literature and maps on the second. (Also see *Special Places* in THE CITY.)

Across Washington Square, at the intersection of School and Washington Streets, is the *Old South Meeting House* (formerly the *Old South Church;* phone: 482-6439), a structure steeped in history. It was here that an overflowing crowd of colonists met in December 1773 to discuss what to do about three British tea ships docked in the harbor. The multimedia presentation "In Prayer and Protest" re-creates the deliberations prior to the Boston Tea Party. On Saturday evenings in the summer, you can watch costumed players reenact a town meeting. Open daily; admission charge.

Just around the corner, at 17 Milk Street, is the site where Ben Franklin was born in 1706. His devout father bundled Ben up at the tender age of three hours and took him around the corner to the *Old South Church* to be baptized.

Now return to School Street and follow it up to the *Old City Hall* building on the right (there's a statue of Benjamin Franklin on its west side). *Old City Hall,* an intriguing granite building erected in 1865, was for years the undisputed domain of James Michael Curley (he served four four-year terms as mayor between 1914 and 1950). He referred to his office on the southeast corner as "Agony Corner." The building is now home to *Maison Robert,* an elegant restaurant serving fine French fare (see *Eating Out* in THE CITY). A more moderately priced café is downstairs (phone: 227-3370 for both).

Ramble along City Hall Avenue, a charming alley on the east side of Old City Hall, where the Josiah Quincy statue is. Just past the *Kirstein Business Library* is Pi Alley, evidence that the phalanx of streets in this area, though arbitrarily placed, were not arbitrarily named. A jumble of great American newspapers and magazines got their start in this area, thus the alley was named "pi," a printer's term for a jumble of type. (Other street-name trivia: The nation's first schoolhouse building was located on School Street; an old courthouse stood on Court Street, which was called Prison Lane when a grim jailhouse, said to have once held Captain Kidd, stood there.) Pi Alley is now home to a motley assortment of vendors. *Ties Only,* with many silk ties for under $10, is worth a look.

Backtrack to School Street via City Hall Avenue and walk in the direction of Washington Street. On the right is Province Street, at one time called Governor's Alley because it ran behind *Province House,* the official mansion of the royal governors. The granite steps leading up to Bosworth Street connected the mansion to its garden, stables, and coach house. There's an intimate and traditionally Bostonian restaurant and bar, appropriately called *Governor's Alley* (42 Province St.; phone: 426-3333), across the street. Try the scrod or the lobster pie.

Just up the steps on Bosworth Street, a picturesque lane that looks a little like the French Quarter in New Orleans, is the *Marliave* (10 Bosworth St.; phone: 423-6340), an eating establishment that dates back to 1875. French Huguenots, fleeing religious persecution, built a small church at the corner of Province and School Streets in 1707, and this area was a French enclave when the *Marliave* gained fame as a French Bohemian–style hotel and dining room. Today, the restaurant serves Italian food that is quite good. There's a glass-enclosed patio overlooking Winter Street in the rear.

Continue down Province Street, taking a left on Bromfield, which leads to Washington Street. Having weathered Boston's past, reward your efforts with some very modern-day shopping in the city's retail district. Turn right onto Washington Street; *Filene's* (426 Washington St.; phone: 357-2100) is at the end of the block, on the left. "The World Famous *Filene's Basement,*" as the sign says, an unforgettable shopping experience, is below (phone: 542-2011).

Those who shop religiously will find it fitting that Boston's first church, the "Old Brick," was located just about where *Jordan Marsh* (450 Washington St.; phone: 357-3000), New England's largest department store, now stands. The blocks branching out of the intersection of Washington and Winter Streets are closed to automobile traffic, forming a pedestrian shopping area known as *Downtown Crossing.* The area is known for its footwear stores.

Walk up Winter Street to Winter Place, about mid-block on the left. Sitting in the corner, reserved and proud, is the *Locke-Ober Café* (phone: 542-1340), a legendary Boston restaurant with traditional ambience and extremely traditional (read "conservative") values. (See *Eating Out* in THE CITY.)

Return to Washington Street and turn right at the corner. Two blocks down on the right is West Street. The three-story, early-19th-century row house at 15 West Street was the home of Elizabeth Peabody, an educator, bookstore owner, and the city's first female publisher. She published the *Dial,* a literary magazine for which Ralph Waldo Emerson served as editor and Henry David Thoreau as assistant editor and writer. Peabody also was responsible for publishing Thoreau's essay "On Civil Disobedience." Her home was a gathering place for the authors and intellectuals of the time. The building now houses the *West Street Grill,* a multi-storied bar/restaurant (see *Eating Out* in THE CITY). *Fajitas 'n' Ritas* (25 West St.; phone: 426-1222) serves up *fajitas* and margaritas that are remarkably good for New England; it even lets patrons scribble on the walls when they're feeling poetic.

The *Brattle Book Shop* (9 West St.; phone: 542-0210) is unquestionably Boston's best secondhand bookstore. Spend some time perusing its shelves, which reach to the ceiling, and leafing through its impressive collection of vintage *Time* magazines, old and rare books, and autographs. The books on the racks outside are $1 apiece.

Follow West Street to its intersection with Tremont Street. Ahead is *Boston Common,* the visitors' center, and the end of this walking tour of downtown Boston.

Walk 7: North End

Any thoughtful Bostonian will admit that there is more to the North End than heaping bowls of linguine with white clam sauce and cup after tiny cup of espresso. They'll say there's also cannoli, calzone, calamari . . . Bostonians (and this includes area suburbanites as well) are guilty of literally feeding the stereotype that everything in the North End revolves around its Italian restaurants. Most non-residents visit the North End only to assuage their cravings for some of the finest Italian food this side of Firenze. But after the last cappuccino, they head in the direction of Boston's glistening skyline and disappear into the night.

The habits of these itinerant diners suit North Enders just fine. They come, they spend, and they leave. It is the "guest" who doesn't leave that has the North End's predominantly Italian population mildly concerned. This section of Boston, the city's oldest, has suffered what is known here as gentrification. This phenomenon is best defined as the movement of the upper middle class professionals from the suburbs into the heart of the city. In the process, townhouses are restored and condominiums are carved out of formerly family-owned buildings. The locals benefit from higher property values, but also suffer from rents that sometimes price longtime residents right out of the neighborhood. Perhaps North Enders went wrong when they let word get out that their neighborhood is the city's safest: The close-knit community certainly helps keep the crime rate down.

The present ethnic dynasty is only the latest of several in the area; the North End is, after all, Boston's oldest residential neighborhood. The Puritans were the first to arrive, making their way from Charlestown, when they found the water was contaminated there. The area was home to clergyman Cotton Mather and Paul Revere; later, it was a meeting place of Samuel Adams and the Sons of Liberty.

After the upper crust moved to Beacon Hill and then to the brownstones of Back Bay, the North End became primarily a commercial center. Mariners disembarked from its nearby wharves. In the mid-1800s, wave after wave of immigrants came ashore here to find housing and jobs. In chronological order, the North End became home to Irish, Jewish, and Italian immigrants. But while the Irish and Jewish communities eventually moved on, the Italians have held their ground here for more than 60 years.

The North End walking tour (it will take about three hours) begins in the Blackstone Block, Boston's oldest cluster of buildings, dating from as far back as the 17th century. Just north of *Faneuil Hall,* the block is best reached by turning left in an alley just west of the swank *Bostonian* hotel on North Street, a short distance from the Haymarket stop on the *MBTA*'s *Green Line.* On Friday mornings and Saturdays, this area looks like a Turkish

bazaar, thanks to *Haymarket,* a farmers' market held on nearby Blackstone Street.

Walk straight on the Blackstone Block, stopping to read a rather skimpy exhibit outlining the history of the block on the right. Farther on is Marshall Street and, to the right, set into the foundation of what is now a shop of kitschy souvenirs, is the *Boston Stone.* The three-story red brick building just across from the stone was built by John Hancock for his younger brother, Ebenezer, a paymaster for the Continental Army. The house was one of four that Hancock built along what used to be a creek, which made the North End an island in the early days. (For more information on the Blackstone Block, see *Special Places,* North End, in THE CITY.)

Walk along Marshall Street to Hanover. Turn right on Hanover, then walk a short block to Blackstone Street. Six days a week, this is a malodorous little thoroughfare, home to several slovenly fish markets and a grubby pizza joint, littered with spent vegetable or fruit crates with rotting contents, and made even more unpleasant by the central artery rumbling loudly and spouting noxious exhaust fumes overhead. But on market days, it becomes a Garden of Eden. There are colorful displays of plump, dirt-cheap vegetables and fruit, presided over by portly merchants who fully expect to haggle over price. Watch out: They don't let you choose your own produce, so even though the fruit on display looks great, newcomers often walk away with a bag of rotting goods. On Saturday nights, all the refuse from the market is swept into giant heaps, wonderful scavenging sites for those so inclined: Two well-dressed women recently were spotted scaling the heap and extracting edible heads of lettuce with what sounded like victory cries. (For all their pretensions and the mystique of old Yankee wealth, Bostonians can be real penny pinchers.)

At the end of Hanover Street, walk across Blackstone Street. Be on the lookout for the whimsical bronze sculptures of *Haymarket* debris imbedded in the street. There are apples, vegetables, a fish, a banana peel, even the front page of the *Boston Globe.* The work is known as *Asaroton,* from a Greek word meaning "unswept floors."

Follow the Freedom Trail, marked by a red line, into a grim tunnel under the Fitzgerald Expressway, or Central Artery. Fortunately, the days of the eyesore above you are numbered. After years of bureaucratic wrangling, the groaning beast will be replaced by an underground highway 8 to 10 lanes wide and 7 miles long, in a project that will take a decade. Imagine the waterfront free of the ugly green monster that consumes so much space and causes such a racket, restored to the beautiful and bustling area it once was. Enjoy the thought of this scenario—thanks to the dynamics of federal funding, you'll probably be paying for it.

After passing through the tunnel and a parking lot, follow the Freedom Trail to the right, down Cross Street to Hanover. Even if the Italian grocery stores on Cross Street hadn't tipped you off, you'd soon know you were in the North End because of the dramatic change in ambience. Suddenly hand gestures are more animated, oregano permeates the air, pistachios are sold by the huge bag, groups of men discuss the latest soccer scores in rapid-fire Italian, and buildings are bunched closer together. Most noticeable is the energy: The North End bristles with it.

As you forge your way up Hanover Street, notice the church at the bend far in the distance. That is *St. Stephen's,* Boston's only remaining church designed by Charles Bulfinch. There'll be time for a closer look later. There are a number of points of gustatory interest along Hanover Street. The *European* restaurant (218 Hanover St.; phone: 523-5694), on the left, is known for its tractor-tire-size pizza, exhaustive menu, and late hours. Most locals, however, swear by the crunchy, crusty pizza down the street at *Circle Pizza* (361 Hanover St.; phone: 523-8787). Next to the *European* is *Paolo* (216 Hanover St.; phone: 227-5550), which serves northern Italian fare in an elegant little subterranean room. Across the street is the cozy *Mother Anna's* (211 Hanover St.; phone: 523-8496). Nearby, *Ristorante Nicole* (54 Hanover St.; phone: 742-6999) serves heavenly homemade pasta dishes. If you just want a demitasse of espresso and a tasty sweet, stop at *Caffè Dello Sport* (308 Hanover St.; phone: 523-5063) or *Caffè Roma* (241 Hanover St.; phone: 723-1760). Farther up Hanover Street is the *Daily Catch* (323 Hanover St.; phone: 523-8567), formerly known as the *Calamari Café,* a petite, moderately priced closet that is the ultimate in intimate dining. Its specialty is—what else?—calamari (squid) with various sauces. Similar in spirit but less well known is *Giacomo's* (355 Hanover St.; phone: 523-9026). Another nearby restaurant is *Ida's* (3 Mechanic St.; phone: 523-0015), a small, home-style eatery noted for a fiercely loyal clientele and for authentic Italian dishes cooked to order.

On Fridays, Saturdays, and Sundays during the summer, Hanover Street and its environs are the site of Italian street festivals, each honoring a saint (the *St. Anthony Festival,* usually held on the last weekend in August, is the largest). The festivals mix religious custom (there is a procession in which statues of the honored saint and the Virgin Mary are carried through the streets) with the usual trappings of an outdoor fair: food concessions, musical performances, craft booths, games of chance, and a generally exuberant air.

Turn right on Prince Street. On the northwest corner of Hanover and Prince is *St. Leonard's,* New England's first Italian Catholic church. The next intersection is Garden Court Street. Two doors down on the right is No. 4, the birthplace (in 1890) of Rose Fitzgerald, later Kennedy—wife of Joe Kennedy, Sr. and mother of JFK, RFK, Teddy, et al. Rose's father, John F. "Honey Fitz" Fitzgerald, is a North End legend. His father was a grocer on Hanover and North Streets. The Fitzgeralds, like the Kennedys, had fled the Irish potato famine in the mid-1800s for Boston, settling in a North End that was predominantly Irish at the time. Honey Fitz lived in this house for eight years in the late 1800s, while he built a political base that took him first to the US Congress and later to the mayor's office in Boston's *City Hall.*

Honey Fitz always called his home base the "dear old North End," and his North End followers "dearos." He could be seen along these very streets around campaign time, performing the "Irish switch"—shaking the hand of one person while talking to another—and talking rings around everyone on most any topic. His gift for gab was so well known that he inspired a new word in the lexicon of Boston politics: "Fitzblarney." Continue walking down Prince Street to *North Square.* This was home to Boston's most impressive mansions during the late colonial period. One such mansion was owned by Royal Governor Thomas Hutchinson. In 1765, when the then lieutenant governor was suspected of supporting the Stamp Act, angry colonists pillaged the place, smashing furniture, draining the wine cellar, and scattering pages of his history of Massachusetts, a work in progress. Hutchinson was later the colony's last royal governor.

To the right is the *Paul Revere House* (19 North Sq.; phone: 523-1676 or 523-2338), a popular North End attraction. A Son of Liberty, friend of Samuel Adams, master silversmith, creator of church bells and cannon, artist, messenger (he rode to New York and Philadelphia to tell of the Boston Tea Party), and family man (he had 16 children), Revere would have been a noteworthy patriot even if Longfellow had not immortalized him in *The Midnight Ride of Paul Revere.* His medieval-style home was built just after the great fire of 1676. Its design—an overhanging upper floor, shingled roof, and lead casements in the windows—predates what is generally thought of as colonial architecture and gives the building a brooding feel. The tour of the house is self-guided, but the knowledgeable caretakers are happy to answer questions. Revere bought the house in 1770, shortly before the Boston Massacre. He owned the place for 30 years but lived here for just a decade, later renting it to others. Ninety percent of the structure's framework is original. Closed Mondays January through March; admission charge (phone: 523-1676). Also see *Special Places, North End,* in THE CITY.

Next to Revere's home is the *Pierce-Hichborn House,* one of the city's oldest brick buildings. Built about 1715, it was owned by a cousin of Revere's. Open 12:30 to 2:30 PM for tours; closed Mondays. Admission charge (phone: 523-1676). On the way back to Prince Street, the *Mariner's House* is on the left. This is an inn for seamen and merchant marines with stopovers in Boston; there often are a few ancient mariners dawdling out front as they attempt to regain their land legs.

Across the square, at the corner of Sun Court Street, is the *Sacred Heart Italian Church* rectory. Here Methodist minister Edward Taylor once preached to sailors. A former seaman himself, Taylor was so dramatic and eloquent that sailors spread his fame around the world. Charles Dickens insisted on attending one of his services during a visit to Boston; he and the poet Longfellow were ushered to side aisle seats by a one-eyed, lame mariner (the center aisle was reserved for sailors). Ralph Waldo Emerson called Taylor "the Shakespeare of the sailor and the poor."

Two of the more peculiar incidents in Boston history happened nearby. On an unseasonably warm day in January 1919, a four-story silo of molasses ruptured on Commercial Street, sending a 50-foot wall of molasses flowing down the street at a rate of 35 miles an hour, destroying buildings and crushing bridges in its path. All told, a dozen people died and many more were injured in the incident. The horses of mounted police that wandered into the morass became so inextricably stuck that they had to be shot. North Enders swear that on hot days they can still detect a hint of molasses in the air. And on the east side of Moon Street, just ahead, was a dwelling owned by a sea captain who was put in the stocks in 1673 for "lewd and unseemly conduct." The infraction apparently occurred when the captain kissed his wife on his doorstep after returning from a long voyage at sea.

Return to Prince Street, walk back to Hanover, then make a right. Two blocks up Hanover on the right, at the corner of Clark and Hanover Streets, is *St. Stephen's Church,* built by Charles Bulfinch in 1804. *St. Stephen's* has been a Catholic parish since 1864. It was restored to its original appearance in 1965, regaining its plain glass windows, white walls, chandeliers, red carpet, and gilded organ pipes.

Across from *St. Stephen's* is the *Paul Revere Mall,* a.k.a. the Prado. The centerpiece of this quiet neighborhood park is Cyrus Dallin's lively equestrian statue of Paul Revere. There are a number of plaques on its south side that recount the lives of famous North Enders.

Ahead is the *Old North Church* (193 Salem St.; phone: 523-6676), Boston's oldest house of worship, built in 1723. Before visiting this landmark, however, notice the three-story brick building on the left at 21 Unity Street. This is the *Ebenezer Clough House.* The home of a mason who helped build the church, the house (ca. 1712) is the only survivor of its era in the North End. It is not open to the public. A similar brick building, the only property Benjamin Franklin ever owned in Boston, once stood next door (now the courtyard behind the church). Franklin's sister lived there. The *Old North Church*—officially called *Christ Church*—is best known for the fabled lanterns Paul Revere arranged to have hung in the church's steeple—"one if by land, two if by sea"—to warn the people of Charlestown of British troop movements. Once inside the church, look for the nation's first memorial to George Washington, located in a niche near the altar, the brass chandeliers that were made in England in 1700, and the oldest clock still running in an American public building. (Also see *Historic Churches* in DIVERSIONS.)

The next stop, following the Freedom Trail up Hull Street, is the *Copp's Hill Burying Ground,* Boston's second-oldest cemetery. Named after its first eternal occupant, William Copp, a shoemaker from England who had his house here, this is the highest point in the North End. Oddly enough, the oldest gravestone here dates back to 1625, five years before the Puritans came to Boston. The discrepancy is due to the fact that the remains (and apparently the gravestone) of Grace Berry, who died in Plymouth in 1625, were brought to Copp's Hill by her husband when he moved to the North End sometime later. Also buried here are the Mathers—Increase, Cotton, and Samuel—a succession of ministers who held sway over religious conscience in the heyday of Puritanism. Their tomb can be found about 20 feet from the Charter Street gate. Some of the *Copp's Hill* gravestones retain the marks of musket balls, scars from the days when Redcoats stationed nearby used them for target practice. The shooting appears to have been indiscriminate, with the exception of Captain Daniel Malcolm's gravestone, which took a heavy pounding. The marker reads, "A true son of liberty."

Leave the cemetery from the Snow Hill Street side. Just over the rooftops, the rigging of "Old Ironsides," docked in Charlestown, can be seen.

At this juncture, the tour offers a choice of two (equally pleasant) alternatives: a visit to *Boston Garden* and a well-deserved ale in a brewery/bar nearby, or a stroll through the heart of the Italian neighborhood via a network of small streets and narrow byways.

Those who opt for the Italian neighborhood walk should head south (away from the water) on Snow Hill Street to Prince Street. Turn left on Prince, then right on Salem Street down to Cooper Street, then turn right again into a tangle of interlocking streets that have an authentic feel of Italy. When you have finished exploring, return to Salem Street, turn right, and head straight across Cross Street and back through the tunnel under the Central Artery.

Sports fans with a hankering to see the fabled *Boston Garden* should descend Snowhill Street to the north, to Commercial Street, near the water. Proceed left on Commercial Street (which turns into Causeway Street after two blocks). Pass under the Fitzgerald Expressway; *Boston Garden,* home of the *Celtics,* and the famous parquet floor, and the *Bruins,* is on the right. (Also see *Quintessential Boston* in DIVERSIONS.) Tours are offered during the off-season (phone: 227-3200). The final stop on the tour is the *Commonwealth Brewery* (138 Portland St.; phone: 523-8383), for some of the finest beer in New England. Continue past the *Garden,* then turn left on Portland Street to Merrimac. Just a peek at the mammoth brass beer tanks, visible from the sidewalk, makes one a little parched. The proprietors brew about 11 different types of beer in their continuing effort to uphold their noble motto: "Let no man thirst for lack of real Ale."

Cambridge-Lexington-Concord

Drive: Cambridge, Lexington, Concord, and Lincoln

Concord and Lexington may sound like familiar names, places you learned about in your eighth grade American history class. The site of the battles that started the Revolutionary War took place here in 1775; today, the towns take such pride in their history that plaques abound, and stories about the legends—the midnight ride of Paul Revere, the Minutemen, the shot heard round the world—still echo through the streets.

But there's much more to this area than a history lesson. This drive will appeal to anyone who appreciates classic New England towns, period homes, and rural landscapes. We start outside Harvard Square in Cambridge, on a street of historic Tory mansions, and travel west to the snug little town greens of Lexington and Concord, with their white churches and colonial homes. Several of the old structures have been restored to period house-museums, giving a visitor a quick insight into all the glory—and grittiness—of colonial times. By the 19th century, the fighting men of Concord were gone or subdued, replaced by creative talents whose works spoke louder than cannon. Long after Paul Revere had stabled his horse, this became the home of Emerson, Hawthorne, and Thoreau. Walden Pond, Thoreau's famous woodland retreat, is on this tour, as is Louisa May Alcott's home, which was the setting for *Little Women*.

The drive begins in Cambridge at Harvard Square, the spiritual heart of these four areas. A singular center of learning and culture since 1636, when Reverend John Harvard set aside 400 pounds sterling to found a "schoale or colledge . . . to advance learning and perpetuate it to posterity," today the square is a center of singular traffic jams, where pedestrians delight in weaving among cars in a death-defying game. Driving here is definitely hazardous to your health. Better to park at a safe distance (the *Charles* hotel in the Charles Square complex has an underground garage) and explore on foot.

Harvard Square is a loosely defined area emanating from the *Out of Town News* kiosk. On one side is the *Harvard University* campus; on the other sides are shops, movie theaters, restaurants, coffeehouses, and, especially, bookstores—about three dozen of them at last count. Worth noting are *Schoenhof's Foreign Books* (76A Mt. Auburn St.; phone: 547-8855), which boasts the largest collection of foreign books in New England, and the *Schlesinger Library* at *Radcliffe* (10 Garden St.; phone: 495-8647), one of the country's foremost libraries on women and women's history. Brochures outlining a walking tour of Cambridge may be picked up at the *Cambridge Discovery* kiosk near *Out of Town News.*

If you prefer to avoid the hassle, start this drive on Memorial Drive, at the intersection of JFK Boulevard. The Larz Anderson Bridge is on the left, and the hustle and bustle of the square is just a short block to the right. Drive northwest on Memorial Drive. This curving, tree-lined section of roadway was slated to be a major highway in 1963, but a group of citizens, led by Edward Bernays, the father of public relations, staged a save-the-sycamore-trees protest; the city took note and the scenic, narrow roadway was preserved.

At the rotary, follow the signs for Route 2, which curves to the right. At the large intersection with Mt. Auburn Street, take the right fork (*not* the sharp right turn), which continues out Route 2, or take one of two interesting detours. The first is the *Mt. Auburn Cemetery* (580 Mt. Auburn St.; phone: 547-7105), the country's oldest garden cemetery. You can drive through the cemetery, but bikes and motorcycles are prohibited. This is the final resting place of several notable people; if you want to find their graves, ask for a map at the cemetery entrance. (See also *Special Places* in THE CITY.) To get to the cemetery, turn left on Mt. Auburn Street, then left again to the entrance. After a stroll among the headstones, rejoin Route 2 by turning left out of the cemetery entrance, a right on Aberdeen Street, right on Huron, then left onto Route 2.

An alternative is to take a side trip down Brattle Street, one of the country's first mansion-lined streets. In colonial times, it was known, scornfully, as Tory Row, since most of the rich and famous residents were British supporters. Take a right on Mt. Auburn Street, then a quick left and right again to reach Brattle Street. Most of these fine old homes are privately owned, but their exteriors are worth a look. Two open to the public are the *Longfellow House* (No. 105) and the *Hooper-Lee-Nichols House* (No. 159).

Built in 1685, the white Georgian *Hooper-Lee-Nichols House* is the oldest home in Cambridge. Its low-slung frame now has a discernable sag, and its huge central hearth, low ceilings, and wide-planked floors are all graceful indications of its age. Now home to the *Cambridge Historical Society,* it is more interesting for its architecture than any collection of artifacts, but look for the antique dollhouse and the circa-1850 wallpaper. Open Tuesday and Thursday afternoons year-round and Sunday afternoons from May through October; guided tours are provided. Admission charge (phone: 547-4252).

For nine months in 1775, the yellow clapboard *Longfellow House* served as General George Washington's headquarters. Built in 1759 by John Vassall—a wealthy Tory who fled for his life during the Revolution—the home was bought in 1843 by Henry Wadsworth Longfellow's new father-in-law and given to Longfellow and his wife. Longfellow lived here until his death in 1882; here he wrote many of his poems, most notably *The*

Midnight Ride of Paul Revere. On display are Longfellow's books, furnishings, and art collection as they were when he lived here. Open daily; guided tours available; admission charge (phone: 876-4491).

Other homes worth noting are the *Vassall House* (built in 1746), at the corner of Hawthorne and Brattle Streets, which was built by Henry Vassall, the uncle of the owner of the *Longfellow House.* The house was the center of the *Army Medical Corps* during the American Revolution.

Close to Harvard Square is the *Dexter Pratt House* (built in 1808). Pratt, the village blacksmith, was immortalized in Longfellow's poem. Both the tree and the smithy are gone; the building is now owned by the *Cambridge Center for Adult Education,* which runs the *Blacksmith House* bakery (56 Brattle St.; phone: 354-3036) on the first floor.

Finally, the modest yellow frame house at 42 Brattle Street was originally owned by William Brattle. In this city of zealous patriots, it's odd that the street retains his name: Brattle was the commander of all British troops in the colonies.

To rejoin Route 2, go west on Brattle Street, turn right onto Lexington Street, then left again onto Huron Avenue. Drive three short blocks and turn right onto Route 2, or Fresh Pond Parkway, as it's called here. Follow the road as it curves alongside the Fresh Pond Reservoir, which supplies much of Cambridge's water. Continue following the signs for Route 2 for about 2 miles (and through three rotaries). Then relax—the road becomes a highway and the driving gets easier.

The first stop is downtown Lexington, which was founded by a few farmers from Cambridge in the late 17th century and was called, appropriately enough, Cambridge Farms. By 1713, it had a population of 450 and was incorporated as the town of Lexington. About 4 miles after the road widens to eight lanes, take the exit for Route 4 and Route 225. Turn right off the exit ramp to Pleasant Street. Follow this street north as it turns into Massachusetts Avenue. Continue north about 1.5 miles past the Route 4/Route 225 exit to 2A (or Marrett Road) to the *Museum of Our National Heritage,* a modern brick museum erected in 1975 by the Masons (33 Marrett Rd.; phone: 861-6559 or 861-0729).

The museum has changing exhibits on American culture and "Let It Begin Here," a permanent exhibit that is a good introduction to local history. The title echoes the words of one Captain Parker, commander of the American Minutemen at Lexington Green on April 19, 1775. On the evening of April 18, 1775, a British force began a march out to Concord to seize the stores of weapons held there and possibly to capture patriots and rabble-rousers John Hancock and Samuel Adams. But some 77 Lexington Minutemen assembled on the green to meet them. As the British approached, Captain Parker told his men: "Stand your ground. Don't fire unless fired upon. But if they mean to have a war, let it begin here." The British were also under orders not to start firing, but somehow, someone fired the first shot—just who it was remains a mystery—and so the war began. Parker's quote is now inscribed on a plaque on the town green and included in a narrated six-minute slide show at the museum. Accompanying exhibits are peopled with cutout characters that illustrate what life was like in colonial times. The museum is open daily year-round; there's no admission charge.

On leaving the museum, return to Mass. Ave. and continue north through the center of Lexington. After passing several blocks of shops and restaurants, you'll come to the Village Green, the site of the first pre-war skirmish in 1775. If you're lucky, you may even walk into the fray. Every April 19, the townsfolk don red coats and colonial garb and reenact the famous battle. The ritual starts at 6 AM, when a Paul Revere character rides through town, yelling (what else?), "The British are coming" (the actual ride occurred at 2 AM, but the annual reenactment takes some liberties with the timing for the sake of everyone's sleep).

The first thing you'll see as you approach the green from the south is the statue of Captain Parker, a.k.a. The Minuteman. On its base are inscribed the words spoken by Samuel Adams on April 19: "What a glorious morning for America." Boston embraced Adams's sentiments, and continues to celebrate the date as *Patriots Day.* A statewide holiday, it is more stirring today because of another competition: The *Boston Marathon* is held on the weekend closest to that date. Fans by the thousands line the city streets or cheer the runners on from windows and decks. Any way you look at it, it's a great day to be in Boston—but a lousy day for anyone hoping to drive through town.

Park near the Village Green, also called Battle Green, for a short walk to the major sites in the area. (There's some on-street parking available, and a municipal lot around the corner on Meriam Street.) Stop first at the visitors' center and look at the diorama of the battle on Lexington Green. Open daily year-round, it also offers brochures and maps (phone: 862-1450).

The handsome yellow house next door is *Buckman Tavern.* It was here, on April 19, that nervous militiamen waited for the British, who, as Paul Revere told them, were coming. The tavern has been restored to its original state, but it's strictly a museum, not a working tavern. Open daily from mid-April through October. Guided tours are available; admission charge (phone: 861-0928).

Walk north from *Buckman Tavern* up Hancock Street. The *Minuteman Memorial* sculpture, with the gunmen carved into a rock, is on the right. Farther up the street is the *Hancock-Clarke House,* built around 1698. Here Revere alerted patriots Samuel Adams and John Hancock that the British were on their way and warned them that they might be taken prisoner. The two escaped and lived to harass the Brits another day. Today, the house is a museum of the Revolution. Open daily, mid-April through October. Guided tours are available; admission charge (phone: 861-0928).

Walk back toward Battle Green and turn right onto Harrington Road. One block over is the stately *Harrington House.* History (or legend) records that Jonathan Harrington, the fifer of the Minuteman corps, crawled back to his home after being wounded in the battle and died on the doorstep—in front of his wife. It is now a private home.

As you may have surmised, the people of Lexington are quite proud of their history and their beautiful town green, with its two churches and its well-spaced, historic homes. But as you walk along Harrington Road, you may notice a small plaque that points out that it wasn't always so. As the plaque reveals, it wasn't until 1956 that a historic district was created to preserve the stately homes surrounding the green. In fact, it wasn't until the *Centennial* celebration in 1875, when 100,000 people from all over the country, led by none other than President Ulysses S. Grant, descended on Lexington, that its citizens recognized the historical significance of their town and the need to create facilities for visitors. The *Historical Society* was soon formed, and the town now plays host to more than 80,000 visitors a year. Emblazoned in gold letters across the front of the massive flagpole in the middle of the green (which was erected for the *Bicentennial*) is the phrase "Birthplace of American Liberty."

Follow Harrington Road just past the green to the *Old Burying Ground* on the right. Here you can find the grave markers for Captain Parker and for a nameless British soldier who died in *Buckman Tavern*. The oldest gravestone here dates from 1690.

Return to the green and note the small obelisk marking the graves of the Minutemen. Erected in 1799, it is the oldest Revolutionary War monument. Toss a penny on their gravestone, like so many others have before you, and read the stirring words praising this courageous fight by many so heroic Americans.

Continue around to where a path leads up the hill to an authentic-looking reproduction of the *Old Belfry,* whose bells roused the townsfolk on that fateful morning. The view over the green is well worth the five-minute climb.

Across the street is the *Cary Memorial Library,* with its portraits of George Washington and Paul Revere, both copies of works by Gilbert Stuart, and a painting of the *News of Lexington* by Emanuel Leutze. Also here are reproductions of the engravings of Amos Doolittle, recounting the battles of Concord and Lexington. Done in 1775 and based on eyewitness accounts, these engravings have served as a key source for historians trying to re-create the battles.

The municipal parking lot is just across Mass. Ave., but before going back to your car, enjoy a pleasant suburban phenomenon: Step into the street in a crosswalk and watch the cars come to a screeching halt. Ahh. You're not in Boston any longer.

Before driving on, you might want to make a stop at one of the many restaurants in the town center. *Café Bellecoeur* (10 Muzzey St.; phone: 861-9400) has classic French food; *Sweet Peppers* (20 Waltham St.; phone: 862-1880) is a sophisticated Italian bistro; and *Bel Canto* (1709 Massachusetts Ave.; phone: 861-6556) serves great deep-dish pizza and wonderful calzone.

For all the local hoopla about the Minutemen, it's easy to forget that they lost that first skirmish. They were badly outnumbered—some 77 to 700—and completely unable to put up an effective front. After a few shots were fired and the field became confused with gunpowder smoke and the cries of the wounded, the Minutemen retreated. With a whoop, the British continued their march to Concord. But the accidental battle took on new significance later, when the militia from surrounding towns converged on Concord, seeking revenge.

By the time the British got to the town, the assembled populace—some 300 to 400—were ready for a fight. They stopped the British forces at the Old North Bridge in Concord (more about that later) and the British began a retreat to Boston. It was here that the Brits' luck really ran out. Harassed by townsmen all along the road to Boston, they met their match at Meriam's Corner, where the Americans attacked and killed eight of their men. The retreat ended with some 73 British dead, 147 wounded, and 26 missing, from a total force of 1,800. On the American side, an esti-mated 3,500 men—almost all the able-bodied men in the area—took part at some point or another. Of that number, some 49 were killed, 41 wounded, and five missing.

Be aware that this "history" was recorded by Americans, not British, so it emphasizes the courageous patriot action and the retreat of the British soldier. The present-day *Minuteman National Historical Park* surrounds several miles of the roadway that the British traveled. To reach it, rejoin Massachusetts Avenue on the north side of the Lexington Green. Follow it west for about 2 miles, going over Route 128. When it dead-ends into Marrett Road (Route 2A), turn right until you see the signs to the park. The first sign is for a turnoff to Fiske Hill, which has a parking lot, picnic tables, and a standing map of prospective sites in the area. From here, a nature trail leads to the remains of the *Ebenezer Fiske House.*

The *Battle Road Visitor's Center* is just ahead on the left in a landscaped park, complete with picnic tables. Besides the usual brochures, this center has several good exhibits and a short movie about the British incursion. It's open mid-April through mid-November; there's no admission charge (phone: 862-7753).

A half-mile farther up the road is a disquieting clash of legend and real-ity. A large stone plaque marks the site where Paul Revere was captured by a British patrol on the morning of April 19. His companions, William Dawes, who took a different route from Boston, and Dr. Samuel Prescott, who started his ride in Lexington, were both able to escape the patrol. Revere was detained and wasn't released until the next morning. While he was able to warn the town of Lexington, he never made it to Concord.

About a mile farther, take the right-hand turnoff that leads to Battle Road. This short detour leads along a narrow, wooded road, past two Revolutionary-era homes. Immediately on the right is the *William Smith House,* home of the captain of the Lincoln Minutemen. This restored home is a traditional New England saltbox, typical of a Revolutionary-era farming homestead. Next is the *Hartwell Hearth,* which is nothing but a wood frame over a huge, central fireplace—the house burned down in 1968. Still, it's worth a stop to marvel at just how huge and how central that 18th-century heating system was. Eight fireplaces and numerous nooks and crannies, including a basement storage area, are set in and around the brick structure, which seems to take up a quarter of the living space.

Farther along Battle Road is the *Hartwell Tavern,* an important watering hole in the late 1700s. The wood saltbox has a simple floor plan. An exhibit is open to the public during the summer months.

Continue along the curved, wooded road to 2A. Take a right and head for Concord (2A soon becomes North Great Road). At the fork, stay to the left, which takes you into Concord center. At the intersection of the Old Bedford Road is Meriam's Corner, the site of the Minutemen's first attack on the retreating British soldiers. Just before the intersection is *Willow Pond Kitchen* (phone: 508-369-6529), a classic seafood shack, where inexpensive seafood, sandwiches, and pizza are served in a no-frills setting.

About a half-mile from Meriam's Corner is the first evidence of Concord's past literary glory. On the right is *Wayside,* a rambling yellow Victorian home with three huge chimneys and a large wraparound porch (455 Lexington Rd.; phone: 508-369-6975). It was the home of Nathaniel Hawthorne from 1852 until his death in 1864, and its subsequent owner, Margaret Sidney—author of *The Five Little Peppers and How They Grew*—kept Hawthorne's study intact. You can park in the lot on the left-hand side of the street. Tours are available April through October; closed Mondays. Admission charge.

Orchard House (399 Lexington Rd.; phone: 508-369-4118), one of the homes of the Alcotts, is just a bit farther down the road. The Alcott family lived here from 1858 to 1877, and this is the home Louisa May Alcott described in *Little Women.* The rooms have been carefully preserved, capturing the life of the period. Louisa's father, Bronson, was a noted philosopher, a friend of Emerson and Thoreau—and a starry-eyed, irresponsible dreamer, which accounts for the family's frequent moves. Several of the family's city homes are noted on the Beacon Hill walk (see *Walk 5: Beacon Hill*). Bronson Alcott founded his school of philosophy at *Orchard House,* after an earlier attempt to found a Utopian community at *Harvard* had failed. Open daily April through October and on weekends in March and November. Tours are available; admission charge.

Next to *Wayside* is the yard of *Grapevine Cottage,* where you can see the original grapevine of the Concord grape. The headquarters of Welch's—the jam and juice company and the biggest promoter of the local fruit—is in Concord. The house is not open to the public, but a plaque on the fence briefly describes grape harvesting.

About a half-mile farther, the *Concord Museum,* a red brick Georgian house, graces the triangle of land created by the fork of 2A and Cambridge

Turnpike. Take the small cutoff to the left before the fork, or make a sharp turn to reach the museum's parking lot on Cambridge Turnpike. The museum's core is the 1,500-piece collection of Cummings E. Davis, a poor tailor who moved here in 1850 from Brooklyn, New York—and began collecting other people's unwanted furniture, tools, and other items. One of the first to recognize the value of preserving these artifacts, he opened a museum in 1858. Davis donated his collection to the city of Concord in 1886; following this bequeathal, the local antiquarian society was founded. Today, the museum has more than 30,000 pieces, and an addition to the building has doubled the exhibition space. Be sure to look for the "two if by sea" lantern, one of the rustic lanterns with a single candle that hung in Old North Church and provided Revere with a warning signal. Ralph Waldo Emerson's study is here, preserved intact, as are many of Henry David Thoreau's artifacts. (While you're in town, do as the locals do and just refer to him as "Henry David.") Open year-round; closed Mondays. Tours are available; admission charge (phone: 508-369-9609).

Walk across the street to *Emerson House,* the writer's home from 1835 until his death in 1882. Today, it houses many of his books, personal effects, and furniture. Open Thursdays through Sundays, mid-April through mid-October. Tours are available; admission charge (phone: 508-369-2236).

Leaving the museum parking lot, turn right onto Lexington Street and continue another 0.4 mile into Concord Center. Halfway there, look for the *Visitors' Information Booth* on Heywood Street (on the left); it offers maps and brochures during the summer months. In the winter, the same information is available at the *Chamber of Commerce* office, housed in *Wright Tavern,* just one block farther at the intersection of Main Street (phone: 508-369-3120).

The huge white church next to *Wright Tavern* is the third incarnation of the *First Parish Meeting House.* The two earlier structures were destroyed by fires. The First Provincial Congress of 1774 was held in the original building; with John Hancock as president and William Emerson as chaplain, it's not surprising that the delegates to this historic meeting voted to resist British tyranny. The town of Concord had little sympathy for Tories. On January 10, 1774, every man in town and five women affixed their signature to a letter to the city of Boston agreeing to support them in their ban of the East India Company's tea. On September 26, 1774, the town voted to raise two companies of men who were willing to stand at a minute's warning in case of alarm: thus, the term "Minutemen."

Across the street, you'll notice a hill dotted with gravestones. This is the *Old Hill Burying Ground,* where several Revolutionary families are interred. In early Concord, except for going to and from church, graveyards were the only places "proper" families walked on Sundays. Since so many families wandered the graveyards, tombstones tended to be decorative and carried suitable moral messages. The raised tombs with large flat stone slabs on top had space for the longest messages, and so were reserved for ministers, deacons, or magistrates. The earliest stones have death heads with wings on them, which denote immortality.

You are now in the center of town, as marked by the flagpole and the small green strip of land. Park your car and walk along Main Street, with its many unique shops selling everything from jewelry to toys. If you arrive in the afternoon, stop in at the *Colonial Inn* (48 Monument Sq.; phone: 508-369-9200) for tea, complete with scones and silver service—you'd think the Tories had never left. The original part of the inn was built in 1718. Today, it has 54 modern and moderately priced rooms decorated in simple colonial style. Traditional (and moderately priced) American fare is served in the dining room, and there's an atmospheric pub. A parking lot is at the rear of the inn.

From the *Colonial Inn,* you can take a side trip to *Sleepy Hollow Cemetery,* the final resting place of some of the town's leading literary lights. Louisa May Alcott, Thoreau, Emerson, and Hawthorne have graves on "Authors' Ridge." It's open weekdays (phone: 508-371-6280). To reach the cemetery, turn right onto Bedford Street from Monument Street, which runs in front of the *Colonial Inn.*

The Old North Bridge is about three-quarters of a mile from here. Depending on your energy and the weather, walk or drive north on Monument Street for about a half-mile to *Old Manse.* This was the home of Concord's early ministers, notably one Reverend William Emerson, leading patriot and grandfather of Ralph Waldo. From its windows, Emerson, Sr., watched the battle of Old North Bridge. Nathaniel Hawthorne once rented the house for about three years. It's open except on Tuesdays mid-April through October; tours available; admission charge (phone: 508-369-3909). The Concord River flows right behind *Old Manse;* if the weather permits, a pleasant way to explore the surroundings is to rent a canoe from the nearby *South Bridge Boat House* (496 Main St.; phone: 508-369-9438), which is open April through October.

Just past the manse, the parking lot on the right is the starting point for a short walk to Old North Bridge. It was here, on this small wooden structure over the Concord River, that the British expeditionary force met with the American Minutemen for the second time, on April 19, 1775. The British had set fire to stores in the center of Concord and traveled on to the bridge, because they thought—quite rightly—that more guns were stored in the fields beyond. The local militia, on the west side of the bridge, saw the flames and, imagining their town burning, approached the oncoming forces. The British fired over the river and the patriots returned fire, with a "shot heard round the world." At the old bridge today, you can see Daniel Chester French's famous Minuteman statue and a battle monument. When the weather is good, talks are given here on the area's history.

Continue by foot across the bridge to the *Old North Bridge Visitor's Center* (174 Liberty St.; phone: 508-369-6993), or drive around by continuing along Monument Street and turning left onto Liberty Street. The center features exhibits and a short film that illustrate the North Bridge battle. Its hilltop location also affords visitors a splendid view of the bridge. You can picnic in the shade of its great trees. Open daily year-round.

This route now heads to Walden Pond, Thoreau's famous retreat. From the visitors' center, turn right onto Liberty Street, then left onto Lowell Road, which brings you full circle to a flagpole. Turn right onto Main Street. If you're a Thoreau fan, you'll want to visit the *Thoreau Lyceum* (156 Belknap St.; phone: 508-369-5912). To get there, turn left on Thoreau Street; Belknap Street is just past the snug white clapboard buildings of *Concord Academy,* a proper New England prep school, which counts Thoreau as one of its early graduates. (Less often noted is that he also taught here for under a year, resigning in protest after being forced to beat several students.) The *Lyceum,* an unremarkable shingle house on an unremarkable street, is the international headquarters of the *Thoreau Society,* and houses some of the philosopher's papers. It's open daily, March through December; there's an admission charge.

If you want to go directly to Walden Pond, go to Main Street and make a quick left onto Walden Street. Follow that for about a mile, past the intersection with Route 2, and you'll see the signs for Walden Pond. In the summer, the clash between past and present couldn't be greater. A replica of Thoreau's small house sits in the parking lot of this state park, which is usually jammed with screaming kids, strutting teenagers, and sun worshiping singles. It's a far cry from the philosopher's solitary, wooded home, where he went to "live deliberately, to front only the essential facts of life and see if I could not learn what it had to teach . . . to drive life into a corner and reduce it to its lowest terms." Now, the contest seems to be to drive as many lives as possible into a corner of the pond, where the beach rests. For a bit of solitude, take the second path to the right and look for the cairn that marks the original site of Thoreau's cabin. Then continue around the pond on the wooded path and hope to find an unoccupied inlet.

On the way home, we recommend a stop at the *Gropius House* and the *DeCordova Museum,* for a one-two punch of modern life. At the exit of the Walden Pond parking lot, take a right onto Route 126 South to Lincoln. After 0.7 miles, make a left at Baker Bridge Road. In half a mile, on the right, is the dramatic white *Gropius House* (68 Baker Bridge Rd.; phone: 259-8843). This was the first American project of architect Walter Gropius, head of the Bauhaus in Germany from 1919 to 1928. After he emigrated in 1937, Gropius built his home from materials from catalogues and building-supply stores. The clean, modern lines—revolutionary at the time—dramatically illustrate the Bauhaus philosophy of form following function. Open Fridays, Saturdays, and Sundays from June through mid-October and on the first weekend of the month from November through May. Admission charge.

To go to the *DeCordova Museum,* turn right out of the *Gropius House* driveway. Turn right again at the dead end; the museum entrance is on the left. Though it showcases one of the area's best collections of modern and contemporary art, the museum's most appealing feature is on its grounds. The turreted red brick mansion sits like a medieval bastion amid 35 acres of rolling gardens, among which are scattered 20 to 30 pieces of sculpture. There are great, expansive arcs of steel, twisted bronze shapes, and rounded pieces of concrete; most are abstract shapes, some are recognizable objects, and all blend remarkably well with the rolling hills and landscaped gardens.

To return to Boston from Lincoln, turn left out of the *DeCordova* driveway. Take the first left at Old Bedford Street. At Route 2 (the first major intersection) turn right. Head east to Fresh Pond, then to Memorial Drive. Instead of going to Harvard Square, return directly to Boston via Storrow Drive.

A COLONIAL NIGHT

If you want to spend the night in colonial country, a short detour to the west leads to *Longfellow's Wayside Inn,* just off Route 20 in Sudbury (phone: 508-443-8846). The building, which dates to the early 1700s, was purchased and restored by auto magnate Henry Ford in the 1920s. The inn has just 10 rooms, beautifully furnished with authentic antiques, and priced under $100 a night for a double room (reserve well in advance). Or just stop by to visit the restaurant, which serves moderately priced New England fare, or the *Old Bar* tavern. The tavern was built in the 1680s and, almost 200 years later, was Longfellow's favorite watering hole; the poet would tell stories here that later became part of *Tales of a Wayside Inn.* Among the memorable lines were (you guessed it) "Listen my children and you shall hear, of the midnight ride of Paul Revere." Also on the grounds are three other colonial-style buildings: a little red schoolhouse moved from its original site by Ford, and a chapel and working gristmill that Ford had built. To get here, go south on Route 126, past Walden Pond. After about 5 miles, turn right on Boston Post Road (Route 20). Signs for the inn will appear after about another 5 miles.

Index

Index

Notes

Notes

Notes